# The Role of Technology in Distance Education

Edited by
A.W. BATES

CROOM HELM
London & Sydney

ST. MARTIN'S PRESS
New York

©1984 A.W. Bates
Croom Helm Ltd, Provident House, Burrell Row,
Beckenham, Kent BR3 1AT
Croom Helm Australia Pty Ltd, First Floor, 139 King Street,
Sydney, NSW 2001, Australia

British Library Cataloguing in Publication Data

The Role of technology in distance education.
    1. Distance education — Audio-visual aids
    I. Bates, A.W.
    371.3'07'8    LC5800

    ISBN 0-7099-3224-3

St. Matin's Press, Inc., 175 Fifth Avenue, New York, NY 10010
First published in the United States of America in 1984

Library of Congress Card Catalog Number: 84-40035

ISBN 0-312-68942-X

MAR 29 '85

Printed and bound in Great Britain

# CONTENTS

# ABOUT THE CONTRIBUTORS

**TONY BATES** is a Reader in Media Research Methods and Head of the Audio-Visual Media Research Group, in the Institute of Educational Technology at the Open University. One of the first staff to be appointed to the Open University (in 1969), his duties include research into the use of audio-visual media in the Open University, and evaluating the potential of new audio-visual technology for the Open University's teaching system. He has worked as a consultant for UNESCO, the World Bank, British Council and the Open University itself on educational media projects overseas, and is the author of "Broadcasting in Education: An Evaluation" published by Constables, and (with John Robinson) "Evaluating Educational Television and Radio", published by the Open University Press.

**PAUL LEFRERE** is a Lecturer in Educational Technology at the Open University, an editor of the journal Instructional Science, and a member of the Institute of Educational Technology's Textual Communication Research Group and the university's Computer-Assisted Learning Research Group. His recent publications reflect his work with other research group members and course teams on applications of computers in the university, including word processing, computer-assisted learning, and quasi-intelligent advisory systems. He has advised and supported almost all of the Open University course teams which have used word processing.

**STEPHEN BROWN** is a Course Manager in the Technology Faculty of the Open University for which he has produced distance learning materials in a variety of media. He has conducted research into the educational effectiveness of different media components used by the Open University and the feasibility of a video-cassette loan scheme for Open University students. His research interests include the extent to which the skills involved in learning from television can be enhanced. He is currently working on the Open University's first educational interactive video-disc.

**KATHLEEN FORSYTHE** is Executive Director, Learning Systems for the Knowledge Network of the West Communications Authority in British Columbia, Canada. A graduate of the Open University, she has been involved in the development of North Island College, an open learning community college, and the Knowledge Network. She has published articles on a variety of aspects of learning systems including new professional roles for tutors, learning to learn and the loneliness of the long-distance learner.

**ROBERT G. FULLER,** a Professor of Physics at the University of Nebraska, was co-author of The Puzzle of the Tacoma Narrows Bridge Collapse videodisc and served as a consultant on interactive video at the Open University during 1982-83. He also served as an author of the physics lessons in the Interactive Videodisc Science Instruction packets for the Nebraska ETV Network, an Annenberg/CPB Project.

**ANN JONES** is a lecturer in the Institute of Educational Technology, and currently vice chairperson of the Computer Assisted Learning Research Group. She joined the Open University to work on the ACERO project and has since worked on various CAL projects. Her research interests include the application of Artificial Intelligence and Cognitive Science techniques in education and educational technology, and, specifically, modelling learning processes.

**HANS U. GRUNDIN** is a Senior Lecturer at the Audio-Visual Media Research Group of the Institute of Educational Technology, Open University, Milton Keynes, UK. His main area of research in this group is the collection and analysis of student feedback on educational media with regard to instructional charactersitics, as well as problems of 'media logistics'.

**NICOLA DURBRIDGE** is a Research Fellow in Media Research Methods in the Institute of Educational Technology at the Open University. After carrying out research into tuition and counselling, she transferred to the Audio-Visual Media Research Group, where she has evaluated the use of audio-cassettes, video-cassettes and broadcasting at the Open University. She has also been an OU part-time counsellor for several years on the Arts foundation course.

**DAVE GREENFIELD** joined the Open University as a student in 1971. In 1975 he became a course tutor, a lecturer in 1976 (course team chairman of PET271, Technology for Teachers) and since 1980 has worked as a project officer, being involved with several technology course teams and a research group. His industrial background has been in engineering design and prototype development work, followed by wide teaching experience in both secondary and tertiary education.

**BERNADETTE ROBINSON** is a Staff Tutor in the Open University's School of Education, based in the East Midlands Region. She is a psychologist with a background in teacher education and training. Since joining the Open University her research has been into the use of telecommunications for educational purposes and the application of research findings in developing training materials. She is currently working on a project on the effect of the media on tutoring.

**DAVID McCONNELL** is at present a Consultant in the Institute of Educational Technology at the Open University, having completed two years as Research Fellow on a British Telecom-funded evaluation of the use of CYCLOPS, the OU's own 'shared screen' distant tutoring system, in the East Midlands region. He has a Ph.D. in educational technology from the University of Surrey, where he focussed on evaluating laboratory teaching of physiology. He also worked as a teacher and as an educational technologist at Murdoch University, Australia.

**ZVI FRIEDMAN** has been a systems analyst with the Open University since its early days, and was responsible for the design of several of the University's major student administration computer systems. He is a member of the University's Distance Education Research Group, and is particularly interested in studying the application of information technologies to the administration of large distance teaching institutions.

**PETER ZORKOCZY** is Senior Lecturer in Electronics at The Open University, United Kingdom, where his academic work is on electronic systems (computer, telecommunication and computer systems). His research interests centre on the application of these systems to distance education, as well as on systems of advanced information technology.

**PAUL BACSICH** has worked at the Open University since 1972. Currently he is Senior Project Manager (Information Technology) in the Technology Faculty. His activities include the Cyclops project (audio-graphic teleconferencing), Optel (a private viewdata system), as well as telesoftware, electronic mail, and computer networks, and Cable TV implications for the Open University. Also, he has recently worked on the OU's Local Area Network Planning Group. His external activities include representing the University on the Milton Keynes Information Technology Users Committee, as well as serving on standards committees and advising organisations on design of viewdata systems.

**RUDI DALLOS** is a psychologist who is working as a Staff Tutor in the Faculty of Social Sciences, The Open University, and is involved in the implementation of distance teaching in the South West region. His research background is in learning theory and currently he is undertaking research involving a consideration of learning and communication, within a systems theory orientation, in long term social groups.

**ROY TOMLINSON,** after early experience in County Libraries, moved into academic librarianship, firstly as an Assistant Librarian at the Loughborough College of Advanced Technology and then as Tutor Librarian at the Percival Whitley College of Further Education in Halifax. The new Library Resources Centre, opened in 1979, is well equipped to meet the library, video and computer needs of Open University students using the College Study Centre. He is himself a graduate of the Open University.

**JOHN J. SPARKES** is a Professor of Electronics Design and Communications and for ten years has been Dean of the Faculty of Technology at the Open University in the United Kingdom. His participation in the preparation of many distance teaching courses has led to his interest in clarifying the educational capabilities of different forms of educational communication.

# PART 1

## INTRODUCTION AND OVERVIEW

# 1. THE GROWTH OF TECHNOLOGY IN DISTANCE EDUCATION

Tony Bates
Reader in Media Research Methods, Institute of Educational Technology, Open University

## Introduction

When the British Open University was established in 1969, it was a radical innovation in many ways. In particular, the teaching system was based on a combination of broadcasting and specially written printed texts. Harold Wilson's concept of 'the University of the Air' was a major factor in bringing the Open University to the forefront of public attention, ensuring widespread publicity and the heavy enrolments essential for its political survival in the early years. From its inception, the Open University was technologically based.

The concept of the Open University was always more complex than the notion of "broadcast courses" (although this is still a popular misconception). The founding fathers recognised early in the planning stages the inappropriateness of basing a University primarily on broadcasting; for a start there would not be enough transmission time. By the time then that the first 25,000 Open University students began their studies in 1971, broadcasting contributed no more than 10% of a student's study time, the most heavily used medium being the correspondence text, supported by a system of part-time tutors and counsellors (see Perry, 1974, for a full account of the establishment of the Open University).

Nevertheless, the teaching model was still relatively simple, in media terms. Text, broadcast television and radio were the main delivery media. In the 13 years that the Open University has been operational, its budget has increased from £2.25 million to £60 million, its students from 25,000 to 100,000, its range of courses from 4 to 150, and its television transmission time from just under four hours a week to over 35 hours a week. Throughout this period, though, for virtually all its courses, the printed text has remained paramount.

## Developments in Distance Education

Nevertheless, while the Open University's basic teaching system has changed surprisingly little over the last 13 years, there have been some major developments in distance education, paralleled by important technological changes.

Kaye and Rumble (1982) have identified a number of different models of distance education. Basically though, there have been two major variations from the national, centralised, high-resourced, high-population, autonomous distance teaching model of the original Open University. The first is the development of a number of smaller, more modest autonomous open universities. In Canada there is Téléuniversité, in Québec; Athabasca University in Alberta; and the Open Learning Institute in Vancouver. There is the Open University of Sri Lanka and the Allama Iqbal Open University of Pakistan in Asia; the Fernuniversität of West Germany, UNED of Spain, and the Everyman's University of Israel in Europe; UNED of Costa Rica and UNA of Venezuela in South America. These are smaller, relatively low-cost institutions, relying even more heavily than the Open University on print as the main teaching medium.

The second development is not really new at all. Distance learning - even at a higher education level - did not start with the Open University. In particular, in the USA, Soviet Union, East Germany, India, Canada, France, Australia and New Zealand, campus-based universities for many years have offered extension services for part-time off-campus students. Recently, full-time enrolments in higher education institutions have been reduced in many countries, with a consequent increase in low-cost, part-time off-campus activities, and this tendency is spreading even to Britain (see Spencer, 1980).

However, both in the smaller autonomous open universities and in extension services of conventional institutions, the use of media other than print and the peripatetic or local tutor is still extremely rare. Unlike the Open University, where nearly every one of the 150 different courses has a television component, few of the other distance teaching institutions use broadcasting extensively, nor are other less expensive audio-visual media generally used.

The low use of less expensive media is rather surprising. While distance teaching projects have become smaller and more flexible, the range of relatively low-cost media available over the last few years has also increased dramatically. Despite its widespread use of broadcasting, it is still the Open University though that is experimenting most with these new technological developments. There is then considerable scope for other institutions to increase their use of low-cost audio-visual media.

## Developments in Technology

Developments in technology since the establishment of the Open University have led to four major trends:

1. A wider range of media is now becoming available for use in the home. To broadcast television, radio and home experiment kits can be added audio and video cassettes, video discs, cable and satellite TV, the telephone, microcomputers, viewdata and teletext systems. When the Open University was established, decision-making regarding the use of media was relatively simple. In essence, the choice had been made before the University opened. The texts would provide the "core" material but television and radio would be available on every course to provide support for the texts. The University and the BBC/Open University production centre were staffed and equipped accordingly. The actual number of programmes made each year is still determined largely by staffing and financial considerations rather than by academic necessity, the latter being extremely difficult to determine. The proliferation of new media though raises a number of issues. Choice now becomes more real and more difficult to make. Are some media more "effective" than others? What do we mean by "effective"? Should new media replace existing media, or should they be used in addition (and hence become an add-on cost?) How should academic staff be made aware of the potential and limitations of new media? Who should advise on choice of media? Who knows about choice of media?

2. There is a greater diversity of access to new media. The three original media - broadcast television, radio and printed text - were not chosen by accident for the Open University. Virtually every home in the land could be accessed through these media. Thus no-one in Britain should have been prevented from enrolling for the Open University because of difficulty in getting the teaching material. However, two things have happened in the last 15 years. The principle of universal access regarding broadcasting at the Open University has been eroded, because not all students can watch or listen at the times at which programmes are broadcast. Secondly, most alternative media (video-cassettes, cable TV, etc.) are not universally available in all homes, nor will they be by the end of this decade, if at all. This raises questions of social equity. Should distance teaching institutions use media that are not universally available? Since units costs are lowered if students can share equipment - for instance, through availability at local study centres - to what extent should distance teaching be home-based or local centre-based?

3. Costs are coming down for new media. A C60 audio-cassette, containing one hour of material, can be delivered to an

Open University student for less than 50 pence. This cost covers everything (copying, materials, packaging, post) except design and production, and the student can keep the cassette. Similarly, a 25-minute television programme can be delivered on video-cassette for 75 pence per student - or for just over £2 for an hour's material - if the student returns the cassette for re-use at the end of the course. 16K microcomputers are now retailing for less than £100, and a 48K microcomputer at £125. A video-disc player retails for under £400, and a video-cassette player can be rented in Britain for less than £12 a month. All these prices will move lower - relative to inflation - rather than higher in the future. In comparison, print costs are rising faster than inflation and Open University broadcast television productions were averaging over £35,000 a programme in 1983. Developments in some areas of technology mean that even institutions with low budgets can afford to produce and distribute some non-broadcast audio-visual media, if they wish.

4. <u>New media are giving students greater control over their learning and greater interaction</u>. This is a most significant pedagogic development. While broadcasting is uninterruptible by the student, new media provide greater opportunities for revision, in-depth thinking, and integration. New media increase the amount and level of interaction between a student and learning materials, and in some cases give more opportunity for <u>human</u> interaction. This means that audio-visual media should in theory become more effective in developing learning. But in turn this raises the question of what likely effect the use of different technologies will have on cognitive thinking.

## The Purpose of the Book

These are some of the questions that this book deals with. It does not attempt to provide comprehensive answers, nor a general theory of media selection (although the last two chapters do examine some of the conceptual issues arising from these technological developments). It does attempt though to deal with practical matters arising from the use of various technologies in distance education. The book then has two principal audiences. The first is staff working in the steadily growing number of "specialised" distance teaching institutions around the world. The second target group is the equally growing number of staff in conventional institutions who are now considering the possibilities and the practicalities of off-campus teaching.

Again, in the space available, we cannot deal with any single medium in depth, but we do hope that the chapters will stimulate distance teachers to consider or reconsider the appropriateness of a wider range of media than hitherto, or to treat with caution some of the more flamboyant claims made for some technologies. Each author has attempted to provide appropriate references for those who wish to follow up certain areas.

Given the speed of technological development, and the pressure to use technology for its own sake, caution is essential. Nevertheless, audio-visual media are not sufficiently used in distance teaching, primarily because academics and administrators are generally unaware of their potential, inexperienced in their use, or frightened off by their imagined costs. I hope that this book will help remove some of these misconceptions, or provide some realism where it is needed.

## References and additional reading

BATES, A.W. (1982) "Trends in the use of audio-visual media in distance education" in DANIEL J. et al, Learning at a Distance. Edmonton: International Council for Distance Education/Athabasca University.

COFFEY, J. (1978) Development of an Open Learning System in Further Education. London: Council for Educational Technology.

KAYE, A. and RUMBLE, G (eds) (1981) Distance Teaching for Higher and Adult Education. London: Croom Helm

LEWIS, R. (1983) Meeting Learners' Needs Through Telecommunication: A Directory and Guide to Programs. Washington DC: American Association for Higher Education.

PERRY, W. (1974) Open University. Milton Keynes: Open University Press.

RUMBLE, G. and HARRY, K. (1982) The Distance Teaching Universities: London: Croom Helm.

SPENCER, D.C. (1980) Thinking About Open Learning Systems. London: Council for Educational Technology.

# PART 2

# MEDIA IN COURSE DESIGN

## 2. TEXTS AND WORD PROCESSORS

Paul Lefrere

Lecturer, Institute of Educational Technology, Open University.

## Introduction

> 'Even the best typist occasionally transposes lettres, or repeats
> themmm, or just hits the wring key. While you check for typing
> errors you realise - no, that's not what I meant to say. I'll
> just move a few paragraphs around and reword the odd sentence
> or three.'
>
> (Hudson, 1981, page 218)

What is the difference between a word processor and a conventional
(or an electronic) typewriter? How does a word processor work? Does
it really save time or money? What can it do besides help with
typing? Is it easier to write course material with a word-processor?
What is the best kind of machine for my work? Can I use it to
produce camera-ready copy? To drive a typesetter? To update a
course? These are just some of the many questions which Open
University staff have asked over the years at seminars and
demonstrations of word processing, questions which this chapter will
attempt to answer.

## What Can Word Processors Do?

Word processors can do many things which typewriters cannot. For
example, the machine I used to type the first draft of this chapter
has a key which corrects any transposition errors I notice; other
machines go further and automatically check spelling word-by-word,
as text is typed. With a word processor, material which has been
typed in can be altered at a later date quickly and easily, without
using correcting fluid or cutting-and-pasting.

Those alterations can range from insertions and deletions to the
reordering of sentences. In every case, alterations can proceed without
any unnecessary rekeying of parts which do not need changing. Once
a piece of text has been typed on a word processor, it may be copied
from one document to another and used many times; administrative

applications include the 'personalised' letter, which is assembled from a library of standard paragraphs.

In offices with much repetitive typing, word processing helps typists do more or do the same amount faster and more easily. It is easy with a word processor to change from single spacing to double spacing. If multiple copies of a manuscript have to be sent out, yet only some of the recipients need a double-spaced version, some reprographic savings are certainly possible. On an Open University course, whose drafts may have a circulation list of dozens or more, those savings might amount to £1000 per year.

Word processors may also reduce the cost of copy typing when material is redrafted. But if the only purpose of buying a word processor is to make a typist more productive, then at the moment it is cheaper to employ many typists, each with an electric typewriter, than to employ a smaller number, each with a word processor. If conventional typists spent all their working hours completely re-typing drafts of course material, the gain in a typist's productivity by using a word processor might well be enough to 'save' several thousand pounds a year. Those notional savings are still less than the capital cost of many models of word processor. In reality it will take several times longer - perhaps four to six years - to amortise such equipment, unless staff costs change relative to capital costs.

One way of influencing staff costs is to change working practices. Producing a distance teaching text is akin to producing a book: the parallels are not exact, but in both cases the material must be drafted, typed, redrafted, retyped, edited, illustrated and prepared for printing. Also, some means has to be found of ensuring a smooth flow of material to the printer. In Britain, word processing is rarely used to support more than a small number of these tasks (Oakeshott and Meadows, 1981), but it can help with each of these aspects of producing a text, as we shall see.

Not all working practices are easy to change. For example, in Britain it is common for material which is to be printed to be sent to a printing house in typescript. That typescript is then completely retyped by staff who operate phototypesetting equipment and who belong to a particular trades union. Technically, it is feasible to connect a word processor to a typesetter and so avoid completely rekeying the text. Some word processors even have a program which inserts typesetting codes (a task long seen as the province of print industry workers). To avoid inter-union demarcation disputes it may be necessary to negotiate over the tasks which each group of workers can undertake, before work can pass freely from one person's machine to another.

Savings on partial or complete rekeying, while usually welcome, may be but a small part of the production costs of the textual component of a distance teaching course; luckily, the purchase of a word processor can lead to a direct or indirect reduction in other costs. This is because material which has been typed into a word processor is often stored in a form which can be 'read' and accessed by other programs, either on the word processor itself or on a computer. Similarly, material which is on a computer can be transferred to a word processor. The result can be synergistic: a word processing program becomes more worth using if it can use data from another program, or from a variety of sources, and this effect becomes more pronounced when several non-word processing programs are available. Consequently, academics, administrators and clerical staff can not only reduce the time spent on existing activities but can also undertake tasks which would normally be impossibly time-consuming.

For instance, word processing can be helpful when it comes to keeping the production of a new course on schedule, which is desirable to avoid a rush in editing, design, printing, mailing and so on, as well as to avoid knock-on effects on other courses. In the Open University, some administrators already use word processors to produce letters reminding authors when their drafts are due and to indicate the effects of delays, so assisting other authors in making prompt decisions on alternative courses of action if problems do arise. Also, if all drafts are produced on a word processor, the number of words in each draft can be counted automatically, making it possible to monitor accurately the total page usage by a group of authors and so anticipate any need for more (or fewer) pages than they had planned.

Word processing can have significant benefits for authors, especially while they are drafting their material. The most obvious benefit is being able to compose on the word processor in a more flexible manner than is possible with any other writing medium (Fluegelman and Hewes, 1983). This can help overcome writer's block and also sustain a good writing rhythm. Also, you do not need to be a touch typist (or even a fast typist) to benefit from its use. Writers who cannot type or who do not have access to a word processor may not appreciate the importance of this point. Interestingly, authors I have spoken to who have their own machines (and so can experiment on the word processor with how they present their ideas) claim that this reduces their tendency to make changes to a printed galley. By contrast, authors with little or no direct experience of using a word processor and whose typing is done for them, often ask for more changes between drafts (and sometimes for more changes to a galley) once their secretary has a word processor.

If a word processor can do more than manipulate text, it can provide further ways of cutting the cost of academic time in originating a course. For example, once you have drafted a manuscript, you can use a text processing program to generate quickly an index or a glossary of all technical terms in the material as well as a handover note with details of any need for action by others, such as applying for copyright clearances.

Potentially more significant savings arise when courses are produced by teams. Team members work together less effectively if they are unclear about what is required of them and what other people are doing. Word processing can offer an additional way of improving the flow of information in a team, some of whom may be working at home. This is possible by interlinking each author's machine, either through an interconnecting cable (e.g. between offices on a campus) or via a telephone line (e.g. from home to work). Those links can be used for a kind of 'electronic mail' (e.g. to exchange drafts) and for annotating others' drafts (as in 'computer conferencing'). They can even be used by an author to 'think aloud' by 'conversing' with a program which draws out one's ideas, argumentation and beliefs about a course topic (Eden, 1982).

How does a word processor work?

Word processors have a keyboard (to key in a text and give the machine commands), an electronic storage medium (to record one's keystrokes while the machine is switched on), a permanent means of external storage (disks) and a computer of some kind (with a program which does the 'housekeeping' associated with word processing).

Word processors can use disks of diameter 3.5", 5.25" or 8". Most word processors also have two or more disk drives. On the majority of those multi-drive machines, the disk drives are identical, so just one size of disk can be used. Each disk drive can store and quickly retrieve hundreds or, on the newest machines, thousands of pages.

Most word processors have a television-like visual display unit (VDU) which can show at least 20-30 lines of text. I drafted this chapter on one which can show 25 lines of large characters (useful for proof-reading) or 50 or more lines of smaller characters (useful when judging how a printed page would look). The draft was edited on another word processor which has two displays - one of which is as big as an A4 page and can show an entire A4 page at once, exactly as it would look if it were printed, while the other display shows a single line containing additional information (e.g. what were the last twenty characters typed?).

When material is typed into a word processor, there is no need to interrupt your typing (and your train of thought, if you are composing material) to hit the return key when you approach the end of a line if a word will not fit on the current line, the machine will transfer it to the next line. This is called 'word wraparound' or 'wordwrap'.

'Hard copy' is the jargon term in word processing circles for typing on paper. When material is typed on a word processor keyboard, it does not appear on paper immediately. Rather, it is recorded temporarily on an electronic equivalent of a sheet of paper: the word processor's memory. That memory is far easier than paper to amend. A copy of the information stored in the memory can be sent to a printing mechanism and committed to paper at any time, most often after making any corrections. The printer can be part of the word processor or - more commonly - is a self-contained unit some distance from it.

## What does word processing cost?

The capital cost of all parts of a word processor except the printer is considered in the next section. It will take longer to type material on a typewriter than a word processor, and so the word processor will cost less to type on, unless (a) what you are typing is short, unique and will not be redrafted; and (b) you do not make mistakes or change your mind while you type. The cost of printing material out on a word processor is often higher than on a typewriter, both because the ribbons on word processors cost more and because many users of word processors find it is quicker for them to print out a complete and up-to-date top copy of a manuscript following a small change, than to find the old top copy and make a correction to it.

The cost of printers and the cost of printing varies widely. With machines costing less than about £400, the printing mechanism will print a legible but rather crude outline of each character, by using a number of tiny hammers in the form of a rectangular matrix; the shape of a character will determine which combination of hammers will strike the printer ribbon. The legibility of such matrix printing depends on the number of hammers in the matrix and on how close they are. For £1000 or more, a matrix printer can have a fine enough matrix to provide correspondence quality printing. The speed of a matrix printer varies from 40 to 400 characters per second. Most matrix printer ribbons are reusable (inked fabric) and so the cost per page of output is low - less than one penny. Many matrix printers can type in a variety of type styles on the same page and can reproduce line drawings. If this is important, but higher quality and higher speed are required, you can use laser typesetting (at £80,000 or more for a Monotype system, plus about 10 pence per camera-ready page), 'ink-jet' printing (at £6000 upwards for a system from

IBM, plus one to two pence per page) or laser xerography (at £20,000 upwards from Xerox, plus one to two pence per page). Typesetting offers the best quality. Laser xerography offers acceptable quality and is also much faster than typesetting, allowing you to reproduce a page in about one second; it is used commercially for short-run publishing by University Microfilms, who can print single copies of books and theses on demand at five to ten pence per page.

This chapter was produced using another kind of printer, a 'daisy wheel' costing almost £2000 and printing at 50 characters per second (say, a minute per page). Daisy wheel printers are available for less than £500, but their speed is only 12-16 characters per second. A daisy wheel printer produces fully-formed characters, like a typewriter. Those characters are arranged on the spokes of a wheel and bear a marginal resemblance to daisy petals. The wheel is removable, like the golfball on some typewriters. This allows you to produce camera-ready, proportionally-spaced typescript (as with this book) in one or more typefaces, possibly including different sizes, italics and scientific symbols. High-quality ribbons are used in such printers and so the cost per page is between one and two pence.

Conventional typesetting and printing offers greater legibility and quality than is possible by using any kind of word processor printer. However, such advantages are costly, particularly for courses with a low print run. Low print runs will be called for if you anticipate low enrolment or a need to make changes to the material (e.g. because it will date). With print runs of just a few hundred, it may be worth using conventional printing machinery to reproduce material from camera-ready copy; if there are many courses for which fewer copies are required, laser xerography may be worth considering. What is not sensible or worthwhile is to dispense with paper as a means of sending students their course material: the disks used in word processors do offer a relatively cheap way of storing text, at under a penny per page, but not a good way of distributing it, for students do not have suitable 'replay' facilities, nor can they study as well from a VDU as from paper.

Equipment options

At the Open University (OU), computers and word processors have been used for drafting some of our course texts since the mid-70's. While word processors are still far less numerous than typewriters in the OU, by 1982 over two hundred academic and administrative staff had access to word processing facilities, either directly or through their secretaries; a significant number of authors had purchased further machines for home use. This might be termed the 'Tower of Babel' approach to word processing: many incompatible machines are used, which makes it hard to transfer material between them. We have experimented with combinations of word processors and other devices. Our combinations are drawn from six main types of equipment:

- upgraded typewriters

- optical character recognition

- portable microcomputer-based 'notebooks'

- dedicated word processors

- microcomputers with word processing programs

- large 'mainframe' data processing computers.

The features of each type of equipment are considered individually below.

1. Better typewriters. Electric typewriters can be upgraded or replaced by electronic typewriters. In the former case, it could be very useful to retain existing typewriters yet not have to retype any material unnecessarily. This would be possible if material typed on them could be fed into the memory of a word processor or computer, ready for any potential redraft. Typewriters can be converted to do this. In one kind of conversion, a secondary keyboard is placed under the existing one; the new keyboard is linked to a special-purpose microcomputer which can record each keystroke on a floppy disk. That microcomputer can record keystrokes from several typewriters at once. If the disks it produces are incompatible with those used on a particular model of word processor, the contents of the 'typewriter disks' will need to be transferred to the word processor via a 'communications program'.

Considering capital costs alone, modifying your existing typewriter may be cheaper than buying a new, electronic typewriter, and will be cheaper than buying a word processor from an office equipment manufacturer. Quoting 1983 prices, converting a 'Golfball' typewriter costs about £200 (and rather more if the typewriter has a 'Typebar' mechanism). The cheapest screen-based word processor which is suitable for lengthy drafts costs about £2,500 (excluding a printer), while one which can cope with scientific notation costs nearer £10,000. Comparable systems based on general-purpose microcomputers cost about £1,200 and £5,000 respectively, but may not be as quick or as easy to use as those designed by manufacturers of office equipment. Electronic typewriters range in price from under £500 to over £2,000. With many of those typewriters, as with modified electric machines, it is possible to record keystrokes and/or send them to a word processor.

Modifying existing machines is a short-term alternative to buying electronic typewriters. Since electronic machines have few moving parts, they must eventually cost less than traditional typewriters. Already, they can improve a skilled typist's productivity. For example, one electronic typewriter costing less than £900 automates the following operations:

> paper feed; carriage return; paragraph indentation (as here); sub- and superscripts; centring (between margins, between tabs or even between words); underlining (word-by-word or with solid underlining); line framing (producing vertical lines around tables); pitch selection; alignment of numbers and words in columns; and numeric punctuation (punctuating whole numbers with a comma or a space every third digit).

Where drafts are long and undergo many small changes, a word processor can provide greater improvements in productivity than even the best in electronic typewriters. However, a typewriter has some advantages: while you can indeed do more with a word processor, you need to learn to use the extra features, which precludes their effective use by the infrequent typist. Since even electronic typewriters are relatively cheap, it does not matter if they are unused for periods of the day. Similarly, until the cost of a word processor becomes comparable with a typewriter, it is a waste of a word processor to use it mainly for jobs which can be done on a typewriter, such as copy typing.

    2.   Optical character recognition.  Optical character readers, or OCRs, are devices which can 'read' typed or printed text and turn it into signals which a word processor can recognise, so avoiding typing that material into the word processor. OCRs are complementary to word processors, not alternatives to them. One application of OCRs to course production arises if material for a new course comes from several sources (e.g. from different authors, using different typewriters or incompatible word processors; from a previous version of the course, which was not word processed; and from material published elsewhere, which is to be reproduced in whole or in part).

Two types of OCR are marketed: programmable ones, costing over £50,000; and very limited ones, costing £5,000-£10,000. The latter cannot read printing at all, and often cannot read typing unless it satisfies some stringent criteria. An example of a more sophisticated, programmable OCR is the Kurzweil Omnifont, which has none of the limitations of the first OCRs. It can read both typed and printed text, in any format or fount. It can also cope with photocopies. The high capital cost of such flexible machines has led to the establishment of OCR bureaux, to which work can be brought for conversion to a given word processor format or to a given phototypesetter format. Typical charges work out at perhaps two-thirds of the cost of manually retyping the material. The economics of purchasing one's own machine become attractive if several hundred pages of typing are to be processed daily or if material has to be put on to a word processor very quickly.

3. Transportable microcomputer-based notebooks. This is the keyboard equivalent of a pocket dictation recorder. It is battery powered, so can be used outside the office. Like an OCR, it is complementary to a word processor, not a substitute for one. Authors may find such a machine very useful. One such system in use at the OU (the MicroWriter) costs about £300 and is held in one hand. It has a six-key 'chord' keyboard rather than a conventional QWERTY keyboard. To type a letter or a number, several keys must be pressed simultaneously. Learning the alphabet and the system commands takes only an hour or two, while to reach handwriting speed takes a few days. The system has a small screen, which can show just part of a line, but this is sufficient for text entry and for a limited amount of text editing (including changing the number of characters per line, or the page length). Its internal storage capacity is just a few pages, but text can be stored on a domestic cassette recorder or sent to a computer or a word processor.

Another portable system in use at the OU has a full-size QWERTY keyboard, costs £500 and fits into a 4lb, A4-sized package. Built into it is a printer, a 4-line by 20-character display and, as a long-term memory, a microcassette drive which can store about 20 pages of text for subsequent transmission to a word processor. Other full keyboard systems in this price range replace the integral printer with a display which is wider and which has more lines (e.g. 8-lines by 40-characters); similarly, the microcassette is lost in favour of a larger internal memory (able to store ten to twenty pages of text even when the machine is turned off). The contents of that memory can be sent to a word processor or computer by cable or, in some systems, by an infra-red link.

Both the hand-held system and the full keyboard system have uses in course production. For example, with the former system an administrator can take notes unobtrusively during a course team meeting and convert them shortly afterwards into minutes of the meeting. With the latter system, which has a larger screen and a larger memory, an author can be independent of a mains powered word processor for days at a time; uses include jotting down ideas for drafts (while travelling or while in the garden or even while in bed) and for copyright clearance (the machine can be taken into a library and can prompt an author for all requisite details, once he has found a piece he wants to quote). A variant on the latter system, which has not been used in the OU, is the Sony Typecorder (about £1000), which can record both typing and speech.

4. Dedicated word processors. A 'dedicated' word processor is a computer which is purpose-built for word processing; that is to say, it can normally only be programmed for word processing. This generally means that the keyboard does not have to serve different applications, so certain keys can be reserved and labelled for specific functions such as 'delete sentence', 'centre heading', etc. Further, the program can be tailored to the particular screen, disk and memory size of the word processor, and special circuitry can be added, all with a view to making the system faster than a multi-purpose machine. This shows in the price, which is often two to three times the cost of a comparably powerful general-purpose computer.

Each dedicated machine has its own word processing program, whose facilities and commands will be peculiar to that system. Further, the program will be written to help with specialised activities such as generating a letter from a set of standard paragraphs, which is more appropriate to copy typists and clerks in ordinary offices than to the other categories of staff found in distance teaching institutions.

A minority of dedicated word processors can do more than process words. For example, one advanced dedicated system (the Star, from Xerox), is particularly easy to use, and can cope with both line and tone illustrations as well as text in a variety of founts. With its laser printer and associated supporting electronics, a basic two-terminal system could cost the best part of £100,000.

At the cheaper end of the market for dedicated machines (i.e. £2,500 to £10,000), few systems can handle even the simplest block graphics, partly because the printers in such systems are incapable of providing the requisite fidelity of output. However, some manufacturers will provide additional programs, comparable with those on the most expensive machines, which can:

-       process records (e.g. search for all the tutors who meet particular sets of criteria, then send each of them an appropriate letter)

-       calculate (e.g. if you are editing a document with columns of figures and you have to make a change to one figure which has repercussions elsewhere, the program will do all the recalculations automatically and insert the correct amounts)

-   check spelling, either once a document has been typed or as it is being typed.

One problem with most dedicated systems is their lack of flexibility: often, no means is provided for writing even the simplest programs to cope with local needs, nor is it possible to use any of the thousands of programs available for home-based microcomputers. A few manufacturers recognise the importance of this and offer an option which allows you run such programs (thus blurring the distinction between dedicated systems and general-purpose computers).

Partly for commercial reasons, there is little compatibility between the ways in which information is stored on the disks of different manufacturers' dedicated word processors (or even between different models in the same range). This problem is made more difficult to surmount by manufacturers who will not divulge how what you type is stored on their disks. The need for such documentation is rarely appreciated until you try to use a machine in conjunction with machines from other manufacturers.

The main consequences of being unable to establish a machine's storage format are as follows: it may be impossible to transfer typing between one dedicated machine and another maker's system; if transfer is possible, it can be time-consuming, inconvenient and expensive and may involve some retyping once the material has been transferred. This is shown by the experience of producing this book. Several authors drafted their chapters on different machines. Another machine, a dedicated word processor, was to be used to edit each chapter. To the machine it was edited on, a third machine had to be used as an intermediary. That third machine was a mainframe computer (a Digital Equipment DEC 20/60). With the document transfer program supplied with the word processor, the transfer process to or from the mainframe removed underlining, subscripts and superscripts and other layout instructions, so creating extra work. In one case, the instructions which were removed included codes for changes from upper to lower case, so the whole of that chapter was converted during the transfer to upper case; since no reconversion facility existed, that chapter had to be retyped on the word processor. A further disadvantage was that the authors' machines and the dedicated word processor were linked to the mainframe using standard British Telecom telecommunication circuits and so could not transfer data to it at their maximum potential rate of 1-3 minutes a chapter. The transfer of a chapter at the maximum allowable speed could take a marginally-acceptable 10-20 minutes at the best of times. When the mainframe was overloaded, transfer could take an hour or more, often preceded by a half-hour wait to get onto the mainframe. This precluded the transfer of material during normal working hours, since the machine connected to the mainframe could not be used for word processing (or anything else) either whilst queueing or whilst material was being sent to or from the mainframe computer.

A less fussy arrangement than document transfer via an overloaded mainframe can be adopted if you know how textual and layout information is stored on your disks. The source disk can be put into a machine which can copy its contents directly, in a minute or so, on to a second disk; that second disk can have a different diameter and a storage format which you can choose. Such a machine costs between £2500 and £5000 depending on the range of disk types and formats required. Such a conversion carried out by a bureau costs about £10 per disk.

   5. Microcomputers with word processing programs. Increasing numbers of Open University courses are being produced with the aid of microcomputers, rather than dedicated word processors. This is not just because the cost of microcomputers is far lower; the computing power and storage capacity of many microcomputers is now at least as good as a dedicated word processor. For example, many dedicated machines cannot print one document at the same time as editing another; only a handful of those machines can simultaneously display both a word processed document and data from another program, such as messages being received from someone on another machine. The current generation of microcomputers can offer a greater degree of concurrency: a single machine can simultaneously carry out word processing, printing and several other tasks (e.g. communicating with a mainframe, sorting the contents of a file into alphabetical or date order and compiling statistical information). One variant of this allows you to suspend a process, switch to some completely different program and, when the time comes to switch back, know that the microcomputer will pick up exactly where it left off.

Microcomputers can be classified according to whether or not they are readily transportable (and so suitable for use at home as well as in the office). Transportable microcomputers are roughly suitcase-sized, but offer a full desk-top specification system packaged in a way which allows it to be taken with little fuss to where the work needs to be done. An increasing number of OU authors now take such systems home when they are drafting material. For such a purpose, the minimum suitable storage capacity is 100 pages of text. The majority of systems show at least 24 lines of 80 characters, but cannot show graphics. The screen size, measured across the diagonal, should be between 7 and 11 inches; machines with smaller screens in my opinion strain one's eyes. Most systems have two disk drives.

Typically, a transportable system will weigh 15-20 lb and cost about £1500. Many transportable systems have a built-in telephone communication link, which cannot be used legally in the UK. Elsewhere, such systems are popular with authors because they can be used for electronic mail (e.g. exchanging drafts or sending comments on a draft to another person's computer to be read whenever they start work).

Non-transportable microcomputers suitable for office use have a full-size screen 11-15 inches across the diagonal. A typical machine will weigh 45 lb (just light enough to be taken home on occasion by determined OU authors) and will cost between £1,200 and £2,000, depending on its manufacturer. Lower cost systems of comparable or higher capability are just becoming available, as with the Elan microcomputer which, at £750, has two disk drives and a screen which can show a full page of text in a variety of type styles. Above about £4,000, microcomputers begin to offer word processing which is integrated with graphics. Perhaps the most usable microcomputer with graphics is the Apple LISA (at about £8,000), which compares well with much more expensive dedicated systems such as the Xerox Star and which, with its large screen, would be more appropriate than a dedicated word processor to designers and editors.

A microcomputer is only as good as the programs that can run on it. The most common word processing program for microcomputers is WordStar. This was used to draft this chapter and has been used to produce several courses in the OU. It takes at least a day to master but has similar facilities to those on many of the cheaper dedicated word processors. Broadly comparable microcomputer programs include Select and Memoplan, both of which contain a self-instructional course and are easier to learn than WordStar. More powerful programs include EdWord, FortuneWord, Perfect Writer and The Final Word. These and other programs are evaluated in Naiman (1983).

Like most of the programs on dedicated word processors, WordStar permits you to view and make changes to only one part of one document at a time; several of the other programs listed above allow you to compare and alter two or more parts of the same or different documents, which can speed up writing and editing. They also have other handy features. For example, with EdWord (a £400 program available on the £4,000 Corvus Concept microcomputer), you can save work done so far on a draft, knowing that next time you work on that draft, the 'context' of the work will be re-established exactly as before, with all bookmarks in place and also taking you to where the last change was made. Also, all alterations made to text are invisibly logged. By retracing the log, a single UNDO key lets you backtrack on the changes you have made; if required, you can restore the text step-by-step back to its original state. Further, it takes just a fraction of a second (rather than the several minutes of some systems) to compare pages in different documents, or to move from the beginning of a course-length text file to the end; this makes a big difference when copy-editing full drafts.

6. Large 'mainframe' computers. If there is spare capacity on a computer, and a suitable word processing program is available, it may be possible for dozens of people to use that computer simultaneously for word processing, with only marginal effects on other users. The advantages include low cost and the possibility of more facilities than on a run-of-the-mill dedicated word processor. The cost can be low per additional user for two reasons: first, they will share existing, centrally-sited printers and require just a terminal at their place of work; also, there may be economies of scale on training, documentation, maintenance and other forms of user support. If the mainframe computer is not overloaded, it can carry out a given task faster than can a smaller system, particularly when working with lengthy documents. Further, as we see later, a mainframe computer can have additional 'text processing' programs which are helpful in course production, but which cannot run on the majority of smaller machines.

Major disadvantages of using a mainframe for word processing are that if the mainframe needs maintenance, all of its users are affected; some of its non-word processing users may slow the machine down for hours at a time with special jobs and may take priority if access to the machine is limited; the screen display is updated with unpredictable and possibly disconcerting delays following each change which you make to a document, unlike the instant screen updating of a microcomputer or a dedicated word processor; there may be conflicts of interest over resource allocation between those running the large machine and those, often in another department, who are responsible for word processors; and most word processing programs available for mainframes need to be augmented by the text processing programs referred to above, before a mainframe can offer better facilities than a dedicated word processor or a microcomputer to an editor or a designer.

From experience at the OU, at least two word processing programs should be available simultaneously on a mainframe: one program should be suitable for occasional users or other users with limited needs, while the other should be for more advanced users. Ideally, the two programs should be compatible to the extent that common word processing tasks should be carried out identically with either program, so reducing training needs; such compatibility is rare. The 'simple' program should have a small set of commands (to make it easy to learn), while the other program should have both a large basic set of commands and allow features to be added by users. A commercial example of the former, costing about £8,000 for a site licence, is MUSE; this is suitable for simple copy typing and copy editing. While the main users of MUSE at the OU are secretaries, many authors who use a mainframe computer for other purposes tend to use more powerful extensible programs such as MIT's EMACS (which may be supplied free to educational establishments). With EMACS, you can view and edit more than one document, or more than one part of a document, at once.

## More applications of word processing

At the time of writing, the majority of word processors in distance teaching establishments are used by secretaries and clerical staff for administration and for copy typing. As we see below, designers and editors who are based outside the UK do already make use of this technology, as do authors outside distance teaching. The time savings for those non-secretarial users can be immense. Further time and financial savings could result from adopting an integrated course production system containing the equipment described earlier. In such an integrated system:

- first drafts could be typed by authors, possibly at home, or typed by secretaries from handwritten drafts or audio tapes;

- redrafts could be produced by authors with the help of secretaries and editors;

- final drafts, whether intended to be camera-ready or printed, could be merged with computer-processed artwork and made ready for reproduction without the need to rekey the text or to paste-up illustrations;

- in addition to conventional long-run printing, single copies of the course material could be printed on demand in various formats, if a laser xerographic printer were incorporated;

- essential administrative tasks could run in parallel (such as arranging for circulation of drafts to all involved in producing a course and also to external assessors of the course; and monitoring the length and stage of readiness of drafts, for such purposes as course costing and allocating designers and editors to a course).

A fully-integrated, computer-aided course production system is technically feasible and could offer significant recurrent cost savings compared to current labour-intensive methods of producing courses. Those savings could not be achieved without staff cooperation, since the implementation of a fully-integrated system in an existing institution would affect the work practices of most staff and hence the staffing levels.

As an indication of what has been achieved outside distance education with components of such a system, US Navy staff (Braby and Kincaid, 1981) found that it took just $2\frac{1}{2}$ hours of an author's time to produce 154 pages of typeset training material, rather than the man-weeks that would be required with a conventional system. The material was fairly stereotyped, but its redundancy was not much higher than in some components of OU courses (for example, parts of computer-marked assessment material and guides for using OU computers, outside library facilities or OU home experiment kits). The US Navy material took the form of self-study pocket booklets aimed at mastery learning of weather symbols and their definitions. Each part of each booklet had:

- an introduction with the learning objective and a discussion of why students had to know the information;

- a criterion test;

- a description of the organisation of the material in relation to the learning objective;

- directions for study, presentation of the symbols and their definitions with memory aids, practice exercises with the new symbols and with previous ones, a self-test and criterion tests;

- reinforcing statements and study suggestions;

- an index.

The US Navy has found it worthwhile to use their computer-based authoring system for increasingly complex tasks, such as producing self-study manuals on the procedures involved in operating and maintaining particular kinds of equipment. One interesting feature of their system is that it can help increase the readability of the teaching material. Their programs can quickly flag and suggest replacements for passive constructions, long sentences and sentences containing uncommon or overused words or phrases, as well as misspellings. Similar programs have since become available on mainframe and microcomputers which use Bell Laboratories' UNIX computer operating system (Thomas and Yates, 1982). For example, at Athabasca University they use UNIX on a large minicomputer (a Digital Equipment VAX 11/780) connected to a Linotron 202 phototypesetter. Such a configuration can be used by many people at once but costs well over £50,000. A single-user UNIX system such as the Fortune microcomputer could cost between £5,000 and £8,000 and could also be connected to a phototypesetter.

A simple example of the way in which a UNIX-based system can save time and money is the task of checking deviations from a house style on spelling, the use of quotations and the style of citations. At Athabasca, an editor can use a UNIX program to check a course-length (250,000 word) corpus for consistency and correct any spelling variants in less than 30 minutes. Further savings are possible at the design stage, where staff can dispense with a final proof of most manuscripts in paste-up, before printing. With older technology, other institutions find that final proof stage is essential, although it is a laborious step in producing printed copy. It is technically possible to use a computer to process the parts of manuscripts which have visuals and complex tables, but Athabasca find that it is currently cheaper and easier to retain the final proof stage for such items, which they deal with by hand.

Conclusions

Using dedicated word processors just for copy typing and for input to typesetting equipment can save time and money. Further savings can result if microcomputers with word processing programs are made available to all staff in their normal place of work (which may be at home, for some) and if it is possible to send material freely between those machines and word processors.

References

BRABY, R. & KINCAID, J.P. (1981) "Computer-aided Authoring and Editing." Journal of Educational Technology Systems, Volume 10(2), 109-124.

COWPER, D.W. & THOMPSON J.R. (1982) "Text Processing: the revolution in word manipulation," in J.S. DANIEL, M.A. STROUD & J.R. THOMPSON (eds.), Learning at a Distance: a world perspective, Athabasca University & International Council for Correspondence Education.

EDEN, C. (1982) COPE User Guide. Bath School of Management, University of Bath.

FLUEGELMAN, A. & HEWES, J.J. (1983) Writing in the Computer Age: Wordprocessing skills and style for every writer. London: Century Publishing.

HUDSON, P. (1981) "Word Processing Applications," in Word

Processing: selection, implementation and usage into the 80s. Northwood, Middx.: Online Publications.

NAIMAN, A. (1983) Word Processing Buyer's Guide. Peterborough, N.H.: BYTE & McGraw Hill.

OAKESHOTT, P. & MEADOWS, J. (1981) The current use of word processors by British Publishers. Leicester: Primary Communications Research Centre, University of Leicester.

THOMAS, R. & YATES, J. (1982) A User Guide to the UNIX System. Berkeley: Osborne/McGraw-Hill.

## 3.    BROADCAST TELEVISION

Tony Bates
Reader in Media Research Methods, Open University

### Broadcast Television in Distance Education:    A World-Wide Perspective

If you thought that broadcasting and distance education are synonymous, you would be wrong. By any generally agreed definition of a distance education system, the organised provision of two-way communication between student and tutors is an essential feature of distance education (see for instance Keegan, 1980). Many educational broadcasting initiatives do not include such provision; many distance-education systems that do have two-way communications do not use broadcasting. Thus, of the 14 autonomous open universities operational in 1982, only two made use of more than five hours a week of "through the air" terrestrial transmission (the British Open University, with 35 hours a week, and the Chinese Central Television University, with 32 hours a week). Another two (Téléuniversité and Athabasca University in Canada), made use of between 9 and 12 hours a week, but nearly all on cable. The other 10 made no or minimal use of broadcast television.

Even in the U.S.A. where local forms of broadcasting are more prevalent, the use of television for off-campus teaching is not common. Lewis (1983) found in a nationwide survey that only 21 colleges, a further 9 consortia of colleges, and five broadcast stations offered post-secondary distance education via broadcast television, and even some of these projects did not provide organised two-way communication.

One reason for the low use of broadcast television by distance teaching institutions is the relatively small number of enrolled students for any particular course. Only six of the 14 autonomous distance teaching universities for instance had more than 50,000 students in total. Even at the Open University, no course with television has more than 7,000 students, and two-thirds of the 127 courses have less than 500 students. It is difficult to convince managers of national broadcasting organisations of the need for good quality transmission times for such small numbers, no matter how crucial a teaching role the broadcasts may play.

It is not surprising then that in most countries broadcasting tends to be used more for "stand-alone" or "broadcast-led" continuing education, rather than linked to an integrated, comprehensive distance teaching system. In this sense, the Open University is very much an exception, although in recent years there have been several interesting co-operative ventures, where broadcasting organisations and other agencies have combined to provide individual multi-media projects in which two-way communication has been provided by the non-broadcast agencies. Funkkolleg in West Germany, the "Take it Easy" and "Start" English-language courses in Sweden, and the adult literacy project in Britain, are good examples of such co-operative ventures (see Bates, in press, for a detailed discussion of the use of broadcasting in adult education).

## Educational Roles

When broadcast television is used in distance education, what are its appropriate educational roles? In the following discussion, it will be assumed that broadcasting is one of several media available to the course designer (another common feature of distance education). Secondly, it is important to distinguish between television as a means of encoding messages, and broadcasting as a means of delivering messages. In this chapter, I will concentrate on the broadcast aspects of television, using "through the air" terrestrial transmission. The unique characteristics of recorded television in video cassette and video-disc form, and the potential of satellite and cable distribution, will be dealt with in subsequent chapters.

There are three educational characteristics of all forms of television:

- distributional and access characteristics;

- student control aspects;

- structural and symbolic aspects.

For distance teaching, effective distribution and universal access to learning materials for all students is essential. Broadcasting still has distinct distributional advantages over other forms of television (cable, satellite, cassettes, discs). In many developed countries, almost every household can receive the through-the-air terrestrial transmissions of the national networks (in Britain the figure is 98%). Secondly, for the student the cost of broadcast distribution is free, since nearly every student will already have a television set. Even for the institution using broadcasting, transmission costs for national distribution can be very low. Broadcasting then is more consistent than other forms of video distribution with a policy of enabling all in the community who wish to benefit from home study to do so.

Universal access to broadcasting brings four major educational benefits to distance teaching systems:

(a)     the programmes can carry essential teaching material, since all students should be able to access the broadcasts;

(b)     broadcast programmes publicise the educational opportunities offered by a distance education system, hence boosting recruitment;

(c)     the programmes, by using the attractive and interesting forms of presentation common to television production, increase motivation and interest in students who are otherwise generally working in isolation;

(d)     they add to the cultural milieu by offering alternative programming for the general public.

However, these distributional advantages of broadcasting depend essentially on suitable transmission scheduling, so that programmes are available at times appropriate for these goals. The difficulty of obtaining transmission times that are suitable for distance education students is a major limitation of broadcasting.

The second educational characteristic of television is the extent of control it gives both students and teachers over the learning process. Compared with other forms of video distribution, broadcasting is very weak with regard to student control. Broadcasts are ephemeral, cannot be reviewed, are uninterruptable, and are presented at the same pace for all students. A student cannot reflect upon an idea or pursue a line of thought during a programme, without losing the thread of the programme itself. A student cannot go over the same material several times until it is understood.

With regard to teacher control, production of even educational programmes is mainly in the hands of professional broadcasters, because in most countries broadcasting is managed and operated by separate broadcasting organisations, and because high technology and professional skills are required to make broadcast programmes. While this professionalism helps to exploit the full potential of the unique presentational characteristics of television, it can also result in distancing the teacher from the design of programmes, with consequent problems of integration with other media. This can also be a problem with other forms of video production, but it tends to be more acute with broadcasting.

The third educational characteristic of television is the way it represents knowledge and presents meaning, through the symbol systems it uses and the way it structures meaning. Salomon (1979) discusses the differences between media in their use of different symbols to present or represent knowledge. He argues that television is a particularly rich medium, because it uses a wide variety of symbol systems - moving and still visuals, words, music, and increasingly text. All media, I believe, have two qualitatively different educational functions: to present knowledge and to develop skills in using that knowledge. Learners need knowledge to be presented in a variety of symbolic ways for "deep" understanding of a concept or an idea (see Bates, 1981 for a fuller discussion of this issue). At the same time, as Olson and Bruner (1975) have argued, while knowledge can be presented or represented through any medium, media differ in their facility to develop different intellectual skills in appropriately using and applying that knowledge.

The symbolic systems of television are common to all forms of television, whether broadcast, or on video-cassette or on video-disc. However, the way knowledge is structured can radically differ according to the format. At the moment, video-cassettes and even video-discs tend to be merely recorded versions of broadcast programmes, but it will be seen in the following chapters that moving to these new formats allows video material to be structured quite differently from broadcast television.

A broadcast programme tends to have a continuous seamless flow, to be a unity in itself, to be self-sufficient (even if integrated with other media). The structures common to broadcast television are to some extent inevitable, given the ephemeral nature of the medium. It is the only way a viewer could make sense of a single continuous viewing. At the same time, every broadcast television programme has to be interpreted by the learner, and this interpretation will vary considerably from learner to learner, because of the uninterruptable pace of a programme. It is essential for learners to construct their own meaning from the totality of the programme, and the scope for individual variation between learners is consequently greater with broadcast television than with most other media, due to the inherent structure of a broadcast programme. This has important implications for learning, as we shall see.

Secondly, the way knowledge is structured and presented is crucial to learning. The structure provided by the teacher, the text-book, or the television programme provides for the learner a model of the conceptual nature of the area of study. Furthermore, some forms of structure assist certain kinds of learning and thinking, and inhibit others. The structure of broadcast television programmes is commonly very different from that of a text-book. For instance, documentary-style case studies are a popular form of Open University broadcast. They tend to require a passive response, to be open-ended, neutral, loosely structured, and free-standing - the opposite of most OU correspondence texts. We have found students have great difficulty in using documentary programmes in the way intended (see Bates and Gallagher, 1977). However, such programmes have very important higher education objectives. They attempt to give students the opportunity to practice high-level learning skills, such as analysis, application of abstract principles to real-world situations, evaluation, and generalisation. Such programmes often provide the only chance, outside examination and assignment questions, for students to practice and develop such skills. The alternative is to regurgitate or condense the material given in the correspondence texts. Unfortunately, though, it seems that students need to be given much more guidance in how to approach documentary-style programmes, before they are able to use them to develop such skills.

The combination of educational characteristics commonly associated with broadcast television then suggests that educationally, broadcast television has the following general strengths and weaknesses:

| Good for: | Bad for: |
|---|---|
| Encouraging individual interpretations | Mastery learning |
| Stimulating creative thinking | Feedback/self-evaluation |
| Providing an overview or synthesis | Analysis (of processes or situations). |
| Narrative/story-telling | |
| Demonstrating continuous processes | Storage of information |
| Modelling learning processes | Reflection/deep processing |
| Raising awareness | Presentation of complex ideas |
| Developing skills of evaluation | Development of abstract thinking |

The specific value of broadcast television will vary according to the context in which it is used, but there is no doubt that it can provide distance learners with unique resource material. Complex or expensive experiments, field-visits, microscopic observation, advanced technical equipment, industrial processes, a wide range of social and interpersonal interaction, drama, archive film, classroom situations, and interviews with distinguished politicians, researchers and educators, are just some of the experiences that can be offered to students in their own homes through broadcast television. (For a fuller discussion of the educational strengths and weaknesses of broadcast television, see Bates, in press). What is clear is that for the learner, learning from broadcast television is a difficult process. Students will need a lot of skill in using broadcast television for educational purposes. The programmes themselves need to be structured in ways that help the development of such skills, but making programmes this way tends to be contrary to the production styles generally used in educational broadcasts.

## Production

It is very difficult to write about production because of the differences between various systems. In this sense, the Open University is unique because of its partnership with the BBC. There is a formal agreement between the Open University and the BBC. The BBC will supply the Open University with a minimum of 30 hours a week of television transmission time and approximately 240 television programmes a year (as well as radio and audio-cassette programmes). To do this, the BBC has set up a separate department, BBC/Open University Productions, employing about 400 staff. Purpose-built studios on the campus, costing £5million to construct and equip, were opened in 1981, and paid for by the Department of Education and Science, which also pays the full operational cost of the BBC's Open University activities. In 1983 this totalled about £10 million a year, approximately 15% of the total Open University budget.

BBC producers for Open University productions were specially recruited for their academic qualifications in the areas in which they will make programmes. Many were recruited as academics from other universities. They are full members of course teams, and are encouraged to play a full role in the overall design and development of a course, as well as being responsible for the production of the television and audio programmes. They make on average approximately four to six television programmes a year, plus a slightly larger number of audio programmes. Programmes are made to a high professional standard. Many are all-film programmes, shot on location in Britain or overseas. Others use sophisticated graphics, specially constructed studio models, visual effects or specially constructed experiments or laboratory work. Costume dramas are also sometimes produced for appropriate courses. In this way, broadcasts bring to students unique resource material which it would be impossible to provide in other ways for students studying at home.

The main problem facing course designers at the Open University is to ensure that programmes are integrated with the texts in such a way that students can perceive their relevance. Lack of relevance is the main criticism levelled by students against the programmes. In most cases, the programmes are relevant, but the essential links or bridges between programmes and text have not been made explicit, neither in the programmes themselves, nor in the texts. There are two reasons for this. Despite the producers' membership of course teams, the production process for broadcast television tends to be physically separate from that for the design of texts. Secondly, television production is often on a different time schedule from text production. Where the whole production process for both texts and television has been tightly integrated and reflected in the design of the teaching materials, including direct cross-referencing within the programmes and text, programmes are perceived by students as being more valuable (see Bates, 1982 for a wider discussion of the factors influencing successful use of broadcasting at the Open University.)

As already stated, the Open University/BBC relationship is unique. The Open University's system of television production should be compared with television production at the Chinese Central Television University. Programmes there are mainly lectures, often lasting 50 minutes, written out on a blackboard, at which the camera is pointed. In 1981, 10 producers were responsible for 30 hours a week of unedited production, although now strenuous efforts are being made to improve both technical facilities and the training of staff. Over 300,000 students, however, will be watching any single transmission (see McCormick, 1982, for more details of the Chinese Central Television University).

Most distance teaching institutions using broadcasting tend to use the television production facilities of a broadcasting organisation (see Bates, 1980). The resulting production costs, the dependency on another organisation, difficulties over transmission arrangements and in some cases the difficulty of access to broadcasting for students, are all reasons why these other distance teaching institutions have not made greater use of broadcasting.

Distribution

The average life of an Open University course is about eight years. Allowing for some re-makes and non-course production, it can be seen that in any one year, there will be approximately 1600 progammes to be transmitted (200 x 8). If every 25 minute programme was to be repeated, (i.e shown twice in the same year), this would require over 40 hours a week transmission time, over a 32 week academic year. Course life is a crucial factor in determining the amount of transmission time needed, if the programmes are to last the life of a course (as they must do if they are integrated). Studies by Bates (1975), Gallagher (1977), and Grundin (1980), have shown that repeats are essential for high viewing figures, since there will always be a substantial proportion of students who cannot watch at any single time. With the programme repeated in a different time band, more than 90% of students can watch one of the two transmissions if the two times are of good quality. It will be seen that with only 35 hours a week transmission time, repeats have had to be dropped for many programmes.

High viewing figures though are also dependent on the quality of the transmission times. In 1974, the average Open University viewing figure was 64%. This can be interpreted in two ways: on any course, an average student would watch about two-thirds of the programmes on a course; or for any single transmission, about two-thirds of the students on that course would be watching (Bates, 1975). This average viewing figure on transmission has dropped from 64% in 1974 to 51% in 1982. Thus in 1982, only half the students were watching on transmission, on average (Grundin, 1983). The research indicates quite clearly that the loss was not due to a drop in the quality of the programmes themselves, but to a steady deterioration in the quality of times offered by the BBC over the eight years. (The agreement with the BBC specifies the amount but not the quality of the times it will provide). In particular, the loss of the early evening slots (5.30 p.m. to 7.30 p.m.) has been critical. These losses of quality transmission time have been due mainly to a need felt by BBC management to respond to competition from new services such as Channel 4. As we shall see in the next chapter, the deterioration in viewing on transmission has been largely compensated for by an increase in viewing on cassette - but at a high financial cost for the Open University.

The lesson here is clear for any distance teaching institution wishing to use broadcasting in a central teaching role: it must obtain agreement for quality transmission times guaranteed for the life of the course, in sufficient quantity for each programme to be broadcast twice in the same year.

Costs

Nowhere is there greater variety between distance education systems than in the way broadcasting is costed. In a survey of 12 distance education systems carried out for the International Institute of Educational Planning (Bates, 1981), every conceivable method of costing was found.

One or two distance education institutions are unfortunate enough to be charged market costs by a broadcasting organisation, i.e. what advertisers would pay per minute of transmission. More common is full or total costing. This means that the broadcasting organisation charges for all aspects of production, including overheads such as building and equipment depreciation, studio rental and maintenance, a contribution to a wide range of services, such as copyright, legal services, access to archives, and administration. Marginal costing is based on the extra costs incurred by a broadcasting organisation in the actual making of extra programmes for a distance teaching institution. In such cases, overheads and administrative costs are not usually included, but costs for "consumables" or additional actual expenditure, for actors, film stock, travel, graphics, etc., are charged. A free service was, not surprisingly, the least common cost basis in the 12 institutions surveyed.

These forms of costing are not discrete, nor are they applied consistently or logically. For instance, marginal costing is feasible and logical when spare capacity can be used to make extra programmes. Some services - perhaps a contract producer - may have to be specially provided, but most parts of the broadcast service could take on board the extra work. When, however, the demand for services is so great that a special department has to be set up solely to cater for the demand, then total costing makes sense. However, there are cases of total costing being used for marginal services. In one case, full production costs for the same programme is levied each year for the repeat of that same programme in subsequent years, so that over four years the distance teaching institution is paying four times the total production cost of the same programme

The important point is that it is usually the broadcasting organisation, often in a monopoly position, which sets both the principle of costing and the level of tariffs. Usually distance teaching institutions have little choice other than to decide to take the service or not, at the cost set by the broadcasters. It is extremely difficult for a distance teaching institution to know whether or not it is paying a "fair" price for the service, and it is even more difficult to know whether or not to increase or decrease the amount of broadcasting, because costs will not increase or decrease in a linear fashion. The nature of financial arrangements is a major reason why broadcasting is not used more by distance teaching institutions. They are dependent on another organisation, and the costing procedures are often outside their control.

Because of the variety of costing procedures, it is difficult to generalise from one institution to another. In giving figures for the Open University, it should be borne in mind that the arrangement is based on a total cost principle for production. This means that the grant from the Government to the University for BBC costs covers the full cost of a separate department, building and services devoted solely to Open University productions and transmissions, and includes contributions to services supplied to the University from other departments in the BBC. Thus the cost of the BBC service to the University in no way impinges on the revenue raised through the licensing system. At the same time, the BBC does not gain financially from the revenues, in the sense of being able to use any of the University grant for other purposes. The University also has to pay value added tax of 15% on the BBC bill. All costs given below include VAT costs.

The total cost of a 25 minute Open University broadcast television programme averages around £35,000. This figure is obtained by deducting transmission and audio production costs from the overall figure of £10 million and dividing this figure by the number of television programmes produced each year (around 240). However, this is the total cost. The marginal cost of producing extra programmes beyond this basic figure is between £6,000 - £10,000, dependent on the nature of the production and whether or not extra staff have to be hired. Since the non-graduate, continuing education programme of the Open University has to be self-financing, their programmes are considered as extra productions, and are charged at marginal cost, because they provide extra income. It should be noted that reducing the number of programmes produced each year would save no more than £6,000 per programme, but would considerably increase the average programme cost.

Like most other higher education institutions in Britain, the Open University has had to make substantial savings in the last couple of years. With regard to broadcasting, it has adopted two major policies: it has set an annual cash limit for the BBC, i.e. an annual expenditure which must not be exceeded; and it has encouraged the BBC to make use of spare production capacity for other than Open University productions on a marginal cost basis as a means of increasing revenue which can be set off against overheads. These policies in fact have enabled production levels to be maintained and in some ways even increased.

Transmission of Open University programmes is charged largely on a marginal cost principle, since the network, the equipment, the transmitters and the maintenance are already there and needed for the general service. The Open University programmes are basically added on to the "ends" of the normal transmission schedule. This means that for the Open University, national transmission costs are very low, approximately £250 for one transmission of each television programme.

The Future

Broadcasting is still potentially the most effective way of distributing audio-visual learning materials to distance education students. It costs the students nothing to receive the programmes, all students can be reached through broadcasting, and it can cost the institution very little in terms of transmission charges. There are several valuable educational functions that are best served through broadcast television.

Unfortunately, though, the production cost of broadcasting tends to be high, and as a medium for instruction, broadcasting on balance is less effective than video-cassettes and is unsuitable for a number of educational functions. Above all, programmes need to be broadcast at suitable times for adult learners, but given the often low numbers in the target group, it is difficult for a broadcasting organisation to give such programming high priority against general service requirements.

Given this context, it appears that broadcasting can still provide a valuable service for distance education institutions, but it will need to be used very selectively. There will still be a need for a limited number of broadcast programmes made to be viewed as broadcasts. These programmes will have a dual task. As well as supporting students on courses with large enrolments, they will need to be comprehensible and of interest to a much wider public. This would have three benefits. Such programmes will enable a distance education institution to distribute audio-visual materials economically on courses with large numbers of students; such programmes will provide a shop-window and publicity for the institution, and hence stimulate recruitment; through their broader appeal, such programmes should be able to secure appropriate transmission times.

During this decade, despite the growth in access to video-cassette machines in the home, it will probably still be necessary for a distance education institution to broadcast most of its audio-visual materials, if the aim is for most students to be able to use such material. Those students fortunate enough to have machines can record off-air, but for those without machines - perhaps a majority - transmission will still be necessary at times when students can watch, although for many courses these may be at inconvenient times (e.g. betwen 6.00 a.m. and 8.00 a.m. and/or late at night). Such programmes would still then have to be made in a broadcast format.

By the end of the decade, one could expect most people to have video-cassette machines. Most programmes could then be made in a video-cassette format. Even then, it is likely to be more economical to broadcast such material for recording at home. Since, however, no-one will be expected to view these programmes as broadcasts, they can be broadcast at night-time, using the automatic timing provided on video-cassette machines, and made in a production format that can exploit the features of video-cassette use.

There are substantial educational benefits for distance learners in using television, particularly in a recorded format. However, getting the balance right between broadcast and non-broadcast production and distribution will be difficult over the next few years. It will be particularly important to monitor closely equipment ownership patterns, and utilisation patterns for broadcast and non-broadcast audio-visual media. A "mixed" strategy, regarding both production and distribution, will be necessary, gradually moving from broadcast to non-broadcast audio-visual media. Even then, some broadcasting will continue to be valuable, mainly for recruitment and publicity, but also as a low-cost distribution method for courses with large student numbers.

References and additional reading

BATES,A.W. (1975)  Student Use of Open University Broadcasting Milton Keynes: Open Univeristy (mimeo).

BATES, A.W. (1980)  The Planning and Management of Audio-Visual Media in Distance Learning Institutions.  Paris:  International Institute for Educational Planning.

BATES, A.W. (1981)  "Some unique characteristics of television and some implications for teaching and learning".  Journal of educational Television, Vol 7, No.3.

BATES, A.W. (1983)  "Adults learning from audio-visual media" in Howe, M. (ed.) Learning from Television. London:  Academic Press.

BATES, A.W. (in press) Broadcasting in Education.  London; Constables.

BATES, A.W and GALLAGHER, M. (1977) Improving the Effectiveness of Open University Television Case Studies.  Milton Keynes: Open University (mimeo).

GALLAGHER, M. (1977) Broadcasting and the Open University Student.  Milton Keynes: Open University (mimeo).

GRUNDIN, H. (1980) Audio-Visual and Other Media in 91 Open University Courses: The Results of the 1979 Undergraduate Survey. Milton Keynes: Open University (mimeo).

GRUNDIN, H. (1983) The 1982 Media Survey.  Milton Keynes: Open University (mimeo).

KEEGAN, D. (1980) "On defining distance education" <u>Distance Education,</u> Vol 1, No. 1

LEWIS, R. (1983) <u>Meeting Learners' Needs Through Telecommunications: A Directory and Guide to Programmes.</u> Washington, D.C.: American Association of Higher Education

McCORMICK, R. (1982) "Central Broadcasting and Television University, Peoples Republic of China" in RUMBLE, G. and HARRY, K. (EDS.) <u>The Distance Teaching Universities.</u> London: Croom Helm

OLSON, D. and BRUNER, J. (1974) "Learning through experience and learning through media" in OLSON, D. (ed.) <u>Media and Symbols: The Forms of Expression:</u> Chicago: University of Chicago Press.

SALOMON, G. (1979) <u>The Interaction of Media, Cognition and Learning. London: Jossey Bass.</u>

WENHAM, B. (ed) (1983), <u>The Third Age of Broadcasting.</u> London: Faber & Faber.

# 4. VIDEO-CASSETTES

Stephen Brown
Course Manager, Technology Faculty, The Open University.

## Introduction

Video cassettes are a comparatively recent and still evolving educational medium. This chapter compares the educational advantages and disadvantages of the new medium for distance education with those of its parent - broadcast television. It examines the availability of video cassette technology and discusses likely further developments in its educational use. Throughout it draws upon examples of Open University experience to illustrate how the medium can be used.

## Video-Cassettes as television

The most obvious features of video cassettes are that they are <u>like</u> broadcast television in as much as they combine moving pictures with sound but <u>unlike</u> television in that they can be viewed in ways which are independent of pre-determined transmission times. In discussing the educational advantages and disadvantages of video cassettes it is useful to be able to compare and contrast them with the more familiar broadcast medium which they resemble.

In a distance teaching institution such as the Open University, and in many face to face situations that are subject to limited resources, there is an obvious educational role for television. As already mentioned in Chapter 3, television can be used to provide the student with experiences that would otherwise be inaccessible. In all, 22 different educational functions of this kind have been identified among bids for resources to make Open University television programmes (see Bates, in press, for details). The educational advantages of such television programmes can be summarised as involvement, dramatic impact, dynamic properties and rich symbolic content. These advantages apply equally to cassette recordings of broadcast television programmes or to video-cassettes made ab initio for use as cassettes.

Video-cassettes though, have the advantage over broadcasting of increased student control of the medium. Not only can the student watch when she wants but as often and with as many pauses or partial replays as necessary. The mass media aspect of broadcast television makes it difficult to design programmes which are appropriate for the wide range of skills and ability which are common in many student groups. Inevitably, there will be members of the target audience who find the pace too fast or too slow. The more flexible control characteristics of video-cassettes allow students to adjust the pace of the material to an individually appropriate level by replaying sections that move too quickly or by skimming forward over sections that are too slow.

## Video-cassettes as a back-up to broadcasting

At the time of writing (1983) video-cassettes are a high growth industry. Sales of video-cassette players in the U.K. are doubling annually and video cassette hire shops are proliferating across the country. In April 1982 226,000 video-cassette players were imported into the U.K.; by October of the same year the figure was over 250,000 according to Broadcasters' Audience Research Board figures (Guardian 1983). In March 1983 21 per cent of the U.K. population owned or rented a video-cassette recorder according to estimates by the BBC Audience Research Department (BBC 1983). This compares with 20 per cent of Open University undergraduates with home access (November, 1982) and a further 22% with convenient access elsewhere. Thus, in 1982 42% of OU students had convenient access to video-cassette recorders. It is expected that 50% of all households in Britain will have a VCR machine by 1986 (Screen Digest, 1983).

There are three major formats of video-cassette currently available. The most popular format for domestic purposes in Britain is VHS, or Video Home System. In 1982 VHS machines accounted for approximately 60% of machines in domestic use; the second major format, Betamax, accounted for 30%; the remaining 10% were mainly the obsolescent Philips 1500 series. Another major format is U-Matic, but this is concentrated in the commercial rather than the domestic market. These formats are not interchangeable and in a rapidly developing market it is difficult to predict which format, if any, will eventually provide a standard. Philips have recently introduced yet another new series (V2000) and a compact tape cassette format has been developed (8mm) although it is not yet widely marketed. Finally, new videodisc technology may eventually replace video-cassettes, at least for educational purposes (see chapter 6).

In such a fluid situation it would be rash to make predictions about the general level of availability of video-cassette replay equipment or the costs of distributing appropriate format cassettes of educational material. Instead I shall discuss the experience gained at the Open University through the operation of a pilot Video Cassette Loan Service, looking first at the availability of replay equipment, then at alternative cassette distribution methods.

In 1982 the Open University provided a pilot Video Cassette Loan Service for students on selected courses in response to deteriorations in the transmission times available for Open University television broadcasts (see chapter 3). Cassette copies of programmes on 37 courses (439 different programmes) were made available on a mail order basis to the students studying those courses in 1982 (12,400 students). Each student could borrow up to two cassettes per course at a time, for up to four weeks per cassette. The service, which was provided free of charge to students, was intended as a supplement to the single broadcast slot assigned to each of the programmes on the 37 selected courses. In other words, the cassette loan scheme was used to replace the repeat broadcast transmissions which had been lost due to lack of adequate transmission time. In addition to supplying cassette copies of programmes, the University made available a national network of 311 video-cassette players throughout the U.K. in a variety of different locations, including Further Education colleges, public libraries and Open University regional offices, for those students who did not have convenient access to video-cassette players elsewhere. Of these machines, 243 were rented by the University, at an annual cost of £77,582, including a television set for each player, insurance and TV licences. The remainder of the replay equipment was made available free of charge by friendly institutions. In fact, the replay equipment provided by the University was considerably under used, being regarded as among the least convenient of all the equipment available by those students who used the service (Brown, 1983).

The method of distribution was essentially a mail-order loan system, one programme per cassette. In practice ten VHS copies at a time were generally made of each programme from a U-matic sub-master and then drawn off the shelf to meet requests until all ten were gone, then another ten would be made. Returned cassettes were banked for future use instead of being wiped and re-recorded. This minimised the total amount of copying involved but it maximised the cassette stock and storage capacity required to operate the service. In all, approximately 20,000 E30 cassettes were purchased to meet an estimated demand of 20,000 cassette requests. Although overall demand was somewhat less (16,000 requests in total) the implicit assumption that each cassette would be used only once a year turned out to be correct. Less than one per cent of all cassettes were despatched more than once. The total cost of the scheme, including equipment costs, salaries for the two staff members involved, cassette postage and packing costs, was £183,300 during 1982.

The results of the pilot scheme (Brown 1983) confirm earlier, smaller scale experiments of a similar kind (Marshall and Gallagher 1974; Dickinson 1980). Even though the service was provided as a supplement to programme transmissions and even though only VHS format cassettes were provided, there was a significant demand for cassettes. Nearly 6,000 cassettes were requested by students on the courses within the scheme during the 1982 academic year, February to October inclusive. The service increased the overall viewing rates for included programmes by 16 per cent over the previous year. Moreover, there was a significant difference between the viewing rates of students who borrowed cassettes and those who did not. Of those students who did not borrow cassettes, 50 per cent watched each of the programmes on their course on average. The comparable viewing figure for students who did borrow cassettes was 75 per cent. In other words, simply making television programmes available as video-cassettes as well as single broadcasts resulted in a large increase in the viewing rates for those programmes. In fact, the viewing figures for programmes with cassette back-up were better than those typically achieved when repeats were available. So, at the Open University cassettes are already more effective than repeats in increasing the viewing rate.

When asked, students gave three main reasons for borrowing cassettes through the Video Cassette Loan Service: access, control and level. They took advantage of the flexibility of cassettes to study the programmes at times convenient to them and in phase with their own study patterns. They were able to view the programmes as often as they liked (a majority viewed each cassette at least twice), to interrupt, and to take notes. They were able to adjust the pace of the programmes to suit their own needs as necessary (on their first viewing, on average, two thirds of students watched the programme through non-stop, whereas on subsequent viewings only a third did so).

These findings show, therefore, that even where access is limited to a single format there are considerable educational advantages to be gained from transferring broadcast television material to video-cassettes. These advantages are both quantitative in terms of the effects on programme viewing rates and qualitative in terms of the way students were able to respond to the material. It is interesting to note in this context that of those students who watched programmes as cassettes, 61 per cent rated them as helpful or very helpful, compared with 46 per cent of those who viewed them as broadcasts.

The service has only just entered its second year of operation and it would be dangerous therefore to generalise too much from its performance so far. However, two trends are readily discernible. Even if new courses are added to it (as they have been in 1983) the service will tend to move from being a cassette copying operation to a cassette library. That is, there will be progressively less cassette copying to meet specific demands for programmes as the amount of ready recorded stock accumulates. Secondly, as more courses are added to the scheme so demand will grow. In 1983 the number of courses in the scheme was increased from 37 to 84 and in the first two months of 1983 demand was more than twice that of the previous year.

These trends may tend to push the service in two different directions simultaneously. For courses with large populations it may make better economic sense to broadcast programmes for recording off-air. This will not be a feasible option for some years to come however, as access to replay equipment is much higher than access to recording facilities. A student who can borrow a machine at work for half an hour is likely to find it more difficult to use it for recording as this generally means monopolising it for quite long periods. A more likely scenario in the short-term is for the University to mail two-hour video-cassettes with other course material to students on low population courses. The cassettes would be returned at the end of the course and reissued the following year. This would result in substantial savings for courses with less than 300 students, because the savings on transmission costs will be greater than the costs of physical distribution.

## Video-cassettes as video-cassettes

Transferring television broadcasts to video-cassettes is the simplest use of the new medium and possibly the least effective. Video-cassette copies of broadcasts may alleviate the more obvious disadvantages of the latter, i.e. problems of access, control and level, but they retain features which are characteristic of the broadcast medium and which are unsatisfactory in an educational context. It has been suggested (Gallagher, 1978) that good television in a general service broadcasting context may not be the same as good practice in an educational context. Paradoxically, some of the qualities of television which make it appealing to educators can be counterproductive. The richness of the medium, which derives from the dynamic combination of sound and vision means that a particular programme may be interpreted in a wide range of different ways. This can be advantageous when it permits students of differing levels of ability and background to derive different levels of meaning for themselves. Research has shown however, that students commonly lack the interpretive skills required to derive the intended messages or achieve the intended learning goals of television programmes (Bates and Gallagher 1977, Brown 1981).

What happens instead is that students tend to follow the story line of a programme and concentrate on the factual content rather than attempt to analyse the relationships or underlying messages contained within it. For instance, in the case of a programme which was intended to exemplify a novel approach to house design based on careful analysis of living requirements, materials properties and energy sources, most students thought the programme was about a man and his family who lived in a strange dome-shaped house. They queried the relevance of such a programme even though its conceptual framework was based directly on a set of principles taught in a related text that they had read already (Brown 1980).

This problem is least noticeable in the case of didactic, highly structured and neutral programmes such as laboratory demonstrations where the aims of the programme are explicit, clearly related to the texts, reflected in the structure of the programme itself and where there is no emotional content. It is most acute in the case of documentary style programmes where the material tends to be less structured, more emotive and less explicit in its meaning. In the first type of programme the content very often is the message, e.g. this is how to carry out a titration or this is what we mean by stress and strain in a material. In the second type the content is usually presented as semi-raw material for the student to process in an analytical way. Recent research suggests that students have similar problems even with video-cassette material (Durbridge 1982). In other words, transfer of broadcast material to video-cassette is a necessary but not sufficient condition to enable students to learn more effectively from television.

The majority of Open University television programmes require students to employ relatively high level cognitive skills of analysis and synthesis in the sense defined by Bloom (1956). As we have seen, such skills are not widely distributed throughout the undergraduate population.

Cognitive abilities can be enhanced by appropriate design of video-cassette material itself. In 1982 the Open University launched its first course to employ television programmes designed for use primarily as video-cassettes. Developing Mathematical Thinking (EM235) was a course for school teachers. The programmes contain video sequences of children and their teachers tackling mathematical problems in the classroom. Their main aim is to provide primary source material which the course team later draws upon and uses to analyse and exemplify pedagogical theory and principles.

Although broadcast, EM235 programmes were intended to be viewed as video-cassettes and their design reflects this. Firstly, each programme is divided into short video sequences ranging from two to six minutes in duration. At the end of each sequence students are directed to stop and take notes on, or discuss, what they have seen and heard. Secondly, the programmes are highly integrated, physically and conceptually, with the rest of the course. The course texts are divided into discrete study sessions. Each session explicitly draws upon specific video sequences to develop and illustrate some aspect of educational theory or practice. There are notes which summarise the contents and focus of each of the programmes followed by separate pages of activities for each sequence, including space for comments, mnemonic stills from the sequences, suggested study times for each activity, and reminders to take tape counter readings which serve as implicit invitations to replay and pause where necessary. The crucial differences between these and more conventional broadcast notes for television programmes are their obvious connections with the rest of the course and the way they encourage students to interact with the video material; to respond actively and thinkingly to it both during and after each programme. A number of important findings have emerged from an evaluation study of this course (Durbridge 1982) with respect to the design of educational video-cassettes.

Few students were "video conscious" in the sense that they differentiated between broadcast television and video-cassettes, even when they viewed EM235 programmes on video-cassette only. Video and broadcasting were seen as sharing the same characteristics. Many students though were "video conscious" in the sense that they found its technology inconvenient to use.

Few students manifested "visual awareness" at the time of viewing. That is to say, attempts to note down or comment upon events displayed visually were rare. Most students appeared to focus on the audio track of video sequences. It seems probable that much detailed visual information was lost. Despite the lack of immediate and overt awareness of visual detail, though, students showed good long-term recall of events and characters seen on screen. The mnemonic stills proved effective stimuli in this respect, although less effective at aiding recall of the sound track. There was one noticeable exception to students' aural awareness. Some of the video sequences used a standard "voice-over" technique to direct students attention during the video sequences. These were rarely noticed by students or if noticed ignored or rejected. Students' comments revealed that when they were conscious of voice-over interjections they found them distracting.

Although the programmes were intended to be viewed by groups of students and followed by discussions, roughly half the students viewed as individuals. In most instances, convenience dictated or guided students' choice in this respect, although a small minority expressed a positive preference towards an individual mode of study. There were differences in the way students responded to programmes depending on whether they viewed as individuals or in groups. Overall, the programmes were very successful in stimulating a high degree of involvement, interaction and analysis, particularly in the case of students who viewed in groups.

The conclusion which emerges clearly from these findings is that it is possible to design educational video materials which use the characteristics of the cassette medium in ways which are more effective than simply recording television broadcasts on cassettes. The distinguishing characteristics of such materials are their high degree of integration with other course materials and the high level of student/video and student/student interaction they encourage. Before going on to consider the alternatives of designing video-cassettes for individual or group use, there are a few negative findings from the EM235 study which deserve comment.

The failure of voice-over comments confirms suspicions derived from earlier research (Brown 1981) that the use of voice-over is not especially appropriate to educational television. In general service broadcasting voice-over is commonly used to provide a narrative link between programme components to ensure a smooth flow, even where there is little real connection between the two sequences thus linked. A good commentary for a general service broadcast is thus often one which blurs the joins between different sequences within a programme. Such links are rarely memorable. If the viewer responds casually to voice-overs in general service broadcasts there is usually little lost, but in an educational programme the consequences may be more critical. In educational programmes voice-overs are often used in a quite different way. They frequently serve as cognitive organisers, to summarise what has gone just before, to prepare the viewer for what is to come or to provoke some response from the viewer through questions. It may be, therefore, that "presenter to camera" shots or graphics and typography to reinforce the sound track would be more effective than the more subtle broadcasting technique of a "voice-over". Alternatively, where voice-overs consist of questions, Durbridge encourages authors to think very carefully about how students are to respond to them and to avoid them unless they are absolutely necessary. This recommendation is based on the finding that EM235 students found the specificity of voice-over questions in direct conflict with the more general discussion topics posed in the video notes. Consequently, they were unsure as to the appropriate way of responding to the video sequences.

The two findings related to "video consciousness" suggest that notes and video sequences which explicitly encourage students to take advantage of the interactive potential of video-cassettes would be an advantage, as would suitable equipment. Durbridge recommended the provision of smaller television sets and hand-held remote controls for cassette players to encourage a feeling of personal control and intimacy with the equipment. Lack of visual awareness is a common phenomenon in a heavily literate society (Masterman 1980) but students (and teachers) can be encouraged to develop their visual skills through creative use of the video medium and through activities designed to focus their attention on the visual aspects of the material.

## Individual vs group use

The EM235 study revealed several important differences between the ways in which students responded to video-cassettes, depending on whether they viewed as individuals or in groups. The cassettes were designed primarily for group use. At the end of each video sequence there was a voice-over question which often led to considerable discussion among groups of viewers. The notes on each sequence usually contained guidance on what to look out for during the video plus a more general discussion topic. Again, in groups, the discussion topic usually stimulated a lengthy debate ranging over many issues broadly related to the course. The guidance notes on what to look out for in the video sequences, especially those which recommended note taking, were regarded as helpful by some students but tended to focus attention on recording factual detail at the expense of observation and analysis of overall relationships.

This was particularly so in the case of individual viewers. These students were unable to obtain support and guidance from colleagues in relation to the discussion topics and were consequently more concerned with finding the "right" answers to what were intended to be open-ended questions. They tended to concentrate their attention therefore on obtaining an accurate factual record of what occurred in the video sequences. That is, they tended to concentrate on recording what happened and less on discussing why it happened or what its implications might be. The discussion questions left these students uncertain and it was recommended that video notes for individual students should contain more guidance and feedback on the kinds of responses expected. (Interestingly the device of recommending a particular study time for each activity was counter productive. Generally, students spent either far more or far less time than that recommended.)

These findings raise an important issue with respect to the design of video cassettes: should cassettes be designed primarily for group or for individual use or is a compromise possible? In the case of

EM235, group use was clearly more profitable. Interactions between students and the video were minimised while those between students were maximised. Thus, the video was used as a stimulus rather than a teaching vehicle. The students probably learned as much from each other as from the programme itself. Individual students on the other hand had to rely entirely on their own ability plus the video. It is interesting that individuals made much greater use of the pause and rewind facilities on their cassette players than did groups of students. To some extent this was probably due to the fact that it is easier for an individual to intervene than it is for groups. It was also a reflection of the individuals' preoccupation with factual accuracy and note-taking. Nevertheless, it is an important finding because it suggests that video-cassettes for individual use will result in more student/video interaction than those for groups and that the former should contain more feedback to the student on appropriate responses and performance than the latter. Moreover, these differences suggest that attempts to compromise will be counter-productive. Students working in groups will probably find frequent interaction disruptive and generous guidance and feedback too restrictive. Individual students are likely, as in the case of EM235, to find cassettes with minimal guidance, feedback and built-in interaction too open-ended.

These conclusions suggest two alternative directions of development for educational video-cassettes: highly student-interactive cassettes for individual use; and more open-ended stimulus material for group use.

## Future developments

Despite the recent innovation of video-discs it seems likely that video-cassettes will play an increasing role in distance education for some years to come, and in a number of ways. Firstly an increasing number of Open University programmes will be designed as cassettes rather than broadcasts. In 1982 one undergraduate and one non-degree course used cassettes in this way. During the production year 1983-84, a further 16 courses are planning to design programmes as video cassettes. There will almost certainly be an associated increase in the amount of integration between cassettes and other course components which in turn will affect students' attitudes to video-cassettes. A growing video consciousness and visual awareness may be the result. Another result may be an even more rapid decline in the use made of broadcast television programmes by both students and course teams as their limitations are highlighted by the new medium.

Two distinctive forms of video-cassette design seem likely to emerge. The first, for group use, will stress open-ended analysis and discussion with fellow students or tutors. An example of this form is tutored video instruction (TVI) devised at Stanford University, California in the early 1970's (Gibbons et al, 1977). TVI is a recorded live lecture replayed on video-cassette by a tutor to small groups of students (3 to 10 is best) with frequent interruptions for discussion of the points being made. The tutor's role is to stimulate discussion and tease out misunderstandings rather than to answer technical questions directly. Unresolved difficulties are referred to the lecturer herself, either by telephone during the tutorial or afterwards. The purpose of the recorded live lecture is to provide an entertaining and informative stimulus which can be used by the students watching to discuss new concepts or to interpret aspects of the world in new ways.

This example is similar to the use made of cassettes in EM235 in that it allows students to stop, interrupt and discuss the material as often and for as long as they wish, and in the way it encourages learning through the examination and exchange of ideas among the students themselves. Its main difference is the use of a conventional live lecture format rather than the case study approach used in EM235 and many other Open University courses.

A second form of video-cassette design will be for individual students and will be a move towards more interactive forms of video. These will be much more structured in their design, with frequent questions, guidance and feedback. At a simple level they could incorporate printed text with the video-cassette to form a fully integrated video package. A more sophisticated development would be a combination of video-cassette player plus microcomputer. In the Open University a pilot interactive video package which combines computer aided learning technology with existing television material has already been developed and will be tested in 1983 (see Laurillard, 1982). As student ownership of video-cassette players rises along with microcomputer ownership (currently 15% at the Open University) this development will become quite practical.

As more households acquire video-cassette recorders so new options for the distribution of cassette materials will open up. It will be possible to replace intermediate postal based distribution systems or local cassette libraries with either broadcast transmissions or cable transmissions for off-air recording. If this happens, then video-cassettes will once again resemble television but for reasons which are precisely the converse of those at present. Video-cassette material will be distributed in the same way as broadcast television but it will be very different in appearance.

## Conclusions

The educational potential of video-cassettes is very great and not just for distance teaching organisations. Video-cassettes which are designed to take full advantage of their potential seem likely to play an increasingly important role in the Open University in particular and education in general over the next ten years. Major outcomes of this will be increased video consciousness and visual awareness, and a more analytical and critical approach to television material.

## Acknowledgements

Thanks are due to Professor Sparkes for notes on TVI and to Nicola Durbridge for comments on the EM235 evaluation.

## References and additional reading

BATES, A.W. (1983)   'Adults Learning from television: The Open University experience.' in HOWE, M. (ed)   Learning from Television. London: Academic Press.

BATES, A.W. (in press)   Broadcasting in Education. London: Constables

BATES, A.W. and GALLAGHER, M. (1977)   Improving the use of case-study and documentary TV programmes at the Open University. Milton Keynes: The Open University. (Mimeo).

BBC (1982)   BBC Handbook 1983. London: British Broadcasting Corporation.

BLOOM, B.S. et al (1956)   Taxonomy of educational objectives. Handbook 1: Cognitive Domain. New York:   David McKay.

BROWN, S. (1980)   T101 "2+6" evaluation. Report on the broadcasts and cassette vision packages for Block 1 of the course. Milton Keynes:   The Open University. (Mimeo).

BROWN, S. (1981)   T101 "2+6" Evaluation: Final report on the use of audio-visual media in the first year of presentation. Milton Keynes: The Open University. (Mimeo).

BROWN, S. (1983)   The Open University 1982 Video Cassette Loan Service. Milton Keynes: The Open University. (Mimeo).

DICKINSON, R. (1980)   An evaluation of the use of video-cassette machines in the Regions. January 1979 to June 1980. Milton Keynes: The Open University. (Mimeo).

DURBRIDGE, N. (1982)  Real life film on video.  A case-study of video-cassette usage on EM235, Developing Mathematical Thinking.  Milton Keynes: The Open University. (Mimeo).

GALLAGHER, M. (1978)  "Good television and good teaching: some tensions in educational practice."  Educational Broadcasting International  Vol. 11, No. 4.

GIBBONS, J.F. et. al (1979)  "Tutored Video Instruction: A New Use of Electronics Media in Education".  Science, 195.

GRUNDIN, H.U. (1979)  Audio visual and other media in 91 Open University courses.  Milton Keynes: The Open University. (Mimeo).

GUARDIAN (1983)  TV's Missing Millions,  The Guardian: 11/2/83.

LAURILLARD, D. (1982)  'The Potential of Interactive Video' Journal of Educational Television Vol. 8 No. 3.

MASTERMAN, L. (1980)  Teaching about Television.  London: MacMillan Press.

MARSHALL, J. and GALLAGHER, M. (1974)  Video Cassette Recorder Project.  Milton Keynes: The Open University. (Mimeo).

MOSS, J.R. (1983)  Video: The Educational Challenge.  London: Croom Helm.

SCREEN DIGEST, (1983).  World Video Reports Compendium.  Screen Digest, May 1983.

# 5.   SATELLITE AND CABLE

Kathleen Forsythe
Executive Director, Knowledge Network, British Columbia, Canada.
(with comments on the European situation by Tony Bates)

## The European Situation

Satellites offer the prospects of universal television and radio
coverage within a country, and the easy exchange or "overspill" of
programmes from one country to another.   Where there is also
adequate terrestrial transmission, satellites can result in extra
channels for both television and radio.

However, in Western Europe, each country is limited by international
regulation to five direct broadcast satellite (DBS) channels.   In
addition there are several transponders available for TV transmission
on low-powered tele-communication satellites, suitable for reception
on larger antennas by cable TV companies, etc.   The availability and
feasibility of satellite channels for distance education will depend
very much on commercial and political decisions.   The first United
Kingdom domestic broadcast satellite (DBS) is to be launched in 1986.
The BBC are committed to providing two entertainment channels for
this satellite, and the Government has offered the Independent
Broadcasting Authority the option of allocating two more to
commercial television companies.   The likelihood of satellites being
available for distance education in Britain on an operational - rather
than an experimental - scale though seems pretty remote.   West
German and Japanese plans are more advanced, and Japan in
particular is keen to carry an educational channel on its satellite.

Cable offers the possibility of a major expansion in the channels
available (up to 100).   Such an expansion could make more time
available for educational programmes at more convenient times, allow
"narrowcasting" in the form of programmes directed at quite small
numbers, and possibly reach potential students that are inaccessible
by other means.   With fibre-optic or broadband cable, several
institutions or homes could have full two-way video and/or audio
communication.   Cable has obvious potential in distance education,

particularly for conventional or local colleges wishing to branch out into off-campus distance teaching.

However, in the United Kingdom, despite a government initiative to encourage the cabling of Britain, the growth of cable will depend very much on commercial viability. Educational institutions able to offer cable companies free programming and production may be able to get access to a channel. For instance, the Polytechnic of the South Bank in London is' preparing and producing education and community programmes for Visionhire, the owners of a cable network which passess 57,000 homes in South London (Jinkinson, 1983). However, cable growth in Britain is likely to be piecemeal and cautious, especially given the prior and continuing growth of video-cassette ownership and low-cost cassette rental in Britain. Furthermore, there is no guaranteed access to cable for educational purposes. Two-way video and audio communication is likely to be a long way off, as far as most households are concerned. Fibre-optic cabling will be initially much more expensive and a great risk commercially, although two-way communication with cable television to the home, and telephone links from the home to the television studio, is quite feasible in the short term.

Even in the U.S.A., in 1982 there were only 38 post-secondary distance education projects using cable television, and of these, only one (Berks Community TV, Reading, Pennsylvannia) was truly two-way, in the sense that individuals at all sites could be seen and heard by everyone (Lewis, 1983).

The extent that satellite and cable will be used for distance education will vary from country to country more than any other factor in distance education. U.S.A. and Canada have not yet been limited by international regulation in the number of satellite channels they can use, but because of the enormous land space shared by just these two countries - compared with the huddled masses of Europe - their channel-capacity will be far greater than in Britain, for example.

## The Technology

Communications satellites are now a well established part of the telecommunications infrastructure. They are used for communications over long distances, particularly where normal terrestrial signal transmission is difficult.

Almost all communications satellites (including all INTELSAT and TELESAT-CANADA vehicles) are geostationary, that is, their orbital period around the earth is precisely 24 hours, so they appear from earth to occupy a stationary position in the sky. The great advantage of a geostationary orbit is that earth station antennas do not have to track the satellite, but can instead be mounted in a fixed position.

There has been much discussion of direct satellite telecasting to the home with each house or apartment building equipped with a small, cheap TVRO (television receive only) terminal. However, TVRO's need to be marketed in hundreds of thousands before the unit cost can be brought down within reach of the consumers' pocket book, although the technology is already developed. Domestic satellite aerials, less than one metre wide, are expected to cost about £250 each in Britain, from 1986.

The greatest potential for public services and health though lies in the combination of satellite distribution and cable TV delivery systems. The advent of cable systems provides a leap from three or four television channels to ten times that number. We are then presented with a fundamental choice of what to do with all these channels. There has been a long history of cable television in the U.S.A. and Canada, largely due to the difficulties of home reception of broadcast television due to terrain and distance.

Thus, where political, geographical and financial conditions are right, satellite and cable can have enormous potential for education. The most advanced and exciting prospect in this respect is Knowledge Network, based in British Columbia, on the West coast of Canada, as can be seen from this account by Kathleen Forsythe, the Executive Director.

## Knowledge Network

Stellar music ... a panning shot of majestic mountains, glacial blue and white - magnificent and ethereal. "This is the Knowledge Network..." An upbeat voice announces the station as a stylized electronic tree of knowledge zooms in. Ironically, this image reminds one each time of the humanity behind this exciting satellite-delivered telecommunications network rather than the wonder of its technology.

The startling achievement of communications satellites make telecommunications almost independent of distance, for as the signal travels 35,800 kilometres up to a satellite and then back down again, it makes little difference whether the destination for the signal is a mile away or on the other side of the ocean. Satellites do make all the difference, however, to our ability to be immediately accessible to each other. Two important qualitative changes result from this:

- the cost of long distance communications virtually ceases as an impediment either to exercising organizational control or to consulting and working cooperatively over a distance; however, a new democracy of networking becomes necessary as senders and receivers find the way to work together;

- the technical impediments to widespread "swapping" of television programmes are largely removed. Geographic boundaries are also rendered irrelevant as the images of many cultures filter down like rain; consequently we must make conscious choices about what we will receive.

To complement this "open sky" concept, grass-roots networks of both people and distribution systems are being developed to find humane uses for this new technology. What is the potential for education of these new technologies and where is the human interface between the grass roots and the open sky?

"The difference between George Orwell's 1984 and a hypothetical participatory democracy with widespread sharing of political power lies in the question of who controls the sending and receiving of information in the society." (Parker, 1975).

Education is very much part of the humane vision of 1984, but this will be achieved only if the use of such communication systems is seen as part of a larger learning system that may well be a network of institutions.


## A Working Model

Using ANIK-C, the first space-shuttle-launched direct broadcast satellite, the province of British Columbia has innovated in providing a comprehensive model of how an existing educational system can be integrally linked by high technology carriers such as ANIK-C and the use of broadband cable and community cable television. Through provision of this "electronic highway" all educational agencies in British Columbia are able to be involved in "distance education", and a new hybrid learning system has emerged characterized by decentralized programme development and utilization, all centrally coordinated and electronically delivered (Forsythe, 1982).

British Columbia was one of the first widespread experimenters in using satellites for tele-education. The immense geographic size of B.C. (950,000 sq. km), its small dispersed population (2.7 million) and its bleak, mountainous terrain prohibited the development of a broadcast system using traditional technology. Because of the satellite's position above the earth, geography suddenly ceased to be the main obstacle to access. Every location within the satellite's footprint became equally accessible to the point of transmission.

British Columbia conducted the Satellite Tele-Education Project (STEP) using the Hermes satellite in 1977-78 and experimented with ANIK-B from 1979-80. In 1980, the Provincial Government of British Columbia created the Knowledge Network of the West as the province's Educational Communications Authority responsible for establishing a telecommunications network, using satellite and cable, and coordinating its use. In January, 1981, the Knowledge Network launched a public educational television service, with 98 hours a week of transmissions, as part of a provincial learning system. In January, 1983, when this service was transferred to ANIK-C, it became the first full public "DBS" service for education in the world.

Although satellite development and launching costs are in the millions of dollars, once the satellite is launched, the cost of access is determined by market competition. As the first commercial customer of Telesat Canada for use of ANIK-C, the Knowledge Network will pay C$975,000 (£500,000) in 1983. This is less than C$200 (£100) an hour for carriage of a broadcast quality signal 98 hours a week. (This compares with approximately £600 an hour for Open University "terrestrial" broadcasts - or £700,000 for 35 hours a week.)

In British Columbia, the satellite's signal is received by TVRO's (television receive only dishes). The dish aerials used to receive Knowledge Network's signals range between 1.8 and 3 metres in diameter, and cost between C$2000 and C$10,000 each. Over 95% of these dishes are linked to community cable systems. Thus, the television signal is receivable by 85% of the population. The terrain of British Columbia has meant that cable television is the normal way of receiving television by most home owners and 90% of the province has been cabled. Community cable operators were then able to erect powerful receivers to tune into broadcasts from both Canadian and U.S. stations. The advent of satellite has meant a multiplicity of new television signals and a regulatory nightmare. However, such a satellite and cable-television system should be seen as an attempt to provide as comprehensive a coverage by broadcast television signals as that available in countries such as Great Britain or other parts of North America where the geography of mountains is not as extreme. Since 1980, there has been a movement in British Columbia to provide more than the basic 12 entertainment television channels and to move into television and videotext services for specialist target groups as new tiers of channels are added. Knowledge Network is therefore one of the major outcomes of this policy.

The Knowledge Network also has established a broad-band closed-circuit cable system in the city of Vancouver. This broad-band coaxial system is a complex network which links three major post-secondary educational institutions, five medical teaching hospitals and a number of other sites. This system is capable of carrying over 40 two-way video and audio signals as well as a high speed data network. This system is also linked to the satellite system thus creating a very sophisticated electronic highway throughout British Columbia that can carry video, audio, data and video text signals (Hart, 1982).

## Functions of the New System

Knowledge Network is primarily a service organisation for the various educational institutions in the province. It is thus available to any of the provincial regional colleges, schools, universities, etc., that wish to make and distribute television programmes. In this sense, it is very different from the other Canadian provincial educational communications authorities, such as TV Ontario, Radio Quebec, and ACCESS, Alberta, which are semi-autonomous, and decide their own programming.

Any institution wishing to use the Knowledge Network must first apply for access to the system. The application process stresses the concept of the learning system and prospective users must prove both their ability to design and deliver programs for learning as well as their ability to identify and reach their target student population. The Knowlege Network provides technical facilities and staff, but does not impose editorial control. The educational, production and technical guidelines developed by the Knowledge Network and its users ensure that minimum standards are constantly exceeded. At least three of the institutions who use the Knowledge Network deliver their programs "live" from their own studio facility thus further decentralizing both programming and production in this complex "network" of institutions.

Use of the satellite for tele-education has at least three distinct forms - telecasts of general educational programmes; telecasts of the pre-recorded television component of a learning system; and the "live" telecast of educational learning systems with two-way inter-action by regular telephone. All these uses are comparable to those of terrestrial technology such as broadcast, microwave and cable as means of transmitting visual and audio information. The uses can conform to the production values of public television when the satellite is used as a broadcast carrier or to those of closed-circuit systems or the newer video-conferencing systems when it is used for multi-point visual communication. The advantages of satellite telecast are that it is capable of providing access across large geographic distances and this makes satellite more attractive for relatively specialized populations, such as all engineers in British Columbia. For British Columbians, satellite telecommunications is "appropriate" technology for education, as it provides "equal" delivery to all regions of the province at a reasonable cost.

The emergence of a new "hybrid" learning system such as the Knowledge Network has introduced a transformative factor into a traditional structure. All educational institutions, schools, colleges, universities and even government departments who wish to use this sophisticated satellite and cable television must develop a "learning system" that is cognizant of the needs of their target students and the capability of the system. They all participate with the Knowledge Network in developing guidelines for fair access to, and humane use of, the new Network (Forsythe, 1983).

## Interactivity

Satellite has the strong feature of being able to cover great distances. Conversely, cable can provide comprehensive webs for communication within small geographic locations. Future potential for both technologies lies in their ability to carry video, audio and data transmissions simultaneously and their potential for two-way signal carriage and thus "inter-action". The crucial "human feedback" loop in real time is now a possibility in open learning.

Salomon (1982) has argued that "interaction" may be the key to off-setting the debilitating loneliness of distance education. Certainly technologies such as radio and telephone, audio-cassette and computer have all been explored for their potential in this area; what satellite and cable provide is the potential for interactivity through access to electronic highways that are not dedicated to mass public communication, as is the case with existing broadcast and telephone technologies.

With the decreasing cost of video cassette and video cassette players, it will soon be within reason to provide every student with such specialist communication capability. How then will we use television and telecommunications? The experience in British Columbia is suggesting that the key uses will be for:

- immediacy
- interactivity
- promoting a sense of community and focus

To this end a large portion of the programmes delivered via satellite and cable are produced live and designed to engage students in problem-solving and active questionning. Such programming differs radically from conventional educational broadcasts. It is also not a "cheap" form of television production but a use of telecommunications that focusses on what cannot be delivered in other ways. This is particularly important where the target audience is scattered geographically or where the knowledge changes too fast to "package" it in the normal course development. However, the basic design of the learning system remains the same. The learner, however, is encouraged to actively participate in the "electronic classroom". The key to this idea is involvement at both the send and receive end in providing a human interface. New professional roles are being developed to facilitate access to the new system (Forsythe, 1983). Satellite and cable must be kept in perspective. They are linking and communicating technologies that require human minds to activate and use them wisely.

Many satellite experiments have provided one way video, with audio return connection using remote satellite uplinks from the return communities. However, "uplink" capability is still scarce and expensive and even though the ability to access the satellite with voice only is less expensive it is still not yet economically feasible to offer on a wide-scale. Experiments with a "spacelink" satellite telephone here in British Columbia may change this in the future.

Thus at present interaction means calling back by traditional telephone links. So, although experimentation has amply determined the potential for two way video and audio via satellite, it is not yet commonplace. It is, however, potentially the most significant aspect of these new technologies for learning over distance. There are genuine fears about technological determinism but Knowledge Network's experience on the contrary suggest that these new technologies provide new human and social opportunities that promote co-operation and communication. Open skies, grass roots is a real vision for 1984.

## References and additional reading

BACSICH, P. et al (1982)   The Implications for the Open University of Recent Cable and Satellite Developments.   Milton Keynes: Open University (mimeo)

FORSYTHE, K. (1982)   "The Knowledge Network: New Hybrid Learning System" Distance education, Vol. 2, No.3

FORSYTHE, K. (1983)   The Learning Systems Working Group - A

Democracy of Networking. Vancouver: Knowledge Network (mimeo)

FORSYTHE, K. (1983) "The Human Interface: Teachers in the New Age." Programmed Learning and Educational Technology. Vol. 20, No. 3.

HART, R. (1982a) Academic Uses of the Interinstitutional Network Vancouver: Knowledge Network (mimeo)

HART, R. (1982b) Data Uses of the Interinstitutional Network Vancouver: Knowledge Network (mimeo)

HART, R. (1983) Interactive and Broadcast Video Text Services. Vancouver: The Knowledge Network (mimeo)

STENHAM, R. (1983) and JINKINSON, R. (1983) Evidence to the Public Hearings in Cable. London: Polytechnic of the South Bank (mimeo)

MADDEN, JOHN (1980) "Simple Notes on a Complex Future" Gutenberg Two: The New Electronics and Social Change. Victoria, B.C: Press Porcepic Ltd.

PARKER, E.G. (1975) "Background Report" Proceedings of the OECD Conference on Computer/Telecommunications Policy, Paris: OECD

SALOMON, G. (1982) The Adult Distance Learner: Lonely, Mindless and Helpless or Interactive, Engaged and Efficacious, paper of the Symposium of the American Research Association, New York, March 1982

# 6. VIDEODISCS

## Robert G. Fuller

Professor of Physics, University of Nebraska-Lincoln, U.S.A.

## Introduction

Each new technology generates its own group of enthusiasts who proclaim its virtues and neglect its vices. By now teachers have heard it all and found each new technology fails to bring the peaceable kingdom to education. It is with scepticism that we receive the first laser industrial/educational/consumer product, the optical videodisc.

The sale of consumer videodisc players began in the USA in 1979 and in the UK in 1982. The first regular teaching uses of videodiscs were found in the fall of 1979 in university film criticism courses in the USA. Subsequently specially designed videodiscs were produced and evaluated in a variety of learning environments. The first commercial videodiscs for interactive education were available by July, 1982, in the USA.

The use of videodiscs by educational institutions is just the tip of the videodisc iceberg. The first large scale use of videodiscs placed about 2,000 videodisc replay systems in the automobile sales rooms of General Motors dealers across America. These discs were used to train salesmen and to show customers the features of GM cars. By 1983 other companies, such as Digital Equipment Corporation, were developing interactive videodisc systems for training their sales and service personnel. Yet the civilian corporate uses of videodiscs are probably much smaller than the military training uses of videodiscs.

By 1983, hardly four years after the introduction of videodisc players to consumers, the place of videodiscs in training and education in high technology societies seems assured. The question is: "To what use will videodiscs be put by distance education institutions?" In order to answer that question let us examine several aspects of videodiscs. First, the videodisc hardware will be briefly described along with its attractive features. Second, the cost and availability of videodisc hardware and software will be discussed. Finally, various uses of videodiscs in distance education will be suggested.

## Videodisc Hardware

A videodisc is a brilliant silver coloured disc about 30 centimeters in diameter with a 5 cm hole in the centre. Use of a complex ultra-clean, high technology, laser-based photochemical process enables the videodisc manufacturer to produce a reflective surface master which faithfully reproduces the audio-visual properties of the original programme materials. At this time original programmes are usually developed on 16mm film or 1" broadcast quality videotape. From the master disc plastic copies can be relatively inexpensively produced by moulding or stamping processes similar to those used for producing high quality gramophone records. One can think of a videodisc as a high fidelity gramophone record with pictures to accompany the sound. An educational videodisc in the UK may contain up to 55,500 individually numbered pictures. Since the normal PAL television set displays 25 pictures in a second a videodisc will play continuously for 37 minutes on one side. Consumer videodiscs of movies and rock concerts cost about £20.

The laser videodisc player is about the size of a combination stereo record player and receiver. The player spins the disc at 1500 revolutions per minute and uses a beam of laser light, reflected from the shiny disc, to recall the audio and visual information stored on the disc. The player puts out electrical signals to a standard TV set or to a TV monitor and a stereo amplifier.

However, there are two features of the videodisc player that make it dramatically different from a typical record player. Since only a beam of light is striking the videodisc surface, the disc will last indefinitely. The location on the disc from which the laser beam is receiving information can be changed rapidly and precisely. Because each picture is numbered, the laser beam can be sent to a precise location on the disc. Imagine each note of your favourite symphony with a separate number and if you wanted to hear just the portion after the second chord after the second movement you could send your record player exactly to that location. It is a very different experience from hunting for your favourite passage of music by lifting up the needle stylus, placing it down about where you guess the proper location is, and trying until you find the correct place on the record.

The precise rapid single picture access of the videodisc player makes it possible to step through the whole videodisc one picture at a time. If you looked at each picture for only 3 seconds it would take you 48 hours of viewing just to see every picture on one side of a disc.

In addition to simple picture stepping, the videodisc player offers variable slow motion forward and reverse, and rapid scan forward and reverse in addition to the precise picture location search mentioned above.

At its present stage of development a videodisc will produce an audio signal only while it is being played at normal forward speed. The videodisc can record two independent audio tracks offering stereo music or the possibility of two different narrative sequences. Hence, a videodisc can play 74 minutes of sound.

The locations of the pictures are stored as digital information on the videodisc. Most videodisc players are equipped with an input port to accept digital signals directly from a computer. This combination of computer/videodisc player is the basic interactive videodisc system. This system makes it possible to develop computer assisted learning materials that combine the logical control and flexibility of computer software with the superb audio-visual characteristics of the laser videodisc.

Many of these characteristics can almost be matched by a computer/videocassette player system. The search to individual frames is usually rather slow. A single frame ought not to be held indefinitely to avoid excessive wear of the tape. Slow motion is not generally available. Nevertheless, interactive educational lessons can be devised using a proper combination of a computer and a videocassette player. However, using videocassettes in this way is a clumsy alternative to videodiscs and the still frame picture quality is either impossible via cassette, or requires an expensive cassette play back machine.

As of now the outstanding physical capabilities of the computer/videodisc system far surpass any of the educational lessons that have been developed to use the system. As a result the section of this chapter on the educational uses of videodiscs will have to contain a good deal of speculation, assuming that educators will eventually learn how to use the maximum capabilities of computer/videodisc systems.

Hardware Availability and Costs

Today the educational uses of videodiscs are both disc and player limited. There are very few, perhaps ten, videodisc players in educational institutions in the whole UK. There may be even fewer in the homes of students. At the time of writing (July, 1983) there are no (zero!) videodiscs specifically developed for formal educational use in the UK.

The first educational uses of videodiscs will consist of discs made for specific uses such as at summer schools, day schools or classrooms, where the educational institutions will provide the necessary equipment. Following shortly will be courses for continuing education where the educators will develop the disc lessons and the company, community, or society for whom the lessons are made will provide the equipment. Next the players will become useful equipment for public access and public libraries will have them and begin to have videodiscs available for loan. The OU regional centers will, by that time, have videodisc players for use and perhaps for short term loan to informal self-tutor groups of students. Finally, the videodisc player will become a common piece of home furniture, perhaps with such amenities as videodisc-of-the-month clubs which will send monthly videodiscs to subscribers.

The costs of a computer/videodisc player system can vary over a wide range from £2,000 to £10,000. Below are itemized the present costs of two adequate computer/videodisc systems based upon equipment that can be purchased in 1983 in the UK. The availability of equipment in this area of high electronics technology changes very rapidly and may well be out of date by the time this book is published. Nevertheless, these figures will provide an estimate of relative costs.

An adequate low cost system for interactive education consists of a microcomputer with two disk drives, a computer to videodisc player interface, a videodisc player, and a colour television set. The Open University has selected a system for use during the summer of 1984 that consists of an Apple II computer with UCSD Pascal language software and two disk drives (£1,400), an Omniscan interface (£200), a Pioneer LD1100 Laservision player (£500), and a colour television set (£300). This system enables the OU development team to author their computer software in a transportable language, Pascal, and to show either computer text and graphics, or videodisc images, on a single TV screen, but the computer text can NOT be placed on the screen over a videodisc picture. The total costs of this system is about £2,400.

A more advanced system could use a larger computer and the Philips industrial videodisc player (£1,200) which makes it possible to write computer generated text over a videodisc picture. Such a system would cost upwards from £3,000 depending on the computer power purchased.

I expect by about the time videodisc players become useful public access equipment, say 5 to 10 years from now, the computer/videodisc player will be an integrated package that will sell for about £1,000.

## Educational Uses

Photographic Archives.  One of the first educational uses of the videodisc is as a collection of still pictures accompanied by a printed manual for teaching. The University of Washington, Seattle, Medical School, put their collection of haemotology microphotographs on a videodisc and sold them to other medical schools. The Center for Aerospace Education, Drew University, collaborated with the National Aeronautical and Space Administration (USA) to produce a series of space discs. The first one is a collection of photos and flight simulation films from the Voyager satellite missions to Jupiter and Saturn. The second space disc features the manned Apollo missions to the moon.

For large collections of photographs, say 100 or more, the videodisc seems to be in the educational field all by itself. For distance teaching and with projection television equipment for large lecture halls, it seems to offer low cost, ease of distribution and of use not matched by either 35mm slides or film strips, once the number of pictures gets large. Most of the colour photographs presently used in the art history and architecture courses in the UK could be made available on one videodisc, including several close-ups of portions of each photograph.

The costs to produce photographic archival videodiscs are possible to estimate. If the photographs already exist, as in the haemotology and aerospace cases cited above, then the extra costs are only those required to convert them to the proper format, 1" videotape, at a cost of £3,000. The mastering costs for videodiscs are £1,500 with the additional cost of £30 each for 50 discs or £7 each for 5000 discs. The total cost for 50 discs would be £6,000 or £120 per disc. The total cost for 5,000 discs would be £39,500, or only £8 per disc. If, on the other hand, no photographs already existed for the videodisc, the production costs increase dramatically. Suppose you hire a professor of art and a professional photographer to make a videodisc containing high quality photographs of all the paintings in the National Gallery, including carefully selected close-ups to show individual painters' characteristics. The educational and photographic design work, as well as the supplies, film, and processing would cost about £8 per photograph. Hence, the costs of the original materials for the videodisc would be nearly £500,000  The cost for 50 discs would be about £10,000 per disc and for 5,000 discs about £100 per disc.

Let us pause to think about the costs we have just estimated. They reflect an important aspect of the costs of educational materials and an important aspect of videodisc costs.  First, if a careful analysis of the professional costs for the design and production of good quality educational materials is done, the creative costs far outweigh the distribution costs. For the example above the educational creative costs were ten times the television/videodisc production costs. For a more typical videodisc that would include motion film sequences the educational creation to videodisc production cost ratio is about three to one. For the Open University system the creation to distribution cost ratio is about six to one. This, to me, is the ultimate argument against developing interactive education on videocassettes. The creative costs for good educational materials are so much more than the production and hardware costs that the best delivery system should be used if possible. A random access videocassette player is a poor imitation of a videodisc player.

Second, the cost of using videodiscs is very much influenced by the economy of scale. This characteristic is radically different from many of the other systems used to distribute educational media such as broadcast television and videocassettes. The total cost of broadcast television is constant, independent of the number of viewers. The total costs for videocassettes increases linearly with increasing numbers so the cost per videocassette is nearly constant. The total cost for videodiscs goes up slowly with increasing numbers, so the cost per videodisc drops dramatically as the number of copies increases.

Show and Tell Lessons. This is the present state of most distance teaching (and "close-together" teaching, for that matter!). It frequently features a presenter controlling the flow of the lesson. This type of linear holistic presentation can be done on videodisc but it seems better suited to the lower levels of technology such as broadcast TV or videocassettes. Furthermore, the powerful educational capabilities of the videodisc are wasted on materials that only need an occasional stop, or repeat, to be useful to the viewer. Consequently, nearly all of the present educational media materials are not suitable for putting on to videodiscs.

Individualized, Interactive Lessons. For individualized, interactive education there is no competition to the computer/videodisc. This system has the ability to bring together all of the best features of computer assisted learning and audio-visual media. Once the computer/player systems are readily available the distribution of the educational materials can be quite easily done by mail. Both the videodisc and computer floppy diskettes are reasonably hardy and can be sent through the mail with most of them safely reaching their destination. The availability of this technology for distance education can completely transform our present modes of operation. Now a typical OU course is probably eighty per cent based on printed materials such as course units, tutor marked assignments, computer marked assignments, and final examinations. The interactive videodisc system allows a distance education course to shift its emphasis away from printed materials. Nearly all the pictures, drawings, and graphics for a course could be available on the videodisc system. Even the assignments could be done on the computer floppy diskettes and returned for grading. The videodisc images could be used as the source materials for the final course examination.

## Videodisc for the Open University

The year of 1983 has seen the beginnings of the use of interactive videodisc in Open University undergraduate courses as an experiment. In April two different course teams, one in materials science and the other in engineering mechanics, received University support for the resources necessary to produce videotape masters for videodiscs to be used in their summer schools.

The materials science videodisc has been developed around an existing television broadcast for the course. Additional film sequences and computer control were to be used to transform the television programme into an interactive tutorial lesson. This videodisc was to be available on a free choice basis, alongside the usual materials science computer assisted learning lessons. The interactive videodisc is intended to motivate the students to study, to test their knowledge, and to tutor them on their weak points. It was hoped this lesson would bring together the best insights from Open University BBC producers, computer assisted learning programmers, instructional designers and materials scientists. This complete computer/videodisc lesson will be available for use and evaluation early in 1984.

Every technological change brings stress to existing institutions. The interactive videodisc is no exception. The new ideas for distance education of more than a decade ago added some broadcast television programmes to courses primarily dependent upon printed materials, regional tutorials and summer schools. By now the Open University is quite comfortable with this whole process. The arrival of interactive videodisc lessons on the scene will create some difficulties.

First, the use of videodisc demands some financial resources for mastering the disc and providing the computer/videodisc equipment. From where does the needed money come in these days of tight budgets? Second, the development of interactive videodisc lessons puts the fruits of creative television production under the control of computer logic designed to teach some essential concepts. Such development requires friendly, close cooperation between TV producers, computer specialists, instructional designers and content experts. Even at an institution with a strong course team tradition such cooperation cannot be assured.

Third, an interactive videodisc lesson places computer software in control of video material. This implies a dominant role for computer programmers compared to television producers. For institutions already heavily committed to broadcast television for distance education the growing importance of educational computer software will pose a different challenge. How can their support for computing services be raised to a level comparable to their investment in television?

Finally, interactive videodisc lessons may be able to teach more effectively than some of the present text and/or television materials. The use of this new instructional medium will demand its proper attention from the decision makers of an institution. For the time being institutions can put off this challenge to their organizational structures by treating interactive videodiscs as educational experiments. But when videodiscs have shown their areas of effectiveness, how will these new uses of computers and television in distance education replace existing practices and secure their necessary institutional support?

## Summary

The laser optical videodisc has arrived. Its use for industrial and military training purposes assure us of its continued existence independent of its success in the consumer market. The equipment required to assemble useful computer/videodisc systems is readily available and affordable in the UK. Unfortunately, there are no computer/videodisc educational materials available yet.

The production of interactive videodiscs lessons is expensive, but once we consider producing videodisc courseware for one thousand or more students, then the total costs begin to become reasonable. If our educational goal is such that individualized, interactive education is essential to achieve it, then even the higher costs for producing computer/videodisc lessons may finally be the most cost-effective.

All of this is presently speculation as the ability of the technology is superior to our ability as educators. We hope that the next few years of experimentation with this new computer/videodisc technology will show us how best to use it for education of all types.

## References and Additional Reading

Books:

DUKE, J. (1983) Interactive Video: Implications for Education and Training. London: Council for Educational Technology. Working Paper 22. (A good basic description of the details and educational promises of interactive videodiscs.)

FLOYD, S. and FLOYD, B. (eds.) (1982) White Plain, NY; Handbook of Interactive Video, Knowledge Industry Publication, Inc. (An introductory book that discusses design issues as well as hardware. Several case studies of American projects are included.)

Articles and Papers:

FULLER, R. (ed.) (1982) The Uses of Interactive Videodiscs in Open University Courses. Milton Keynes: (mimeo). (A collection of internal papers that report on the experiences of the materials science videodisc development team.)

LAURILLARD, D. (1982) "The Potential of Interactive Video" Journal of Educational Television. Vol. 8, No. 3. p.173. (A discussion of a computer assisted learning/videocassette lesson and its educational implications.)

ZOLLMAN, D. and FULLER, R. (1982) "The Puzzle of the Tacoma Narrows Bridge Collapse: An Interactive Videodisc Program for Physics Instruction", Creative Computing. Vol. 8, No. 10, p.100. (A detailed discussion of the first interactive videodisc for university teaching commercially available in America.)

Newsletters:

Videodisc Newsletter, British Universities Film Council Ltd., 55 Greek Street, London, W1V 5LR. (A twice a year leaflet to share information among people interested in videodiscs in higher education in the UK.)

Videodisc Design/Production Group News. KUON-TV. University of Nebraska-Lincoln, P.O. Box 83111, Lincoln, NE 68501-0747. (Published about six times a year as a report to public telecommunications personnel and educators.)

# 7. COMPUTER ASSISTED LEARNING IN DISTANCE EDUCATION

**Ann Jones**
Lecturer, Institute of Educational Technology, Open University.

## Introduction

This chapter discusses the use of computers as an aid to teaching and learning. Most of the examples will be drawn from our experience of computer assisted learning (CAL) at the Open University. Using the Open University as a case study, and drawing on other examples where appropriate, it will discuss both current practice and possible future directions for CAL in distance education.

The term computer assisted learning is used here in its broadest sense to include all aspects of teaching and learning with computers, but not teaching about computers.

## Why use CAL at all?

The question of whether to use CAL at all needs some consideration as it is a very expensive medium, one estimate being that it takes about 2-4 professional person-months to prepare a one hour CAL exercise (Scanlon et al, 1982).

The decision to provide CAL at all in distance education may seem strange, but one of the prime motivations for at least some of the CAL at the Open University was to provide students with some additional support and feedback on their work - additional that is to the limited face to face tuition and comments on assignments submitted to tutors. In other words, CAL was seen as a way of reducing the isolation of the distance learner.

The reasons for having CAL at all depends largely on the properties of computers, in particular:

- the capability for interacting adaptively with individual students and providing instant feedback;
- the simulation capacity - enabling students to watch, for instance, computer animations of nuclear reactions;

77

- the ability to store and retrieve large amounts of data, quickly and flexibly;
- input and output devices which make it a usable medium for disabled and blind students;
- motivational: harnessing some of that motivation to educational purposes can make computers a very powerful and exciting educational medium;
- their potential for use at home.

## The provision of CAL in distance education

How can students who are spread out over a large geographical area gain access to computers? There are various ways such access can be provided. The Open University, in 1970, adopted a 'network' approach initially to support computing for the Mathematics foundation course. This network now consists of three Dec System 2040 computers at different sites, each of which has a number of ports enabling simultaneous dial-up access. Students access the computer from one of 250 terminals in study centres, which are usually housed in local educational institutions.

This scheme of regionally accessed computer provision makes use of, and fits into, the existing administrative and tutorial regional bases of the University, and it is this which made the provision of CAL at the Open University (as opposed to the provision of facilities for computing) a relatively small step to take.

It has already been mentioned that this computer network was established to provide computing facilities for the Mathematics foundation course, part of which includes some programming in BASIC. The provision was made by setting up the Student Computing Service (now called the Academic Computing Service) and the service expanded to include not only other Maths courses but most of the other faculties as well.

The existence of the Computing Service and its network for teaching computing skills meant that CAL could also be provided using existing facilities, and this makes it almost impossible to cost the CAL system as a separate item, since the use of CAL at study centres is less than 10% of the total usage of the computing service. CAL at study centres, therefore, makes use of a set up which already exists so that the additional costs (of equipment and phone time) is marginal. Some special facilities have been created. For instance, expensive graphics terminals were purchased recently for CAL at summer school (this type of use will be discussed later.) This usage, however, is only for 6-8 weeks of the year, and the rest of the year the terminals are extensively used for a range of purposes. The general picture, then, is one of CAL making use of, and fitting into, existing provision.

The other high cost, of course, in preparing CAL materials is authoring time. For CAL to be an integrated part of the course, its use needs to be considered early on in the production cycle, and the CAL programs developed alongside other course materials. Unfortunately, most academics have proved reluctant to invest the time and the energy needed to produce good CAL programs, perhaps understandably, as they are heavily committed to writing course units. Nevertheless, the outcome has been that most of the CAL discussed in this chapter was in fact produced by members of the Academic Computing Service. For this state of affairs to continue is not very satisfactory, as it means that the course team is often less involved than it should be, which causes problems for maintenance and up-dating of the CAL materials. This has led to a position where a course team must put forward strong and convincing arguments for the use of CAL in the course. The course team must include the provision of sufficient manpower to produce and to maintain CAL (although some of this manpower, may, in practice, be 'borrowed' from the Academic Computing Service.) Some of these issues are discussed further in Scanlon et al (1982); the main point to be made here is that it is a costly process, both in terms of money and time, and course teams thinking of using it need to be aware of this.

## Types of CAL

The CAL used most at the Open University, can be classed as one of two types: 'tutorial' or 'simulation'. Tutorial CAL is so called because it attempts to simulate the type of dialogue which a student and tutor might engage in. Three tutorial CAL systems are used at the Open University: 'CICERO', 'MERLIN' and 'CALCHEM'.

### Tutorial CAL: Cicero

Cicero was designed to provide students with feedback, diagnostic assessment and remedial help, in addition to the tutorial provision and tutor-marked assignment feedback which students normally get. Cicero tutorials are written in the Cicero authoring language and can be accessed from any study centre with a terminal, and are available whenever the study centre is open.

For each tutorial, a set of 'profile questions', typically multiple-choice questions which relate to a specific block of the course, is sent to students to answer at home; the answers to these diagnostic questions provide information about the student's conceptual strengths and weakness related to specific objectives of the block and course. The student then takes the completed answer form to the study centre, accesses the Cicero program and types the answer in. Further questions may be asked, by the program, to verify the diagnosis made, and, according to the student's answers, advice and remedial help is given.

For the student unable to get to the terminal, a 'postal' version is available, which provides diagnostic advice based on the answers to the profile questions but cannot, of course, enter into further dialogue. To use this alternative the student posts the answer form and receives a printout within a few days. The postal version of this system is similar to the computer assisted feedback systems used elsewhere, e.g. the CADE system in Sweden or that used by TV Ontario with its "TV Academy" courses (see Waniewicz, 1981).

On many of the courses which have used Cicero, it has replaced computer marked assignments, so that the time otherwise spent in doing the CMA's is available for CAL. Cicero has been used in a wide variety of courses ranging from Social Science (macro and microeconomics, statistics) through education (educational psychology) to an interdisciplinary Science course.

### Merlin

Merlin was developed specifically for use by students on a second level physics course. Like Cicero, students attempt to answer a set of profile questions before using the system. Unlike Cicero, however, a human tutor is available at the other end of the phone.

After calling up the tutorial they wish to study students are asked to type their answers to 'profile' questions. These answers enable the computer to draw up a profile of each student and route that student through the tutorial in the way most appropriate to his or her ability.

The human tutor is situated at the telephone switchboard associated with the computer and watches a visual display screen which shows the progress of all the students currently using the program. By typing a suitable command, the display can be made to provide a detailed analysis of any student's answers and to pinpoint his or her 'weak' concepts. If, at any time, a student types the word 'HELP', or if either the program or the tutor decides that the student is doing particularly badly, then the student will be put into direct voice contact with the tutor. This uses the telephone line which until this moment has been the link between the computer and the terminal. At the end of the conversation the student can automatically continue the computer tutorial precisely where he or she left off. The tutorials are supervised (i.e. have a tutor available) on about thirty evenings in the year (ten evenings per computer location), and on the remaining evenings the system operates in a non-supervised mode.

## Calchem

Calchem is used in the Open Unviversity's foundation course in Science and is implemented in the STAF system (Science Teachers Authoring Facility) which was produced by Leeds University's Leeds Author Language (LAL). The programs consist of a dialogue which is a linked sequence of question-answer-comment between the teacher and the pupil. The student may use free-format input and program control of the dialogue is achieved by means of a bank of performance counters. Information fed back to the student is designed to locate any errors or misconceptions and to correct these. Like the other two systems, because of the variety of routes through the questions and answers there is a considerable degree of individualization possible in a tutorial; unlike MERLIN however, there is no tutor contact.

## Simulation CAL

In simulation CAL the computer takes the place of a laboratory or field situation and students are invited to carry out experiments which would otherwise be impossible, or very difficult, due to expense, time, danger, etc. It can allow students much greater freedom in the planning of their experiments than would ever be possible with real experiments, and can considerably enhance understanding of the scientific process.

Simulations usually present students with a number of parameters or variables (e.g. population size or temperature) for which they have to input values. When all the parameters of the model have been set, the program is run and the output obtained, usually in the form of data, either numbers per se or as a plot of some kind. Having interpreted this output, students will often re-run the program, having modified the values for one or more of the variables. Good simulations have some definite goal for which the students are aiming. The goal is usually not explicit in the program itself, but is set by the tutor, by the documentation or, occasionally, by the students themselves. Prior knowledge of the topic is often assumed, and many simulations will be educationally effective only if the students and, where relevant, their tutors are adequately prepared for the task in hand. Students benefit immensely from a well-structured and informed de-briefing session after their interaction with the simulation.

Most of the Open University simulations are provided at day schools or at residential summer schools and are mainly used for science courses, with some also used for social science and technology courses.

## Evaluating tutorial and simulation CAL in distance education

The Computer Assisted Learning Research Group was established in 1979, and not surprisingly one of its first tasks was to survey the use of CAL being made at the Open University. All the CAL described here was available to students on a voluntary take-up basis so one indication of its success is the amount of take-up. Using this indicator, tutorial CAL did not appear to be too successful. For example on one course a little over 30% of the students started off by making some use of CAL, but by the end of the course this figure had dropped to about 13%. A series of evaluation studies set out to discover what students thought about the CAL provision, and to discover their reasons for using, or not using CAL, although it should be noted that these evaluations did not attempt to establish the educational effectiveness of CAL tutorials.

## Methods of evaluating CAL

The evaluation of tutorial CAL used a wide range of methods including

-       an initial questionnaire sent to all students;

-       questionnaires sent with answers to postal tutorials, and questions about the tutorial included at the end of interactive tutorials;

-       interviews of students and staff;

-       final questionnaires sent to students to follow-up answers to earlier open-ended questions;

-       questionnaires sent to tutors.

Spontaneous sources such as letters received from students were also used, and usage figures were available.

The main method of evaluating simulation CAL was observation.

## Findings from the evaluation studies

The benefits which students expected to get from one of the tutorial systems (Cicero) included individualised feedback, self assessment, a means of diagnosing weak points and receiving help, revision, clarification and consolidation of concepts. Students' beliefs concerning the likely problems of using such a system were also realistic, centering around time, travel and booking difficulties and more specific instances often arising from previous personal experience or hearsay. These expectations matched fairly well with students' experiences, but usage declined sharply over time.

Students whom we interviewed who had not used Cicero cued us to the following factors for why they had not used Cicero (these cues also may help explain the attrition rate):

- bad computer experiences and embarrassment at the idea of using a computer terminal with others in the room;

- fear of secret assessment by the computer;

- an instrumental approach to Open University study which ignores anything not perceived to be essential.

The evaluations of MERLIN and CALCHEM tell a fairly similar story. MERLIN however is probably the most successful of the three systems and two points should be noted: first that MERLIN is well integrated into overall tutorial arrangements; secondly that tutors are specifically appointed to deal with CAL. The major conclusions for tutorial CAL, however, is that use does not relate to the educational benefits perceived from using it. Students are realistic about what such a system can provide, and on the whole, what the students thought they gained from using the system matched with their expectations. However, the value of use is traded against the energy input needed; and thus a small amount of extra 'hassle' can discourage a future user for good. Unfortunately, in an institution such as the Open University, the amount of effort needed to use a system like Cicero, for example, is quite considerable, including reading the documentation, thinking about answering the questions, filling in the form, booking a terminal, travelling to it, and for the first-time user, learning to use the system. A lot of the problems of using CAL, such as access, although not necessarily specifically related to distance education, are certainly not easily solved within this context.

The use of simulations at residential summer schools did not critically depend on access to the computer in the same way as tutorial CAL, since a computer was readily available on site. Problems here however centred around the 'support' which was provided. Although there is no evidence that the simulations themselves were in any way less than adequate, their successful use depended crucially on the tutors. For instance, tutors obviously need to know the 'answers' where appropriate and also should know something about the models used to generate the data which their students are asked to interpret. At another level, it is unreasonable to expect tutors, employed for their ability to teach an academic subject, to engage in what is still a relatively novel teaching exercise without more support from the course authors or training in CAL if they so desire. At the most mundane level this must include procedures for 'logging-in' to the computer and instructions on what to do if things go wrong, even though in the majority of instances connection to the computer takes a matter of seconds.

## Conclusion from evaluation studies

A number of issues were highlighted by these students:

- access (both to the computer and program);

- integration (with courses);

- support (documentary and tutorial);

- quality of the program.

Although the situation in the Open University has improved greatly recently, it is still not ideal; using educational institutions as hosts leads to access problems such as long summer breaks and finding caretakers  Access includes the practical difficulties of accessing a terminal and the problem of accessing a program, which for novices include their fear and embarrassment, the problems of logging in and possibilities of the machine malfunctioning.  One alternative is to site terminals in public premises such as libraries; other possibilities of course include using systems like Prestel and Viewdata and the University is now experimenting with such systems (see Chapters 14, 15 and 17).  The real breakthrough here must be in providing home terminals.  Not only would access cease to be a problem, but it would allow a radical re-think about the role of CAL, permitting it to occupy a central role in the learning process, instead of being merely an optional extra.  Access of course also includes getting hold of the program and this should be made as easy as possible.

Secondly, it is important that the CAL element of a course is seen as an integral part of it, both by those preparing the course materials (the course authors) and by any course tutors or counsellors.  One way of emphasizing this is to assess it, otherwise students can easily perceive it to be optional and unimportant.

CAL also needs support in terms of good documentation and tutor training; it is clear that this is particularly important in simulation CAL.  Documentation should be helpful but concise.  Tutors should be properly briefed.  Nervous students can be encouraged to go along with someone more experienced who can provide a helping hand. Induction sessions should also be provided.

Little has been said so far about the educational quality of CAL. This will depend partly on the amount of effort put into CAL, and the amount of effort needed to produce good quality CAL is surprisingly high.

## Overcoming access problems: home terminals and microcomputers

A small-scale experiment on the use of home-terminals was conducted by Whitelegg (1981). In this study six physics students were able to use the MERLIN system from Open University terminals installed in their own homes. The experiment was moderately successful. While many negative access factors were eliminated in that the students made use of the terminals, they missed meeting other students, and students also confirmed the desire for hard-copy terminals rather than visual display units (VDU's) so that they could work through the tutorial later. This study is being followed up by the investigation of various possibilities of home-use. One of the problems with home-use for tutorial CAL is that VDU's are becoming more popular than hard-copy terminals, yet students clearly welcome the addition of hard-copy.

It might seem that the obvious solution to the problem of home access is for students to use home microcomputers, for they are, after all, becoming cheap and very popular. However, there are various problems with this suggestion - at least for tutorial CAL. A study of OU students in 1982 found that 34% of all OU students have access to a microcomputer, either at home or elsewhere, and this percentage becomes much higher when specific areas are looked at: 41% for Science students, 49% for Technology and 58% for Maths (Grundin, 1983). So it would seem that a reasonable proportion of students (at least a third) would have access to some sort of micro, and this is where the first problem lies : there is no evidence that most of these would be the same micro. The Micros in Schools project, which will be discussed briefly later in this chapter, has addressed the problem of providing different versions of software for five different "School" micros. This though is not a trivial task, so any undertaking to provide enough different versions for the large array of home micros is just not feasible.

Thus, one problem is that there are too many kinds of incompatible micros in existence. The second problem is probably greater, at least for tutorial CAL. The type of tutorial CAL which has been discussed here would just not fit on most existing microcomputers. There tends to be a difference in the kinds of microcomputers bought for the home market : Sinclair was the most popular make in the survey of OU students' access (what sort of Sinclair is not stated), but it is probably a fairly cheap, small micro; and PET and Apple were the next - but only 4% of all students had access to one of these. In British schools, however, the microcomputers most likely to be found are probably Research Machines 380Z and 480Z, sometimes Apple micros, and more recently the BBC Acorn computer; the commercial arena will have yet different micros. None of these machines can yet support the type of CAL that we have discussed and which was developed for large main-frames. The Micro in Schools project however does produce in-service courses for teachers, some of which contain small CAL packages, to be used on school microcomputers.

More powerful microcomputers do play a role in OU CAL; some of the programs developed for use at an OU Physics Summers School were developed on a TERAK microcomputer for delivery on a North Star Horizon (Every, 1982). Although this kind of use cannot make use of students' own microcomputers, microcomputers are a convenient and portable tool for use at Summer School and do not require arrangements for 'lines' to the main-frame computer, or dial-up access.

So the conclusion about using students' own microcomputers at present is that the machines to which students may have access are too diverse to provide software for; as yet only a third of our students have such access; and such micros will not support the CAL which the University is already using. The implications of this situation is to consider restricting the software supplied to a range of micros owned or accessed by a particular audience (what the Micros in Schools project does) and to consider different kinds of CAL, and different roles it can play. This will be discussed in the next section.

Future roles for CAL

One of the impacts of the CAL Research group and of the evaluation studies mentioned is a change in some of the CAL being produced at the Open University; a move away from the broad use of CAL wherever possible to specialised high quality 'pockets' of CAL where it is particularly appropriate. In the last section I will outline what I believe to be good models of CAL practice both for now and the future.

Courses with computers as home-kits. The university is rapidly gaining experience in sending out microcomputers to students as part of OU courses. This has so far largely been in courses which teach about computers. A short course for managers about microelectronics includes a microcomputer to introduce them to computer concepts (see du Boulay, O'Shea and Monk, 1981) and this has been followed by a course for engineers. An undergraduate course, 'The Digital Computer', also sends out a microcomputer. In all these instances it has proved more sensible and economical to build an Open

University computer tailor-made to the course than to rely on computers available commercially. One of the results of this progression has been a growing expertise in providing such machines and in testing and debugging associated course material, which is extremely important.

Fraction buggy. Another move has been towards adopting techniques from artificial intelligence research into CAL (see Carbonell, 1970). One course, EM235, 'Developing Mathematical Thinking', includes a computer game which simulates fraction errors made by children, using production rules (see Evertz, in press). Unlike most CAL programs, such programs incorporate simplified versions of the kinds of knowledge representations being developed in Artificial Intelligence research (O'Shea and Self 1983), and are thus more adaptable and 'intelligent'.

Computer awareness and computer education training. The final example is the 'Micros in Schools' project. This produces courses on various aspects of the use of microelectronics in education, including introducing teachers to microelectronics, educational software, CAL etc. (see O'Shea, 1983). The courses are produced in five different versions for different microcomputers. Access to a microcomputer is essential as teachers need to use a microcomputer to do the course. A microcomputer 'kit' is also being sent to the students with two of the short courses.

## Conclusions

At the beginning of the chapter I listed some of the properties of computers which can make CAL a very powerful, exciting and unique form of learning. Experience at the Open University however indicates that there are many issues which require consideration before it can realise its potential in distance education. These include access, integration with the course, assessment, support, and training for tutors. The two questions that are vital are:

- firstly, does the educational experience you wish to offer students require the use of a computer?

- secondly is there enough expertise and time available to produce and maintain the CAL?

Finally, pockets of high quality CAL where it is particularly appropriate is a better investment (and convinces others more) than CAL which is widespread but mediocre.

References and additional reading

CARBONELL, J.R. (1970) "A.I. in CAI: an artificial intelligence approach to computer-aided instruction" IEEE Transactions on Man-Machine Systems, 11 pp 190-202.

DU BOULAY, B., O'SHEA, T., AND MONK, J. (1981) "The Black Box inside the Glass Box : presenting computing concepts to novices". Int. J. Man-Mach. Studies, 14, 237-249.

EVERTZ, R. (in press) "Production rule models (of mathematical competence)" in JONES, A., O'SHEA, T. and SCANLON, E. (eds). The Computer Revolution in Education, Volume 1: New Technologies for Distance Teaching. London: Harvester Press.

EVERY, I. (1981) Graphics and animation in teaching dialogues. Milton Keynes: Open University Computer Assisted Learning Research Group, Technical Report No. 14. (mimeo).

GRUNDIN, H. (1983) Audio-Visual Media in the Open University: Results of a Survey of 93 Courses. Milton Keynes: Open University (mimeo).

OPEN UNIVERSITY (1983) TM222 'The Digital Computer', Milton Keynes: Open University.

O'SHEA, T. (in press) "Teaching teachers to use microcomputers in the Schools". in JONES, A., O'SHEA, T. and SCANLON, E. (eds) The Computer Revolution in Education Vol. 1: New Technologies for Distance Teaching. London: Harvester Press.

O'SHEA, T. AND SELF, J. (1983) Learning and Teaching with Computers. London: Harvester Press.

SCANLON, E. et. al. (1982) "Computer Assisted Learning" Teaching at a Distance, Institutional Research Review, No. 1, 1982, pp 59-79.

WANIEWICZ, I. (1981) "The TV Ontario Academy: the use of television broadcasting and computer-managed learning for adults" Educational Broadcasting International. Vol. 14, No.2.

WHITELEGG, L. (1981) "Home Users Study" in JONES, A. and SCANLON E. (eds). A review of research in the CAL group : A report of the first annual conference, Milton Keynes: Open University, CAL Research Group Technical Report No. 27.

# 8. RADIO

Hans U. Grundin
Senior Lecturer in Media Research Methods, Institute of Educational Technology, Open University

## The nature of the medium 'radio'

'Radio' may seem to be easily defined as a medium since it consists simply of the transmission through broadcasting of an audio signal to a number of listeners - a number which may range from a handful in the case of 'Citizen's Band' radio to several millions in the case of a national broadcasting service.

There was a time, not so long ago, when this simple definition was sufficient, because the only hardware involved at the receiving end was a 'wireless set' which converted the signal to sound (speech, music etc.) at the time it was broadcast, with no possibility to store the signal for the purpose of repeated, deferred or selective listening. Today, however, devices for storing the radio broadcast signal, and hence the 'message' it conveys, are very common. For example, well over 90 per cent of students at the Open University now have access, in their homes, to audio-cassette playback equipment, and nearly all of these students also have the equipment needed to record radio broadcasts off-air.

Any discussion of the use of radio for educational purposes therefore must make it clear whether the material in question is going to be heard directly as and when broadcast, or recorded and used at some later stage. And, if it is to be used as a recording, it is still of crucial importance to determine whether it is intended that it should be played back exactly as broadcast, or with pauses, repeats of parts of the material, etc.

We find then that 'radio' can mean two things: radio broadcasting, solely or primarily, for direct consumption; or recordings of radio broadcasts to be stored and used in much the same way as audio material which has been put directly on to cassettes by the producer, without the intervention of broadcasting.

## The role of radio in the Open University

Since the Open University started in 1971, radio has been extensively used as one of a handful of media in its multi-media courses. In a typical, full-credit course in the early years of the University, a week's unit of study consisted of one text unit, some broadcast notes, one television programme of 25 minutes, and one radio programme of 20 minutes. Ostensibly, radio was an important, if not major, part of any OU course. The radio programmes were intended to be heard directly as broadcasts rather than via recordings off air, and each programme was broadcast twice to give most students the opportunity to hear it at least once, and also to give some students the opportunity of hearing it twice.

In practice, radio never become an integrated and essential component in more than a few courses - mainly in the Arts faculty. Even in the early years, when the transmission times used were still convenient for large numbers of students, the average listening rate was not much over 50 per cent; that is, each radio programme was heard, on the average, by little over half of the students for whom it was intended. And as early as 1974 it was reported that on the majority of OU courses, radio programmes were somewhat peripheral appendages to the printed material (Meed, 1974).

In the last five years, the use of radio in OU courses has been diminishing rapidly, so that in 1983, eight out of ten new courses do not use any radio broadcasts. And the average listening rate in those courses that continue to use radio broadcasts has declined somewhat, to below 50 per cent, in spite of the fact that the use of radio is now much more selective.

It is not easy to establish the prime cause of the decline in OU radio, but in a situation where there were some doubts in the minds of many students - and many of their academic teachers and tutors - as to the value of radio broadcasts, the fact that by 1982 those who wanted to listen usually had to do so either before 7 a.m. or after 11.20 p.m. was bound to have a negative effect on the listening figures.

The recent decline in the use of radio broadcasts in OU courses has been parallelled by a dramatic increase in the use of audio-cassettes which are mailed to the students together with the printed course materials. The effect of this has been that the total amount of audio material provided in OU courses has remained fairly constant.

There has also been a marked change in the way radio is used by the OU students who use it. More and more students who have radio broadcasts in their courses, and who take them seriously enough to want to use them, do not listen to the broadcasts but to their own recordings off air. And even among those who do listen at the time of broadcast, we find that an increasing number also record the programme so that they can hear it again whenever they want to. The net effect of this is that by now over a third of all listening to O.U. radio broadcasts by students is done indirectly from recordings, either made off-air by students themselves, or on cassettes borrowed by students from a library loan service provided by the O.U.

## Student views of OU radio programmes

Given the decline in the listening figures to a level where in a number of courses over a third of the students do not hear any of the radio programmes in that course, one would expect most students to rate the material provided in these programmes rather poorly. There are indeed indications that many students rate radio as a medium fairly poorly, but in doing so they may be influenced by the serious distribution problems, which mean that they have to get up early or stay up late to catch the broadcasts, or go to the trouble of setting up timed recordings off air, which may or may not be entirely successful.

However, when student views on a random selection of 29 radio programmes were studied in great detail in a 1979-1981 study (Bates & al, 1981), it was found that most students who listened rated the programmes favourably. In particular, they generally agreed that the aims of the programmes were worthwhile and that these aims could best be achieved through an audio medium, rather than through, say, print.

## Analyses of programmes in their educational context

Analysis and evaluation of a carefully chosen sample of over 70 OU radio programmes in this study led to the identification of the following major programme formats:

- lecture or 'radio talk' by OU academic or external expert, without accompanying visuals or source material;

- interview/discussion, e.g. a member of the OU course team interviewing one or more external experts and discussing various topics with them;

- source material in the form of talk, usually with comments from an OU academic or expert (such source material could be a sound-recording of historic interest, or a dramatization, or simply samples of spoken language to be analyzed by the students);

- source material other than talk, e.g. music or environmental noise, with comments;

- radio-vision, i.e. a talk illustrated by some kind of visuals (e.g. printed diagrams and pictures, or slides).

Each of these five formats accounted for 15-20 per cent of all the programmes analyzed, and together they accounted for well over 90 per cent of all programmes. Of the remainder, the most common format was a kind of 'tutorial programme', often with an element of radio-vision in that the programme consisted of a tutor's comments on examples, problems, etc. printed in the broadcast notes. This format was used only in courses in the Maths faculty within the sample.

The identification of major programme formats is useful because it provides the basis for a taxonomy of radio in a distance teaching context. It became clear, however, at a very early stage of the research that analysis and evaluation of programme content are not sufficient. Any educational use of radio takes place in a specific context, which varies according to the other media used, the aims, objectives and functions of each particular medium, and the relation of each medium to the overall aims and objectives of a particular course. Consequently, this context has to be carefully analyzed.

Obviously, what kind of programme analysis is most useful will, to some extent, depend on circumstances that are specific to each educational institution. Research into the use of radio at the Open University has shown the following aspects of radio to be important in this particular setting:

- aims/objectives, and explicit statements of aims/objectives in programmes or accompanying programme notes;

- concretization, i.e. the degree to which abstract topics are illustrated by concrete examples ( a factor also found to be important by Trenaman (1967) in his major study of educational television programmes);

- 'didactic mode', i.e. primarily the distinction between didactic discourse (one or several speakers imparting information, analysis, comment etc.) and source material (the sound track conveys material upon which the student is supposed to work, analyzing, comparing, judging, evaluating, etc.);

- didactic organization/structure, i.e. the degree to which the programme or any accompanying notes make it clear to the student - either implicitly or explicitly - what is the nature of the learning activity in which he/she is expected to engage, and how it is intended that the learning should proceed;

- student activity before, during or after the programme; the nature of such activities, how well or ill defined they are;

- integration of programme with other aspects or components of the course; in particular its relation to the printed material (which is usually regarded as the most central component of any OU course);

- utilization of 'medium uniqueness', i.e. the degree to which a programme achieves, or at least aims to achieve, something which cannot be achieved as well, or perhaps not at all through an alternative medium.

A study of the correlations between aspects of programme content and context as outlined above, on the one hand, and overall student ratings of the programmes, on the other, showed that the average student rating of a particular OU radio programme can be predicted with a high degree of accuracy from a handful of observable features of the 'programme in context'. These features were:

- degree to which programme utilized 'radio vision' (the more radio vision the higher rating);

- degree to which the absence of motion picture is a disadvantage, i.e. television or film would have been needed (the greater the disadvantage the lower the rating);

- degree of didactic organization in the programme and/or the accompanying notes (the higher the degree the higher the rating);

- degree to which 'comprehension' is a major aim/objective (the higher the degree the higher the rating); and

- degree to which the programme is explicitly linked to printed course material (again, the higher the degree the higher the rating).

These five variables in an 'evaluator's protocol' can together account for almost 80 per cent of the variance among programmes in terms of student's overall ratings of these programmes.

It is worth noting that 'didactic mode' or programme format (except insofar as the presence or absence of radiovision is concerned) does not figure in this list. In other words, highly successful programmes (as judged by the students) can consist either primarily of didactic discourse, or of what is here called source material, or of a mixture of the two. However, the traditional lecture or 'radio talk' format is much more likely to be successful if it incorporates some element of radio-vision, i.e. specific illustrations, diagrams, tables etc. for the student to look at while listening.

The analysis also shows that the use of a generally successful programme format such as 'radio-vision' cannot in itself guarantee that the individual programme is successful. Whatever format is used, it must be used with a clear aim in mind, to fulfil a specific function in the context of a block or module of study. And the student needs to be made aware of the aim and the function of the programme.


Economic aspects of radio in distance education

Current experience in the Open University shows very clearly that there is a place for audio material in a wide variety of courses, particularly if it is coordinated with visuals (e.g. in printed form) into 'audio-vision' packages. The amount of work, and the costs, involved in developing audio material are likely to be similar to those involved in developing printed material. In fact, even the nature of the work is largely similar at the stages of planning, researching the topics, drafting, editing etc. And as with printed material, the amount of work needed to produce a 'unit' of audio material can vary enormously, from what is virtually an 'off-the-cuff' talk in front of a microphone, to an extensively researched, planned, rehearsed and edited audio 'show' incorporating recordings obtained at great cost on various locations.

The cost of actually recording the 'master' tape will of course also vary depending on the nature of the material, the recording facilities needed, etc., but there is no reason to assume that sound recording is, as a rule, more expensive than 'recording' print on paper - a cost which is also highly variable. BBC/Open University Productions estimate that radio costs are roughly one tenth of those of television.

Once a master tape of a sound recording is produced, there are, as has been noted earlier, two different ways of distributing it: through radio broadcasting or through mail distribution of prerecorded audio-cassettes. If the material is ultimately intended to be used in the form of audio-cassette recordings, the choice of distribution mode should be primarily an economic question. Studies at the Open University indicate that the distribution costs to the University are lower for broadcasting than for audio-cassette production and mailing when the number of students receiving the material is 1,000 or more. For between 700 and 1,000 students the costs are fairly similar, and with fewer than 700 students cassette distribution is less expensive than broadcasting.

It should be noted that the cost to the University is not the same as the total cost. If students record radio broadcasts off-air, they provide the audio-cassettes themselves, at a cost per cassette which is higher than if the University buys them, since students can only buy small quantities. And students who fail to get acceptable recordings may use the OU Library Service to obtain free recordings, thus adding to the University's total cost. On the other hand, cassettes provided by students for their own recordings can be used several times, reducing the cost per programme.

If students provide the recording equipment and the blank audio-cassettes at their own cost, there is no doubt that radio broadcasting is by far the cheapest means of distributing audio material in terms of expenditure by the distance education institution, when there are well over 1,000 students to distribute the material to. In the Open University, though only a handful of foundation courses have very large student populations (3,000-6,000). In its remaining 120 odd courses it is therefore doubtful whether radio broadcasting is at all justifiable in terms of the total cost (to University and students), even if it is in many courses justifiable in terms of the costs to the University only.

That leaves us with the political rather than economic question of what costs should be carried by the education institution and what should be carried by the student. The Open University does not have any consistent policy in this respect. Printed material, for example, is provided by the University free of charge (other than the basic course fee) when it comes in the form of so-called correspondence units, but has to be bought and paid for by the student when it comes in the form of a so-called set book, even if that is also produced specifically for the course by members of the course team. One cannot formulate any general rule for how costs should be divided between an educational institution and its students. It seems reasonable to expect, however, that those who make decisions about the choice of media are aware of the total costs involved, not just the institution's own expenditure.

When judging the cost-effectiveness of radio broadcasting versus audio-cassette distribution, one also needs to take into account the actual effectiveness of distribution. For example, in the OU radio broadcasting has an actual 'take-up rate' of about 50 per cent (ie 50% of the target population actually use each unit of material), whereas the take-up rate for audio-cassette mailing is much higher, about 80 per cent. If it is essential that the material reaches the vast majority of students, then radio broadcasting is likely not to be effective enough, and consequently, the question of cost-effectiveness becomes irrelevant.

If one is prepared to accept the lower effectiveness of broadcasting, one still has to keep in mind that there are situations where broadcasting incurs less expenditure than cassette mailing, but cassette mailing is more cost-effective. In the OU, this is the case when a course has a student population of around 1,500: broadcasting means lower expenditure for the University, but cassette mailing results in a lower expenditure per student user of the material.

## Conclusion

The advantages to students of using audio recordings as and when it suits them, rather than listening to radio broadcasts at fixed, often unsuitable times, are so obvious that they do not need any discussion. It is very much like the difference between having your own copy of a course textbook and using a copy in a library that is only open for a short time once a week.

In any distance educational system catering for groups of students enrolled in specific courses, radio broadcasting can therefore be seen primarily as a convenient means of distributing audio material for students to record off air and use in their studies. This means that the nature of the material broadcast need not have much similarity to what we commonly think of as 'radio programmes'. Since the material is likely to have limited value to non-students, the justification for broadcasting it rather than distributing it in an other form should primarily be economic.

On the other hand, if the target population cannot easily be identified, or if an important aim of the distance education activity is to make the general public aware of what is being offered, then radio broadcasting may be a highly important and potentially very cost-effective means of distributing a wide variety of educational material to large numbers of people.

Regardless of what the role of radio is intended to be, the Open University experience shows clearly that careful monitoring and assessment of the students' use and appreciation of the medium are essential.

References and additional reading

BATES, A.W. (1979), 'Whatever happened to radio at the Open University?' Educational Broadcasting International. Vol. 12, No. 3

BATES. A.W. & al. (1981), Radio: The Forgotten Medium?. Milton Keynes: Open University (mimeo).

BROWN, D.H. (1980), 'New students and radio at the Open University'. Educational Broadcasting International. Vol. 13, No. 1

FORREST, A. (1978), 'Radiovision' in UNWIN, D. and McALEESE, R. (eds), The Encyclopedia of Educational Media, Communications and Technology London: Macmillan.

FORSYTHE, R.O. (1971), 'Radio, Instructional', The Encylopedia of Education. Vol. 7.

GRUNDIN, H.U. (1980), Audo-Visual and Other Media in 91 Open University Courses. Milton Keynes: Open University (mimeo).

GRUNDIN, H.U. (1979), Open University Broadcasting: Results of the 1978 Survey and Overview of Survey Results 1977-78. Milton Keynes: Open University (mimeo).

JAMISON, D.T., & McANANY, E.G. (1978) Radio for Education and DevelopmentBeverly Hills, Cal.: Sage.

JAMISON, D.T., SUPPES, P. & WELLS, S. (1974) 'The Effectiveness of Alternative Instructional Media: a Survey.' Review of Educational Research. Vol. 44, No. 1.

MEED, J. (1974), The Use of Radio at the Open University 1971-1974. Milton Keynes: Open University (mimeo).

MEED, J. (1976), 'The use of radio in the Open University's multi-media educational system'. Educational Broadcasting International. Vol. 9, No. 2

PEIGH, T.D. (1979), The Use of Radio in Social Development. Media Monograph 5. Chicago: Community and Family Study Center, University of Chicago.

SCHRAMM, W. (1977), Big Media, Little Media. Beverly Hills, Cal.: Sage.

THEROUX, J.M. (1978) Techniques for Improving Educational Radio Programmes. Paris: UNESCO.

TRENAMAN, J. (1951), 'Understanding Radio Talks', The Quarterly Journal of Speech. Vol. 37.

TRENAMAN, J. (1967) Communication and Comprehension London: Longmans.

## 9.  AUDIO-CASSETTES

Nicola Durbridge
Lecturer in Media Research Methods, Institute of Educational Technology, The Open University.

First of all, what do audio-cassettes have to offer distance education, and how may one compare their potential with other distance teaching media?  It is perhaps useful to begin by noting that there are two elements embedded in the one word audio-cassette: first a sound element and secondly, the fact that this sound is presented for study on cassette. Each of these elements is worthy of separate comment.

### The Audio Factor

With regard to sound, it is likely to be significant in any teaching context that more often than not what is recorded is the sound of the human voice.  At first sight, this is an obvious point, but one which provides advocates of the medium with some cogent arguments for its use in distance education.  As Marash (1962) points out, the human voice can be modulated, meaning "the correct and artistic use of pitch, sound, pace, pause, phrasing, inflexion, tonal amount and quality".  Thus, a student who is invited to work with a modulated text rather than a printed one can be said to have certain advantages: for example, he or she has access to audible clues about the intended meaning of particular words and phrases in a text, or about the kind of attention he or she should pay to parts within the text as a whole.

Perhaps even more telling for many students is the power of the spoken word to convey enthusiasm, humour and indeed a human touch to their academic study.  An Open University study into the characteristics of effective teaching (Gibbs and Durbridge, 1976) showed an overwhelming stress amongst senior tutorial staff on the importance of personal style; a style categorised as "interesting, systematic, understanding, informal and flexible".  It is a priority paralleled in other research - see Ryans (1960) and Gagne (1972). It appears quite clear that it is a characteristic highly regarded by both appointing personnel and by students. Student feedback on Open University courses for example (Durbridge, 1982) suggests that tutors who adopt a friendly, personal approach in their cassette teaching are very highly regarded. Such a style appears to be educationally effective for the way it can evoke the sense of a one-to-one tutorial for many listeners, and appears to draw even the distant student towards active and participant work rather than passive and unthinking listening. It is then, the fact of <u>modulation</u> which distinguishes a spoken text from a written one and which can provide it with educational advantages.

As compared with a written text, the spoken word can influence both cognition (adding clarity and meaning) and motivation (by conveying directly a sense of the person creating those words.) It is worth considering too whether other sounds have a role to play in distance education. It can be argued that the meaning of much sound is best communicated through its own medium, rather than 'translated' into some other coded system. Music, for example, although it may be described and interpreted by words, consists essentially of a pattern of sound and rhythm, whose autonomous meaning can be distorted on translation. Other sounds too, on a practical rather than a purist level, become relevant to an educational discourse if they are heard rather than described. While it is fairly obvious that the sound of music has a role to play in the direct teaching of its own subject-matter, music along with these "other sounds" can also be exploited to enrich and enhance a spoken sound track. These sounds, such as the noise of certain machinery, or the background hum of daily life, have an associative as well as a pure meaning, which can be used to evoke images or ideas relevant to the main substance of what is being taught. There are, in other words, instances where audio is essential for efficiently mediating certain kinds of information.

## The Cassette Factor

So far, the discussion has made certain comparisons between sound itself and print, and drawn attention to some of the ways an audio medium can achieve more, or certainly different, things from a written one. There are, however, some well-rehearsed arguments against the sound medium, perhaps the most common ones being its ephemeracy and the fact that many students are more experienced at handling (and thus better able to work with) written texts. In passing it might be worth noting that students who are campus-based also suffer from these difficulties, if lectures and tutorials predominate as a teaching method. The present focus however is upon pre-recorded sound delivered in a more permanent form than a transitory lecture, and it is at this point in the discussion that the word 'cassette' becomes significant.

For students, study material presented on cassettes offers considerable freedom. Students can choose to listen at a time and place convenient to themselves and thus use the material as and when it appears most relevant to their individual needs. They can moreover exploit the hardware of cassette-players - the stop, pause and replay devices - to organise their study approach according to personal style and preference. Thus, it can be argued that cassettes provide students with a learning medium which shares many of the advantages inherent in a written text; it is adaptable to such study techniques as skimming and reviewing and listeners can, to a large extent, control the pace and methods with which they engage with particular content. This point alone goes some way towards compensating for the ephemeracy of a sound medium.

## Designing Cassettes

Many Open University cassettes are presented for study in combination with visual material, in the belief that this will help listeners to concentrate on the spoken text, and also provide the potential for simultaneous study activities. Indeed, from the teacher perspective, cassettes can be said to be a very valuable medium for the flexible way they lend themselves to a wide range of teaching strategy, if the educational potential of asking students to pause, replay and so on is borne in mind when a programme is designed. For example, a commentary may be interspersed with questions or activities for students to answer or to carry out, either as they listen or during programmed breaks on the sound track. The function of such activities may be to provide students with comprehension tests, or practice in a range of skills or revision exercises, and in these ways follow-up what has been taught during the cassette lesson.

In-built activities need not be limited to such a summative role however; they may equally well focus on formative tasks. Indeed, one of the main attractions of the audio medium is the way it lends itself, at a distance, to effective formative teaching strategies. The intimacy of the medium and the fact that it leaves students' hands and eyes free combine to provide a context in which teacher and learner can work on a task together. For example, an audio lesson may be interspersed with activities and questions which seek to develop students' awareness of the processes involved in solving various problems; or activities may be inserted which aim to develop practical skills, such as the drawing of graphics and diagrams, or the setting up of equipment. In each case the tutor's commentary can provide an essential and supportive guiding voice as students set about their work.

The kinds of visual material used in combination with such cassette work is very varied. It ranges from maps, geological specimens or chemical solutions in the Sciences, through colour film-strips of paintings or architecture in the Arts, to tables of statistics in the Social Sciences. These data may be used to illustrate a discussion, to provide evidence or to form the focus of an exercise in analysis which students carry out under the verbal guidance of their tutor's voice. For practical reasons these kinds of visual cannot always be located in the main teaching text, but in such cases it is Open University practice for the commentator to refer students (at the start of the lesson) to the materials they will need to hand as they listen. The audio component is, however, usually highly integrated into the main teaching and students are given textual cross-references indicating how and when cassette work fits into their study.

On other Open University courses, the visual material accompanying a period of audio-work is bound into the main teaching text. The Mathematics Faculty in particular has pioneered an approach which combines sound with vision in a rather special way, although the approach lends itself to many disciplines and is also used, for example, in philosophy teaching. In this approach the visuals used are very distinctive and have a number of important design features. Figure One (over) is a typical example; it is taken from a third level Mathematics Course called Introduction to Pure Mathematics.

A cassette lesson consists of perhaps ten pages of numbered illustrations like these, bound into the main text where students should work on them. The visuals are referred to as 'figures' by the commentator. They are clearly delineated and, where print-costs will allow, are presented in colour, usually a clear blue. Each frame provides speaker and listener with a common focus for attention and a structure to the lesson. Each one operates rather like a paragraph of print and contains one basic point or idea which the commentator explores. During the lesson the speaker leads students' eyes forward by picking out the words, images or symbols which appear in each frame, so that students focus briefly on each item in turn.

The lay-out of the frames helps them to do this easily as it is carefully prepared to tie in with a natural reading movement. The handwritten words, and the inclusion of light-hearted touches such as the cartoon-like professor in Figure One, also form part of the teaching strategy. The emphasis is on informality and the aim is to evoke in students the sense of having a private lesson with a personal tutor.

The sound track complements the style of the visuals in that it is directly spoken, as if to one student, and is friendly in tone. This approach has proven very popular with Open University students.

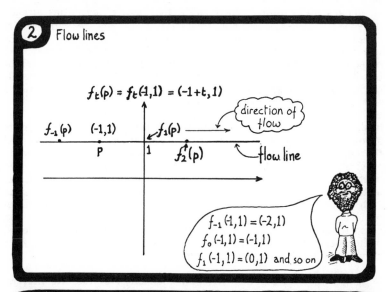

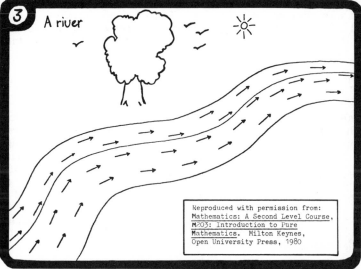

**Figure One**

The method is not just clear but is said to be motivating, stimulating and supportive. It is also flexible, since it can form the basis of an illustrative lecture or incorporate the kinds of activities already described. Hard-core teaching material of the kind described so far clearly needs careful preparation. The content of a cassette lesson will almost certainly be most effective if it is well-integrated with other teaching media; moreover, where sound is combined with vision or is used to build in student activities, it will need to be sensibly organised and paced. In terms of academic time then it is not a soft option but it is an effective one.

It should be added that sound material can be a valuable adjunct to a course of study when it performs a less direct teaching role. At the Open University, for example, audio-cassettes are also used to provide students with educational counselling, to provide enriching (rather than essential) study material, often in the form of traditional lectures, or to provide students with additional reference material, such as primary historical sources for analysis, or sound glossaries of foreign words. Individual tutors moreover may make their own cassettes to provide remedial material for students who have special difficulties with sections of their syllabus or with any written work they may have been asked to submit.

In sum, cassettes, together with the technology of cassette players, provide unique opportunities for encouraging distant students to be mentally alert as they study, and to participate in activities which will probably make their learning more effective and enjoyable, and for giving support with the whole business of studying at a distance.

## Production

The production process of audio-cassettes has various stages. First of all, an academic will usually work on their text and tape at home, with their own recorder. He or she can thus develop an integrated script entirely alone and according to well-developed and individual practice. At the Open University the services of BBC producers may also be used at this stage; for example the producer may collect archive or live recordings which the academic can integrate with the text. When the draft text is ready, it will be discussed and edited in a studio. Roughly two-thirds of Open University cassettes are produced by the BBC; the remainder are recorded by a highly qualified sound technician working in the University's own audio-visual centre.

The master-tape is then sent for fast copying. This can be done externally by commercial copying companies, but the Open University now has its own in-house copying facility. About sixty copies are made per minute, using a reel-to-reel quarter inch tape in a continuous production process. The tape is then cut, packaged into cassettes, and mailed directly to students with their other study materials.

The Open University is now producing over a hundred hours a year of new cassette material in this way. It thus mails roughly 500,000 cassettes per year to students; a marked change from 1977 when cassettes were virtually unused.

## Costs and Availability

The production costs of individual tapes of this last type can be minimal, merely involving the purchase of a blank cassette, its private recording and its postage. The costs, however, of preparing and recording high quality cassette teaching material are likely to be much higher. A rough guide from Open University experience suggests that it can cost between £300 to £3000 to produce one hour of original material and to distribute it in copied form. The higher figure represents all costs from expensive items such as academic and clerical time and the overheads involved in maintaining top (BBC) quality recording facilities, as well as the relatively low costs involved in the copying and distribution process.

It costs the Open University an estimated 50 pence, from master-tape to delivery to a student's house, to provide each individual with one hour's worth of audio material. Moreover, students keep the cassettes they are sent since it is not cost-effective to demand their return and re-issue to other students. This means that one hour of sound (on a C60) providing usually about two to three hours of study material, works out at less than 25 pence per hour of study; it may be an even more cost effective resource if students go back to their cassettes frequently, for revision purposes, for example.

As compared with newer technologies it is probably fair to say that audio-cassettes provide a very cost-effective and problem-free teaching medium. It is Open University experience again which suggests that most students (usually more than 90%) will already own the necessary replay equipment, and where this is not the case, they will either readily purchase or borrow it. Student access to cassette content is not, therefore, seen as a problem, and nor is students' willingness to use it. Most Open University students say that they find audio-cassettes a convenient and easy medium to work with and typically rate them very highly amongst the mix of media they meet on their courses.

Ease of use and wide availability quite probably influence students' high regard for audio cassettes but there is little doubt that other characteristics may hold the key to their success. A teacher who exploits the medium to present a directly spoken and relatively informal commentary which engages students in participative work is likely to be rewarded by attentive and co-operative listening and learning.

## Audio and Video Compared

In the light of the popularity of audio cassettes it is tempting, perhaps, to anticipate that <u>video</u> will prove to be an equally successful educational tool. Clearly, there are similarities between the two media which encourage such thinking; for example, both present information in a cassetted form. Nevertheless, there are some important differences between the two.

Many students appear to find video a more formal medium to work with than audio, and apparently feel less comfortable working with it. It lacks, apparently, the very personal and intimate quality that students using audio-cassettes praise so highly. Secondly, students tend to find video technology rather more intrusive than the small and simply operated audio-cassette player. For this reason too then, students feel less at home with video, and less the master than the tool of the technology. Thirdly, video work involves concentrated watching as well as listening. In this context students are no longer free to carry out simultaneous learning activities without losing information contained in the moving images. Video study is less convenient than audio-casette study. This will remain true until private ownership of video relay equipment becomes as common as ownership of its relatively cheap audio counterpart.

Lastly, the preparation of video material is quite a different proposition from the preparation and production of audio-cassettes. The latter are simple, quick and cheap to prepare and can be drafted by an academic in his own home so that they integrate neatly into a written text. Video, on the other hand, usually requires professional expertise, takes more time to prepare, and is expensive, requiring high capital outlay for overheads alone. It is unlikely, therefore, that an academic will have the same degree of control over the design and production of video material. Such differences are vital ones, and they suggest that, for the time being at least, audio-cassettes are the more valuable of the two media for distance teaching.

It is understandable that more glamorous technologies such as video and microcomputers attract a great deal of attention, but the humble audio-cassette has a great deal to offer distance education, and should not be ignored.

References and Additional Reading List

DURBRIDGE, N. (1982)     Audio-Cassettes in Higher Education:
     Milton Keynes: The Open University, (mimeo)

GAGNE, N.L. (1972)   Teacher Effectiveness and Teaching Education:
     The search for a scientific basis: London: Pacific Books

GIBBS, G. AND DURBRIDGE, N. (1976)    "The Characteristics of
     Open University Tutors" Teaching at a Distance, Nos. 6 and 7

GROVES, P. (ed) (1981)    Series of Audio-Cassettes and Workbooks:
     Hertfordshire: The Royal Society of Chemistry, Letchworth

MARASH, J.G. (1962)     Effective Speaking. London: Harrap

POSTLETHWAITE, S.N.   (1969)     The Audio-Tutorial Approach to
     Learning: Minneapolis: Burgess Publishing Company

RYANS, D.G. (1960)    Characteristics of Teachers: their description,
     comparison and appraisal: Washington: American Council on
     Education

WRIGHT, S. AND HAINES, R. (1981)     Audio-Tapes for Teaching
     Science: Teaching at a Distance, No. 20

Designing Audio-Cassettes - A self-instructional package.   Nicola
Durbridge has prepared an audio-vision package which illustrates a
range of ways in which audio-cassettes are linked to other teaching
components.    The package consists of an audio-cassette, which
contains both a commentary and extracts illustrating different uses,
plus a set of accompanying notes. The commentary draws attention
to the ways each student exploits various characteristics of the
medium and outlines the kind of planning and design decisions involved
in audio-cassette making. It is available from: I.E.T., The Open
University, Milton Keynes, MK7 6AA, England, and costs £90 plus
postage.

# 10.  HOME KITS

Dave Greenfield
Project Officer, Technology Faculty, Open University

## Introduction

This chapter deals with home kits used in distance education.  As there has been very little research on this topic the treatment is very much from a personal viewpoint, based partly on my involvement with course development and partly on my observation within the Open University.  Other influential factors are my experiences as student, course tutor, central academic and project officer with the Open University, together with teaching in conventional education institutions.

## What is a Home Kit?

Home kits, sometimes called home experiment kits, are generally an assortment of hardware sent to each student taking a particular course.  Not all courses at the Open University include home kits.  They are predominantly components of science and technology courses, although they are also part of the odd social science, maths and arts course.  Roughly a quarter of all O.U. courses have home kits.  In most cases, they have to be returned by the students at the end of the course.  The notion of home kit could conceivably be extended to any hardware issued by the University and used at home by a student for learning purposes.  The decision to include them in a course is made by the course team.

Home kits, as the name suggests, are used by students in their homes, or environs.  Each student has a kit for his or her sole use, consisting of essential components not likely to be found at home.  For example, a student taking a science course may be issued with a microscope, but is unlikely to receive a pair of scissors.

The size, complexity and level of sophistication of home kits vary greatly.  The Science Foundation course (S101) uses a typically high-resource kit.  It contains over 220 items, ranging from a spectroscope to a razor blade, a chemical balance to filter paper. In addition, about 60 chemicals are issued with the kit. A low-resource kit, as used by a statistics course, consists of one item only - a random number generator that looks rather like a child's spinning top. Alternatively, home kits might include <u>software</u> which enables students to carry out home-based experiments, such as an audio cassette which talks students through experiments designed to reveal the materials properties of familiar domestic items such as paper cups and plastic vending cups; or a set of fake office in-tray contents to help students to learn how to analyse problems in industrial social systems. Nor do kits have to be inanimate objects. Live chlorella organisms and pickled sheeps brains are just two of the organic specimens used for Open University home kits. (A speedy mail service and home refrigerator are both essential for such home kits )

But high resource kits do not necessarily contain lots of different items. On a course designed to teach microcomputing techniques it was decided to provide every student with their own (identical) microcomputer. This single kit item cost £125 per student at 1983 prices. Similarly, low resource kits need not be restricted to one or two items. Plastic straws, ping-pong balls, tarred string, gridded tracing paper, cheap protractors and dividers are all items which have been supplied in Open University home kits at very little cost.

## What is the purpose of the Home Kit?

The purpose of the home kit, as it exists at the moment, is to give the students practical 'hands on' experience of some aspect of the course. Course units are written to develop a theoretical understanding of a course topic or theme. The home kit complements the course units by allowing the student to observe, explore, analyse a 'real world' situation related to the topic being taught, and to try out the techniques described. The reinforcement of the theory and the development of appropriate skills are major functions of home kits.

For example, a course on thermodynamics may expect students to be knowledgeable about rates of energy transfer by heating. Consequently, their home kit might include equipment that allowed them to conduct cooling experiments. Hopefully the students would then be better equipped to understand the underlying principles, conduct a rigorous analysis based on their own results, and make judgements on how theory relates to practice.

In fact, within this general framework home kits can be used for a great variety of specific teaching objectives. The uses for which Open University kits have been designed include developing aural perception and teaching musical score reading, analysing the composition and evolution of the upper sedimentary parts of the earth's crust, investigation of the inheritance of human traits, observation of stress distributions in photoelastic specimens, measurement of human reaction times to stimuli, development of manipulative and drawing skills, analyses of electronic signals, observation of learning behaviour in fish, and simulation of the air traffic control system at Heathrow Airport.


## How are Home Kits Produced?

The process of planning, designing, developing and producing a home kit can be quite a major task. To think that a home kit is an optional extra simply 'tacked on' to an already prepared course misses the point. To be effective, the home kit needs to be an integrated part of the teaching package, and therefore should be prepared in parallel with the course. Indeed, it may be that the kit is the core item of a course, as in the case of a microcomputer in a course about these devices, with the result that the other course components are designed around the kit. Even in courses where kits are not the main component, it is not uncommon for specific references to be made to a home experiment in a course unit. Course-related television programmes may show some aspect of a home kit being used. In fact, there is a growing tendency on some courses to include home experimental work in the course unit itself rather than as supplementary material.

The course goals form the basis for making decisions about the nature and composition of the home kit. These goals relate to what is to be taught and what students should be able to do as a consequence of experiencing the course. Secondary decisions such as whether home experimental work should be assessed, how much time should be allocated and so on, are also made. All decisions are governed by the overriding constraints of the practicality of the work being done by a student in isolation, at a distance and in their own home. One cannot expect a five-day experiment to be set up on the kitchen draining board, or the postman to turn up with a replacement measuring flask.

The actual effort put into the production of a home kit clearly depends, to a large extent, on the complexity of the kit itself. At one extreme only one or two people may be involved. For example a single academic might design and develop an experiment for his or her part of the course independently of the course team if it were a straight-forward activity using readily available components in a traditional way. The person concerned may then obtain assistance from another member of the course team (either a technical member or another academic) for refining and de-bugging the activity.

At the other extreme, when a more complex activity is envisaged or when a novel approach is decided upon, the majority of the course team, consisting of academics and technical staff, could be involved. Because the prime considerations are educational the initial decisions and inputs are made by the academics. Generally, one of the technical staff, who has an understanding of educational strategies and product design in its broadest sense, has the responsibility of ensuring that the ideas become reality. This person forms the major link between the course team and the producers of the kits, drawing on assistance from technical departments within the University (particularly the home kit section) when necessary. On occasions the linkperson may need to approach external designers and manufacturers to have prototype kit components designed and developed (with a view to production runs) if appropriate items are not commercially available.

Accompanying the kit is instruction on how to conduct the activity. This is usually printed text with illustrations, although audio-visual methods have been used. Generally, the home kit activity is quite tightly structured so that deviation from the intended pathway and failure and frustration on the part of the student is minimised. The aims, recommended time allocation, procedures and information on handling data are all likely to be included in the instructions.

Once the prototype home kit has been completed it is tested out by some of the course team. Generally the activity is carried out under similar conditions to those the students will experience (our own kitchen ). The prototype kit, both hardware and software, is modified and refined, if necessary, until the presentation form of the home kit satisfies the intentions of the course team.

## Educational Advantages and Disadvantages

It would be misleading to claim that home kits used in distance education have radically different educational advantages over similar hardware used by students in 'face to face' learning situations. In common with the tutor in a conventional teaching institution, the distance teacher recognises the benefits to be gained from practical work. Reinforcing the relationships between theory and practice is an aim most teachers would agree on. "Hands on" experience for the learner helps develop course-expected behaviours related to the above aim. Nevertheless, we can examine some of the educational advantages of home kits as components of distance-learning courses in terms of the way that students could benefit from them.

A major advantage is that each home kit is tailored to a specific course. The practical work done by the student relates to the course and is closely woven into the course right from the start. For example, the correspondence between the activity goals and the course goals are made clear. Course unit self assessment questions may be models for the way students are asked to analyse the data they generate for themselves. A television programme might show an industrial process that the students handled on a small scale in their kitchen. A radio programme might contain an interview with a researcher discussing some of the problems related to the work. Integrating the presentation media has a mutually reinforcing effect.

It is certainly an advantage for students to work at their own pace. Although there are specific periods during a course when home kits are to be used, it is possible for students to work without time constraints, as imposed by laboratory-time, for example. Therefore students can allow themselves the time they need to cover the work to their own satisfaction.

Because students retain the home kit for the duration of the course they obviously have continual access to it, thus being in a position to make use of it when and how they like. It is possible for them to use the hardware imaginatively. For example, a student might like to repeat an experiment in a slightly different way, interpreting the new results and making comparisons with the original ones. Another student might feel happier with an 'action replay'. If a set of results is suspect or thought to be outside the expected bounds, that part of the work could be repeated. Having the kit always available permits the student to isolate some baffling aspect of the work and examine it in greater detail in order to clarify an obscure point, thus acquiring a new insight, if need be.

The sense of achievement gained by students who find they can handle home kit activities successfully has a strong beneficial effect on their study attitudes. Many mature students are, initially, anxious about their ability to manage all aspects of the course work, especially the home kit. Learning to manipulate hardware and conducting rigorous experimental work can lead to greater confidence in handling the other parts of the course.

Disadvantages of home kits are not necessarily due to the kits themselves as a teaching technique, but more to do with the students' perception of their role in the study programme. Probably the biggest disadvantage is kit avoidance. It happens that some students tend to make a distinction between credit-award and personal development as reasons for taking a course. If they feel they can gain a pass without using the home kit they are likely to ignore the kit altogether. When home kit work is assessed kit avoidance is not so easy, although in some instances it may be possible to select a pathway through the course where they feel that the home kit work can be regarded as non-essential. Alternatively, the kit may be used in part, depending on a trade-off between effort and results.

The cost of home kits can prove a disadvantage, even from an educational viewpoint. Because of budget constraints some kit components are relatively crude compared with comparable items in a conventional laboratory. Electronic measuring devices, for example, such as oscilloscopes or electronic timers, are generally quite expensive. When these are included in home kits they are likely to be low-priced items which are adequate but not very sophisticated. Consequently, the students' attitude to experimental work could be affected by the performance of their instruments. Unfortunately, naive users are not in a position to know whether the 'fault' is theirs or that of the equipment, if things go wrong.

Provided one takes the above into consideration when designing home kit work the student is not necessarily disadvantaged. Practical work can be treated at an 'in principle' level where an understanding of what is being done is of prime importance. The experience gained would allow the student to conduct the same activity in a better equipped laboratory, thus producing more realistic results, but not necessarily a 'better' student. Moreover, exposure to the difficulties of practical work is a real learning experience, not to be missed

Conducting home kit activities in isolation and at a distance means that there is no 'expert' on the scene. Although it is possible to contact a course tutor for guidance, there is no-one immediately available to help out with an unexpected difficulty. This is a major disadvantage of distance education itself, not just for home kit users. The frustrated student might even abandon the work. On the other hand students tend to form stronger links among themselves to seek solutions to common problems. Although dayschools, tutorials, television programmes and summer schools can be helpful to the student gaining 'hands on' experience, they are no real substitute for the 'craftsman/apprentice' relationship available in the 'face to face' situation. Directed learning can arguably be structured well for distance education. Incidental learning, acquired by watching the 'expert' smoothly carrying out a task, is not achieved by the isolated distance-learner.

Some disadvantages associated with home kits are not immediately obvious. For example, if members of a student's family consider the kit itself an intrusion in the household and show their resentment, the student is likely to be reluctant to use it: what appears to be a logistics problem has an educational effect.

## Friendliness and Convenience

As suggested previously, the effectiveness of home kits in distance education depends largely on how the student perceives the kit and the effect that that perception has on his or her study attitudes. No matter how well conceived the kit may be, it has no educational value if rejected by the student. Clearly it is important for the home kit to be acceptable and to be seen as something from which some benefit is to be gained.

'User-friendliness' is an important characteristic of any home kit. Students generally associate study with reading and talking - something they have been capable of most of their lives. Doing practical work in one's own home may be seen as irrelevant, and even unnecessary. To minimise student resistance to home kit work they should encounter as few obstacles as possible.

A point that needs to be born in mind continually when developing a home kit is the assumption that many students have little or no experience of this type of work. If the intention is to get them to swim it must be obvious to them that the water is not too cold or deep. They should not be expected to conduct tasks that they regard as beyond their ability. For example, the course team may decide to include an already-prepared specimen for, say, microscopic inspection rather than have students prepare their own. That would mean that specimen-preparation was not a goal, no matter how valuable it might be considered to be. Specimen-inspection would be a higher priority goal - partly from an educational viewpoint and partly so as not to intimidate the student. 'Specimen-preparation' could then be included as a goal for a future activity when the success of achieving the higher priority goal has had its effect. Familiarity with kit components makes the work more acceptable to students. If an empty bakedbean can will serve the same purpose as a more elaborate item of laboratory equipment it is arguably preferable, from a psychological viewpoint. (Incidentally, a television programme made in an extremely well equipped thermographic laboratory deliberately made use of a chipped coffee mug and a breadboard, similar to the equipment the students might be expected to use in their own home experiment. The producer was a little upset because 'it didn't look right'. The presenters were quite pleased.) A mixture of the 'new fangled' and the 'homely' can make the home kit less intimidating for the user with little experience.

The mode of presentation of instruction has a strong influence on how home kits are received by the student. Concise instruction, well supported with illustrations, is clearly preferred. The information should be easily extracted and retrieved. The choice is usually between printed material with diagrams and/or photographs and audio-cassette with diagrams, depending on how appropriate each technique is for the type of work the student will be doing. Take the case of one particular course team which used both methods during the home kit development programme, eventually selecting A/V for one home experiment and printed material with illustration for the rest. The A/V method was used for a 'talk through' activity where students did little more than manipulate the hardware and made observations. The tape was made whilst the actual experiment was being conducted, thus producing authentic background noise including comments from the course team members playing the student role. The accompanying diagrams were actual photographs of the hardware being used. The A/V presentation worked well as a deliberate attempt to 'demystify' experimentation and put the student at ease.

'Print with illustration' approach was chosen for experimental work where the procedures were more complex, explanations more detailed and frequent cross-references were required. The procedural steps could then be listed and more easily checked. (This was considered less frustrating than having to search a tape). Explanations did not have be made in the core of the text, but could appear in appendices, available for those who needed them. Consequently, the essential information could be brief and concise, therefore more easily extracted and retrieved. Cross-references were made, if and when needed, by the student - something that could not be handled in a taped presentation.

As with all teaching texts the language should, of course, present no obstacles to the learner. 'Friendly' language can be construed by students as 'patronising', causing antagonism. Use of familiar words may mean that essential information is distorted, whilst jargon, concise and precise and understandable by the experienced, is disturbing to the student. On one particular course, when home kit work was assessed, even some of the tutors were not clear about the language used in one test item.

## Costs

Broadly speaking the cost of home kits can be broken down into developmental, component and maintenance costs. The cost of delivery and return (both borne by the Open University) are relatively minor compared with the other costs. Obviously the number of kits required and the number of years a course will run has an influence on the cost per kit.

The cost of components for a high-resource kit such as the Science Foundation Course kit would be about £200 per student (1983). The kit budget is established at an early stage of course planning.

Developmental costs can be broken down into staff time, both academic and technical, and fees to external consultants, if needed. It would be almost impossible to isolate the amount of academic time put solely into home kit activities. Within the time allocated for the production of a course the academics, individually and jointly, prepare home kits in parallel with other course components. Consequently, how one actually costs academic time would be difficult to say.

Maintenance of home kits is a major cost. The Open University has a large staff in the home kits section for checking, repairing, servicing, recalibrating, replacing, packing and sometimes even modifying kit components. Maintenance extends to renewing expendable stock, such as resistors in electronics home kits or chemicals in science kits.

## Future Availability and Use

The use of home kits in distance education constitutes a major operation, requiring adequate resources and budget. Because they are designed specifically for distance teaching courses, using novel methods to achieve traditional teaching goals, home kits are not likely to be 'off the peg' affairs, readily available to any distance teaching institution that might see a need for them.

Although home kits are by definition intended to be used in students' own houses, this does not prevent their use elsewhere. Open University home kit items have been used successfully in tutored group face-to-face teaching situations. For tertiary level face-to-face teaching institutions hampered by budgetary cuts home kits could offer ways of providing necessary hands on experience at low cost. This could be achieved in two ways. Firstly in some cases it may be possible to substitute simpler items for the sophisticated equipment currently required for laboratories and workshops. This could be backed up by the use of video to show the full scale equipment in operation. Secondly, collaborative development projects among different teaching institutions to devise mutually acceptable kits could result in economies of scale and thus avoid significant deterioration in the sophistication of the devices or procedures so devised.

The same principles could be applied to primary and secondary education. At the time of writing there is continued government pressure for an increase in the amount and level of science, technology and mathematics teaching in schools. At the same time there have been cut-backs in educational spending which make it difficult for schools to respond to this pressure. The Open University has shown that fundamental scientific concepts can be conveyed with the aid of low cost items such as plastic vending cups and an ordinary breadboard, items which are available to any school. Again, by collaborating, schools could take advantage of the economies of scale to devise more sophisticated kits for their own collective use.

In conclusion it seems that home kits have considerable potential, both within the home and without, and potentially at all levels of education.

## Acknowledgement

Thanks are due to Stephen Brown for additional comments on home kits.

## References and additional reading

CORNISH, J.C.L. et al (1981) "External studies in undergraduate physics: self-paced learning with laboratory kits" Distance Education, Vol. 2, No. 2

HOLMBERG, R.C. and BAKSHI, T.S. (1982) "Laboratory work in distance education" Distance Education, Vol. 3, No. 2

KEMBER, D. (1982) "External science courses: the practicals problem" Distance Education, Vol. 3, No. 2

MOSS, G.D. et al (1975) "Practical teaching, the media, and the Open University" in BAGGALEY, J.P. et al (eds.) Aspects of Educational Technology VIII. London: Pitman

# PART 3

# MEDIA IN COURSE MANAGEMENT AND PRESENTATION

# 11. TELEPHONE TEACHING

Bernadette Robinson
Staff Tutor, School of Education and East Midlands Region, Open University.

The last ten years have seen a rapid growth in the use of the telephone as an educational medium. The development of distance education systems, the growth of continuing education programmes for adults, increases in the costs of travel, and new technological developments, have all combined to point to the telephone as a potentially powerful educational tool. During the last decade, teaching by telephone has been used in a number of distance education contexts, and in a variety of ways, with individuals, and with small and large groups. This chapter will, briefly, describe how telephones are used for teaching, examine the technology and the costs involved, and discuss its effectiveness as a teaching/learning medium.

## Uses of the telephone in teaching

Telephones offer two-way, interactive communication across distance. The means of providing the telephone link may be terrestrial wire or cable, high frequency radio waves, micro-waves or satellite. Whatever the method used to provide the link, it means that people who use it can talk to each other, discuss, question and interact with others beyond their immediate boundaries.

Although most familiar in its domestic form, the telephone also has other capabilities. By means of a telephone network, audio, video and data information can be sent and received by individuals or large groups of people. As well as allowing conversation between two people, at two different locations, a telephone network can provide, as additional facilities, multi-point audio teleconferencing (conversation between people at a number of different locations, from 3 to over 100 in number), facsimile transmission of printed material, slow-scan transmission of graphics and photographs on to a television screen, data transmission and computer conferencing.

The use of telephones for teaching comes into what Schramm (1977) calls the category of 'little media' as opposed to 'big media'. 'Little media' (radio, tape-recorders, telephone, film strips, slide transparencies and other visual materials) are less complex and less costly to install and maintain than 'big media' (instructional television, films and computer assisted learning). Hence, when resources are scarce, use of the 'little media' invites reconsideration (Bates, 1982). Telephones in particular provide a readily accessible network of communication using existing and familiar technology.

Telephone communication can serve a number of functions in education and training. It offers an immediate and interactive form of contact which can reduce the sense of isolation experienced by remote or off-campus students, and can help motivate them to persist with their studies. It enables a distant student with a particular learning problem or query to get quick feedback. (Functional communication of this kind is difficult in circumstances where a letter takes two weeks to be delivered and answered). It provides access to courses previously unobtainable in remote areas. It overcomes problems of travel and terrain. When used as an instructional teleconferencing network, it can provide courses which are quicker, cheaper and less onerous to prepare than their printed equivalent, for a wide range of subjects and levels of study, particularly in the field of continuing education. It is a means for separate institutions to share the teaching of jointly produced courses, as well as a convenient way of enriching courses by drawing-in experts or guest speakers who would not otherwise be available. It is flexible in terms of the groupings of participants it can join together.

The terms 'teaching' or 'tutoring' or 'instructing' by telephone cover a variety of usage. They refer to:

- courses and students taught wholly or largely by means of an instructional telephone conferencing network with minimal accompanying printed material;

- courses taught on campus but 'attended' by distant students via a telephone link;

- courses taught partly by correspondence materials, partly by group teleconferences;

- courses taught mainly through correspondence material (perhaps with other media as well, such as television, radio or audio cassette) and which offer supplementary tutorial support by means of telephone (either individual or group);

- courses where telephone communication is an integral part of the teaching event, for example, a live television or one-way video presentation followed by students' telephoned questions, which are both asked and answered 'on air';

- individual telephone calls (occasional or regular) to course writers or tutors from remote students with particular problems in understanding printed course materials;

- individual telephone calls to tutors from remote students needing advice or counselling in relation to educational problems.

The major use of telephones has been in higher education, particularly in North America. However, the number of countries using the medium in one form or another is growing. Current users include the following institutions:

USA:    University of Texas Health Science Centre, San Antonio;
University of Illinois;
University of Wisconsin-Extension (ETN);
Chicago TV College;
Learn/Alaska Instructional Telecommunications Network;
Regents Continuing Education Network, Kansas State University;
Kirkwood Community College, Iowa.

Canada:    Memorial University, Newfoundland;
University of Calgary;
Athabasca University;
Téléuniversité de Québec;
Open Learning Institute, British Columbia.

Europe:    University of Lund, Sweden;
Universidad Nacionale de Educacion a Distancia, Madrid, Spain;
British Open University;
Telekolleg, Federal Republic of Germany.

Australia:    University of Technology, Perth;
Murdoch University, Western Australia.

Elsewhere:    University of the South Pacific;
University of the West Indies;
Universidad Estatal a Distancia, Costa Rica.

Telephone teaching has also been used at the pre-tertiary school level, though to a lesser extent. Such uses have included projects for widening the curriculum in rural American schools, for teaching sick or disabled homebound children, for helping parents in remote communities to teach their handicapped children and for in-service courses for teachers and school administrators.

In addition to its use for teaching, administrative meetings are held by teleconference in an increasing number of distance teaching systems, particularly where an institution has a large regional network, or widely dispersed local centres. Teleconference meetings are held as additional meetings in between regular but infrequent face-to-face meetings involving travel, for committee or working group meetings on a regular basis, or for urgent meetings of people who would otherwise be difficult to assemble. Meetings by telephone are also used for conducting research projects when a team of researchers is scattered over several institutions or countries. It is now comparatively easy to arrange an international conference call bringing together experts from different countries for a seminar or for training purposes.

Telephones are also being used increasingly for 'Dial Access' services which allow users, particularly in continuing education, to dial an audio-tape library for short information items (usually 2 to 4 minutes in length) stored in a central resource bank. It is one of the quickest ways to make specialised information accessible to large numbers of individuals, and topics range from medical up-dating on drugs to agricultural information, from child-care advice to money management.

## The technology

The way in which the telephone is used for teaching varies between institutions not only because of the particular role it is assigned within a teaching system as a whole, but also because of the different kinds of equipment and technology available. The telephone systems run by different institutions are not technologically identical.

Telephone technology falls broadly into two types:

1.  use of a public service network, either with or without additional items of equipment. This can be comparatively low cost, but the quality and performance is highly variable;

2.  use of a 'dedicated' (or private) system, specifically designed for and used by a particular institution. The capital costs can be very high but the quality and performance are good.

1. <u>Teaching by means of a public network.</u> For <u>one-to-one telephone</u> tutoring, the public telephone system is commonly used, with ordinary domestic telephone handsets. Students and tutors are usually at home, or less frequently, at a local study centre. No equipment costs need be involved in this form of use. Costs for the call are borne either by the teaching institution, or by the students or by both (usually depending on the degree of costs involved in the particular country and decisions made by the institution as to how the costs should be borne). It is widely reported that students are at first reluctant to telephone their tutors even when they know costs will be borne by the institution, so tutors are often encouraged to take the initiative in making contact.

As might be expected, the quality of the line varies from country to country and according to the age and frailty of the particular telephone system. One-to-one tutorials with a regular tutor are used widely by (among others) the British Open University and Athabasca University (Canada). At Athabasca they are particularly appropriate for students studying self-paced courses. UNED (Madrid, Spain) runs a general educational advice service and a problem-solving tutorial service for mathematics students ('Consultel'), with costs of calls paid by UNED.

Although there is no special equipment involved, cost is still a factor in the provision and use of one-to-one telephone tutoring and differs from country to country. A recent survey (Observer Business News, Sunday 6 February 1983) showed, for example, that Britain's telecommunications charges are currently among the cheapest in the world, except for local telephone calls which are much higher than elsewhere and which, unlike most other countries, are charged according to duration of the call. Canada, by contrast, is one of the few countries which provides 'free' local calls, but has very high charges for long distance calls.

A relatively inexpensive and simple to install piece of equipment which may be added to the regular telephone line is a <u>loudspeaking telephone.</u> This is an amplifying device which enables a small group of students (up to 10 or 12) at one location to hear and speak to the person at the other end of the line; it also leaves the hands free for taking notes or handling papers or worksheets. This device allows small-group teaching, using a single telephone line.

Another kind of small group teaching can take place by means of <u>teleconferencing.</u> This group telephone call joins between three and nine locations (in Britain) into a network which lasts only for the duration of the particular call. All participants can hear each other and communicate with each other. Students and tutor can be linked in from home. A combination of conference call and study-centre loudspeaking telephones increases the number of people who are able to join in the event, but makes the management of the event more difficult and more formal and the dynamics of interaction more complex.

Audio teleconferencing has developed mostly in the United States (there are currently over 60 systems in operation and 170 organisations using teleconferencing regularly), to some degree in Canada, and to a much more limited extent elsewhere. At the time of writing, there is a growing use of teleconferencing for teaching in Britain. As well as the Open University (currently the largest educational user with between 750 and 1,000 hours of small group conference calls in 1982) it is now being used in trials in medical education in Wales, London and Cambridge, for training youth leaders in Norfolk, for Open Learning groups in Scotland and for teaching music in village primary schools in Cambridgeshire. A small 6 centre teleconference network is currently being planned for use (starting in 1983) in the South West of England, based on Plymouth Polytechnic.

Teleconferencing can take place either by means of a public network or a dedicated one. In the public network service (sometimes referred to as a 'dial up' network because the particular grouping of lines exists only as long as the call itself) the conference call service is provided by the commercial or national telephone company. The company operator joins together up to about nine lines on request by means of a conference bridge. More recently, a conference bridge has been developed which allows participants to dial themselves into a conference call on a pre-arranged date and time. This network enables all participants to hear each other via the public telephone service, usually from home using a domestic telephone handset or at a local centre using a loudspeaking telephone.

Generally speaking (and this is true of the United States, Canada and Britain at least) the quality of service and equipment is variable. Voice quality fluctuates, the bridging of lines is uncertain either because of technical difficulties or lack of operator expertise, and for technical reasons further loss of clarity occurs if loud-speaking telephones are used. While some teleconference calls work well technically, others do not. One frustration of teachers and students in using conference calls through the public network is the unpredictability of performance of the technology. Yet as is widely reported in studies done in several countries, the quality of the technology is a key factor in determining the success or failure of telephone teaching projects. Despite these drawbacks, discussion or tutorial groups by telephone are valued highly by students who are isolated and, depending on the distances to be travelled and the structure of telephone charges in a particular country,

126

teleconferencing can provide a cheaper and more accessible means of contact than a face-to-face meeting.

While the technology described above is adequate for a tutoring or support function, it is generally inadequate for more direct teaching of courses. The quality of the system can be improved by the use of additional equipment at extra cost. Superior conference bridges, capable of linking from 10 to over 100 locations simultaneously, enable very large conference calls to be held, and join the lines together more effectively. These bridges can be purchased and staffed by an institution which then has better control over its use of telephone conferencing. As they are relatively expensive (and additionally incur costs for the staff needed to operate them) they require a moderately high level of use to justify their cost, though they do provide a much improved and more personal service.

Also available are individual microphones and separate loudspeakers, which are more sophisticated technically than the loudspeaking telephone; these significantly improve the sound quality and make it easier for groups of people at different locations to talk to each other than when using loudspeaking telephones. Additions such as these enlarge the scope and variety of possible teaching functions, but also increase the capital equipment and extra staffing costs involved. Decisions about how much to spend on equipment and improvements to the available system are related to what kinds of teaching function it needs to serve and what alternative media are available.

2. Teaching by means of a dedicated network. A dedicated audio-teleconferencing system is a permanently installed network of fixed sites, with lines exclusively available 24 hours a day to the institutions owning or leasing them. It uses a four-wire system which provides much better quality transmission of sound than is possible on the usual two-wire system, where audio signals are both sent and received along the same pair of wires, as on the public networks. It also enables a variety of sub-groupings of locations to be linked together, as well as the joining in of a limited number of public telephone network lines.

Examples of this kind of system are Wisconsin's Educational Telephone Network and the more recently established network of Memorial University, Newfoundland (the only 'dedicated' educational network in Canada). While relatively expensive to install initially, a telephone network of this kind can be financially viable to run where use and costs are shared with other users, and where the system is in continual use. For example, Memorial University Network's installation was supported initially by a Federal Government grant and operating costs are shared by 40 different user organisations.

Once an audio-teleconference system is in place, teleconference lines can also be used for data transmission (often used for medical education courses or diagnosis at a distance), tele-writing (hand-written graphics electronically transmitted to remote screens) or transmitting tones which will automatically call up photographic slides on projectors at participating sites.

While interactive video is often seen as a desirable form of teleconferencing, the costs of it are generally very high, and can outweigh the benefits of being able to see other participants. Audio-teleconferencing, either by itself or with additional graphic facilities, has shown itself to be satisfactory for a large number of communication tasks.

Although satellites are more readily thought of in relation to television broadcasting, they do have other important audio and data applications. For example, they provide a standard long-distance telephone service at lower cost (and of better quality) than through terrestrial circuits. They make possible new opportunities for the development of education and training programmes through audio-teleconferencing, either by itself or in a hybrid media mix.

The availability of satellites to Canada in the 1970s and the decision to designate some of their use for educational purposes have led to a variety of applications being developed for groups who were previously not able to participate in continuing education and training. The possible educational applications of the Australian Domestic Satellite System (ADSS) are currently being considered and planned for use in 1985-7. This system will be complemented by a terrestrial telecommunications network which, by 1990, should increase telephone facilities to 99.7 per cent of Australia's population. This opens up considerable opportunities in Australia for the educational use of telephones at a more realistic cost than at present, for reaching currently inaccessible communities and for providing an improved and more effective service for the School of the Air (see Beare, 1983).

Effectiveness as a teaching medium

In reviewing the rather uneven research into the effectiveness of audio or telephone communication as a teaching medium, one is forced to return to Schramm's conclusion that learning depends on how a medium is used rather than which medium is used. The research and evaluation studies of telephone teaching cover a wide range of situations and include both field and laboratory settings. It is often difficult to draw firm conclusions because of research design problems. The studies, frequently done with very small samples, use diverse measurement methodologies and techniques which vary in reliability. Most of the studies evaluate in terms of user satisfaction;

fewer attempt to measure learning gains because of the difficulties involved in a 'real life' situation. Also many of the studies on teleconferencing were carried out with more primitive equipment than is used today (see Parker & Monson, 1980 for a summary).

In general, the research shows that learning can take place as effectively, and in some cases more effectively, on courses taught by telephone as on courses taught by other means (the usual comparison is with face-to-face). No differences between face-to-face and telephone communication have been found for tasks involving information transmission, some kinds of problem-solving and generating ideas.

It seems that the tasks which most frequently occur in educational settings (giving and receiving information, asking questions, exchanging opinions and problem-solving) are tasks which can be done effectively by telephone. However, tasks such as getting to know someone, or persuasion or negotiation are affected by the medium through which they are done. For example, people who have met face-to-face are judged more favourably than people who have met only by telephone. Broadly speaking tasks in which inter-personal relationships are important are done less effectively by telephone, while those involving cognitive material are done as effectively. Though face-to-face meetings are generally reported as preferred, students rate the value of telephone teaching or tutoring highly when no other options are open to them.

In a British Open University study (Robinson, 1983), telephone tutorials with either individuals or small groups were found to be used effectively for the following tasks:

- to clarify student difficulties in course material;
- to promote student discussion of specific issues and topics;
- to exchange interpretations of a case or thesis;
- to discuss problems of recent written assignments, or strategies for tackling forthcoming ones;
- to check through worked answers to previously-circulated problems;
- to analyse a written text or a musical score;
- to present short case-studies;
- to debate a prepared case for or against a thesis;
- to role-play an exercise;
- to practice and evaluate sight singing on a music course;
- to identify and clarify concepts in genetics using previously circulated diagrammatic material;
- to manipulate symbolic expressions, using previously circulated worksheets;

- to construct and evaluate graphs, using previously circulated worksheets;
- to interpret and discuss previously circulated sets of raw data;
- to negotiate the design of a project in cognitive psychology and monitor its progress.

Telephone tutorials (audio medium only) were not considered effective in the Open University context for:

- lecturing (it was felt to be an inappropriate use of the medium);
- constructing a complex diagram from scratch;
- impromptu tutorials on unprepared topics;
- tasks involving a large number of texts or sources to be consulted in the course of the tutorial;
- groups where the membership is constantly changing and contact with the tutor is minimal;
- some science, technology and mathematics courses which require the exchange or production of spontaneous or dynamic visuals;
- conveying lengthy and detailed instructions.

## The problems of graphics

While providing a satisfactory means of teaching or tutoring for a wide range of subjects and groups, the medium of audio alone imposes some limitations in terms of the use of graphic or visual materials. Teaching strategies can, in many circumstances, circumvent this problem, by for example circulating in advance diagrams with grid or colour coding for easy reference, photographs or worksheets.

Open University tutors have shown considerable ingenuity in developing ways of using graphic material as part of a telephone tutorial (for example, using a series of overlays to build a concept diagram) and for many subjects this is satisfactory. The advantages of these techniques are that they can be used with home-based students, no extra technical equipment is required and they are low-cost (though greater preparation time is involved). The limitations (expressed particularly by Science and Technology teachers) are that the interaction remains at the level of words (even though about diagrams) and two-way graphic exchanges are not possible, thus reducing the amount of checking and feedback than can be done.

Dedicated networks often add a graphics facility; for example, Wisconsin's Statewide Extension Education Network (SEEN) has an electrowriting facility to 23 sites which enables line-drawn graphics to be transmitted via the telephone as they are being drawn by the teacher and received on a television screen. One-way graphics can also be transmitted by the use of slow-scan video or fascimile transmission. But all of them are rather slow in use and teachers express the need for a simple, speedier blackboard equivalent, preferably allowing two-way interaction. One such development which fills this gap is CYCLOPS (described in Chapter 12).

As well as adapting their teaching strategies to compensate for the absence of a graphic mode of communication, telephone tutors or teachers also need to adapt in other ways. They have to learn to communicate with unseen participants without the usual visual cues to ease the transaction or to provide feedback ("how can I pick up puzzled faces by telephone?"). This is usually a beginner's problem which creates high anxiety in the teacher, until he or she quickly learns to translate a raised eyebrow into its verbal equivalent, and to help students to do the same.

The teacher has to re-design the content and format of a teaching or tutoring session, as well as accommodate to the change in teaching role and pacing of the event imposed by the medium. A telephone session, even with a small group, requires more preparation of support materials (such as agendas, worksheets, reading list and diagrammatic material) and a longer 'lead-in' time for setting up the event than would be necessary for a face-to-face meeting. The material chosen, and the topics to be covered, also need to be more specific than for a face-to-face meeting.

The lack of visual contact in a telephone teaching group places the tutor or teacher more firmly in command of the event in the perceptions of other participants than is the case for an equivalent face-to-face group. The tutor takes control of organising the speaking space for all, indicates turn-taking, most frequently takes the initiative in opening an inter-change or in questionning, and is the chief, if not sole, recipient of verbal contributions from others (findings from a study of Open University tutorial groups, Robinson 1983).

This perhaps places the teacher in a more authoritarian role than he or she might find educationally desirable for an adult learning group. However, with conscious planning for a different kind of interaction, and with the growth of familiarity between members of the group, a more informal and interactive structure usually develops, with the tutor moving away from his or her position as the pivot of the wheel.

On the larger instructional networks, the quality and quantity of 'on-air' interactions can be limited because of the size of the groups involved. To meet this problem, use is sometimes made of local animateurs to develop 'off-air' on-site small group discussions as part of a larger-scale teaching event. Whether the telephone teaching group is large or small, conscious planning is needed to facilitate the interaction that is the medium's main strength.

## Briefing and training the users

One of the key factors in developing effective telephone teaching is the kind of induction and training in the use of the medium offered to both students and teachers. Teachers who feel inadequately prepared for an event which research shows to be more anxiety-provoking on first encounter than face-to-face teaching, are unlikely to persist in the use of the medium or to adapt their teaching strategies effectively, even though the technology involved is user friendly (there is no complicated machinery to master before the participant can use it). Successful adaptation to communicating through the medium generally takes place fairly quickly (over the first few sessions) particularly when the group size is small. The development of appropriate teaching strategies takes longer as the teachers or tutors learn to make choices about suitable content and formats, or which media mix to use (for example, what combination of telephone, print, audio-tape, video-tape, slide-transparencies), or what kind of visual or graphic support materials are needed and how to convey them. Many teachers report that the experience of teaching by telephone causes them to re-think their whole approach to teaching both their subjects and their face-to-face groups.

In order to support teachers using the medium a variety of training methods and programmes are being developed by different institutions. In wide use are advisory booklets; audio-tape examples of good and bad practice; simulated workshop sessions using the medium either for teaching purposes or to develop inter-personal and counselling skills; self-evaluation audio-tapes and checklists; face-to-face workshops. For example, Athabasca University uses a workbook on inter-personal communications and counselling skills, together with tape feedback sessions of actual tutorials to help tutors with one-to-one telephone tutorials with students on self-paced courses. The British Open University uses a mixture of the methods mentioned above, including a handbook ('Tutoring by Telephone' 1982) on small group and one-to-one tutorials. Wisconsin's ETN uses a handbook and training programme to advise and guide instructors in the planning and design of the courses to be taught by audio-teleconferencing. Experience and research suggests that teachers who are already effective face-to-face teachers are likely to make effective telephone teachers. Teachers widely report that they learn most of all from 'doing it' and from hearing about and observing other teachers' sessions.

## Conclusions

Telephone technology is not suitable as a means of mass instruction, in the way that radio and television are. To function as an interactive teaching system (one of its strengths as a medium) there is a finite number of locations that can participate. Teaching by telephone is suitable for more limited groups and specialist needs in education and training.

However, there are some cost advantages to this form of distance teaching. While recognising the fact that all media are not functionally equivalent in terms of what they can do as a teaching medium, it is worth noting that the production of courses and training of staff to use telephone teaching systems can cost less than broadcast media such as television, or less than print-based courses for some subjects.

Used as part of a system employing several media for teaching, telephone teaching or tutoring has demonstrated that it can combine effectively with other media, for example, with video, audio-cassette, correspondence and radio. This versatility provides new possibilities for teaching-learning interactions in distance-learning systems.

## References and additional reading

APTED, M.J., and LIVINGSTON, K. (1981) "Teleconferencing via satellite in a distance education programme: the USP experience 1971-81". ASPESA Forum '81 Papers. Australian and South Pacific External Studies Association.

BAIRD, M. et al. (eds.) (1979) Dial Access: A Way to Spread Your Message. Madison: University of Wisconsin-Extension.

BATES, A.W. (1975) "Obstacles to the effective use of communication media in a learning system", in BAGGALEY, J.P., JAMIESON, G.H., and MARCHANT, H. (eds) Aspects of Educational Technology III. London: Pitman.

BATES, A.W. (1980) "Applying new technology to distance education: a case study from the Open University of difficulties in innovation", Educational Broadcasting International, Vol. 13, No. 3.

BATES, A.W. (1982) "Trends in the use of audio-visual media in distance education systems", in DANIEL, J.S., STROUD, M.A. and THOMPSON J.R. (eds) Learning at a Distance: A World Perspective, Athabasca University/ICCE, Canada.

BEARE, H. (1983) "Education by satellite: Australian possibilities" in SEWART, D., KEEGAN, D., and HOLMBERG, B. (eds.) Distance Education: International Perspectives. London: Croom-Helm.

CARR, R.J. and ROBINSON, B. (1978) "Reaching the remote student: tutoring by telephone" in Problems of Education in Remote Sparsely Populated Areas  Scottish Educational Research Association Monograph.

CONRATH, D.W. et al. (1977) "A clinical evaluation of four alternative telemedicine systems", Behavioural Science, Vol. 22.

CONRATH, D.W.et al. (1983) Evaluating Telecommunication Technology in Medicine, Artech House.

FLINCK, R. (1978) Correspondence Education combined with Systematic Telephone Tutoring, Stockholm: Hermods.

FLINCK, R. (1983) "The telephone used in an experiment of distance education at the university level", Pedagogical Reports, No. 4, University of Lund, Sweden.

GENERAL DIRECTORATE OF POSTS AND TELECOMMUNICATIONS, FINLAND (1983) "Human Factors in Telecommunications", Proceedings of the 10th International Symposium, Helsinki, Finland.

GEORGE, J. (1979) "Tutorials at home: a growing trend", Teaching at a Distance, No. 14.

GOUGH J.E. et al. (eds.) (1981) Education for the Eighties: the Impact of the New Communications Technology Day, Deakin University Press.

GRIFFIN, C.C.M. (1981) "Moral ties and satellite networks: creating 'Community' for distance learning across cultures of the South Pacific", ASPESA Forum '81 Paper, Australian and South Pacific External Studies Association.

GRUNDIN, H. (1980) Audio Visual and other media in 91 Open University courses, Milton Keynes: Open University (mimeo).

HAMMOND, S. et al. (1978) Teaching by Telephone: London: Social Science Research Council (H.R. 4487/7)

HUDSON, H.E. (1981) "Teleconferencing Alaskan Style", Technology, Vol. 201, No. 26.

KIRMAN, J.M. and GOLDBERG, J. (1979) "Student teacher telephone conferencing with satellite maps as a monitoring device, "The Alberta Journal of Educational Research, Vol.XXV, No. 4. December.

LA FUNDACION PARA EL DESARROLLO DE LA FUNCTION SOCIAL DE LAS COMMUNICACIONES, Spain (1974) Las Telecommunicaciones y la Ensenanza Universitaria a Distancia, Universidad Nacional de Educacion a Distancia, Madrid.

LA FUNDACION PARA EL DESARROLLO DE LA FUNCION SOCIAL DE LAS COMUNICACIONES, Spain (1979) La Consulta Telefonica y la Ensenanza a Distancia - Proyecto CONSULTEL, Universidad Nacional de Educacion a Distancia, Madrid.

LAUFFER, S. and CASEY-STAHMER, A.C. (1982) "Telecommunications systems for education and training", Educational Media International, 3.

LEWIN, L. (1983) Telecommunications in the U.S.: Trends and Policies, Artech House.

L'HENRY-EVANS, O. (1974) "Teaching by telephone: some practical observations", Teaching at a Distance, No. 1, pp67-9.

MANDVILLE, M.L. (ed) (1982) "A man's reach should exceed his grasp", Distance Education and Teleconferencing at Memorial University. Memorial University of Newfoundland, St. John's.

MONSON, M.et al. (eds.) (1977) A Design for Interactive Audio, University of Wisconsin-Extension, Madison.

MOORE, M. (1981). "Educational telephone networks", Teaching at a Distance, No. 19, pp24-31.

OPEN UNIVERSITY (1982) Tutoring By Telephone: A Handbook. Milton Keynes: Open University Press.

PARKER, L. and MONSON, M. (1980) More Than Meets the Eye: The research and effectiveness of Broadcast Radio, S.C.A., and Teleconferencing for Instruction, University of Wisconsin-Extension , Madison.

PARKER, L.A. and OLGREN, C.H. (eds) (1980) Teleconferencing and Interactive Media, University of Wisconsin-Extension Centre for Interactive Programmes, Madison.

PARKER, L.A. and OLGREN, C.H. (1983) Teleconferencing

Technology and Applications, Artech House.

PARKER, L.A. and RICCOMINI, B. (eds) (1976) "The Status of the Telephone in Education", Proceedings of the Second International Communications Conference, University of Wisconsin-Extension, Madison.

PARKER, L.A. and RICCOMINI, B. (eds) (1977) "The Telephone in Education", Proceedings of the Third International Communications Conference, University of Wisconsin-Extension, Madison.

PINCHES, C. (1975) "Some technical aspects of teaching by telephone", Teaching at a Distance, No. 3, pp39-43.

ROBINSON, B. (1981) "Telephone tutoring in the Open University: a review", Teaching at a Distance, No. 20, pp57-65.

ROBINSON, B. (In press) "Telephone in Education", in HUSEN, T. and POSTLETHWAITE, N. (eds) International Encyclopaedia of Education: Research and Studies, London: Pergamon Press.

ROBINSON, B. (in press) The effect of the media on tutoring (in preparation)

RUGGLES, R. et al. (1982) Learning at a Distance and the New Technology, Educational Research Institute of British Columbia, Vancouver.

RUTTER, D.R. and ROBINSON, B. (1981) "An experimental analysis of teaching by telephone: theoretical and practical implications for social psychology", in STEPHENSON, G.M. and DAVIS, J. (eds) Progress in Applied Social Psychology, Vol. 7 (1), London: Wiley.

RUTTER, D.R. and STEPHENSON, G.M. "The role of visual communication in synchronising conversation", European Journal of Social Psychology, Vol. 7 (1), pp.29-37.

SCHRAMM, W. (1977) Big Media, Little Media: Tools and Technology for Instruction, Beverly Hills: Sage Publications, U.S.A.

SHORT, J. (1974) "Teaching by telephone: the problems of teaching without the visual channel", Teaching at a Distance, No. 1, pp61-67.

SHORT, J.A. et al. (1976) The Social Psychology of Telecommunications, London: Wiley.

TARCOOLA PROJECT (1981)  A Trial in Distance Education Methodologies Using Telecommunications, Education Technology Centre, Education Department, South Australia, 1982.

TUROK, B.  (1977)  "Telephoning: a passing lunacy or a genuine innovation?"  Teaching at a Distance, No. 8, pp25-33.

UNIVERSITY OF WISCONSIN-EXTENSION (1983)  Teleconferencing Directory.  Centre for Interactive Program, University of Wisconsin Extension, Madison.

WILLIAMS, E. and CHAPANIS, A. (1976) "A review of psychological research comparing communications media: the status of the telephone in education, Proceedings on the 2nd Annual International Conference, Madison, Wisconsin.

WILLIAMS, E. et al. (1975)  "Students' reactions to tutoring by telephone in Britain's Open University", Educational Technology, 5, 42-26.

## 12.  CYCLOPS: SHARED-SCREEN TELECONFERENCING

David McConnell
Research Fellow, Institute of Educational Technology, Open University.

The advent of recent technologies in distance education has opened new pathways to the effective teaching of the distant student. One of the most recent of these has been the introduction of Information Technology. British Prestel, Canadian Telidon and other Videotex and Teletex Systems are being applied to the field of distance teaching (eg. see Owen, 1982). Within this context, the Open University's Cyclops telewriting (or audiographics) system has already contributed significantly to our understanding of the potential for Information Technology in education. Cyclops is not a conventional Videotex system, but is a versatile shared-screen technology which can be used over public telephones during live teaching.

### Cyclops in Distance Teaching

The Cyclops distance teaching system is based on the conventional TV set, standard audio-cassettes, micro-computer technology, and telephones. It has been developed by a research team at the Open University in Britain since 1976 (see Liddell and Pinches, 1978; Francis, 1981).

The Cyclops terminal described in this chapter was a medium resolution (320 x 240 pixels) graphics terminal equipped with a 6800 Motorolla processor. There were 48K bytes of RAM (30K of which is used for display), and 14K ROM. The display is 40 characters x 20 lines, with eight colours available. A more advanced version, with greater power and resolution, is being marketed by the manufacturers, Aregon International Limited, toward the end of 1983.

### Cyclops Network

Cyclops has been used since February 1981 to tutor students at a distance in the East Midlands Region of the Open University. This evaluation project, funded by British Telecom, has extended towards the tuition of some 600 students on about 30 courses from all faculties. Fifteen Open University study centres throughout the region - typically local libraries, schools or colleges - have Cyclops in them.

The standard set of equipment consists of a Cyclops terminal, with a light sensitive writing pen and an electronic digitising pad; two telephones, one for voice communication (attached to a hands-free, Doric loud-speaking unit), the other for transmitting Cyclops pictures (via a modem); and a standard TV set (see Figure 1)

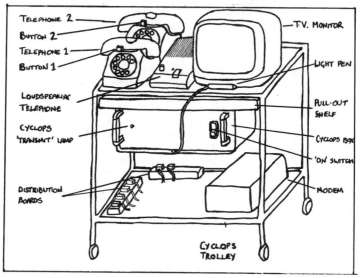

Figure 1

The equipment is secured to a movable trolley with a pull out shelf for laying books or paper on. Dates for the tutorials are fixed at the beginning of the academic year. The study centres are linked together on the voice and data telephones via a separate conference bridge located in the regional office at Nottingham. A 'Cyclops host', paid for by the Open University and located in the regional office links the centres together, welcomes all participants, and monitors the quality of the telephone lines throughout the tutorial. Participants can be linked into the system or disconnected at any time, and up to nine different study centres can be linked together simultaneously. (For more details of the system see McConnell and Sharples, 1982).

## Advantages of Cyclops

There are four main types of teleconferencing technologies:

- audio only;

- audiographic (audio plus slides, etc., at each location);

- slow-scan (or captured frame) video;

- full motion video.

Each of these technologies has certain advantages over the others. Their effectiveness in distance education depends on the degree to which they meet any particular educational needs. However, the common factor in them all is the audio-link.

Cyclops does not fit easily into any of these categories. It is much more than audiographic, but is not video since participants cannot see each other. It is completely interactive, both in speech and in image creation, which is not the case with any of the others. It embodies telewriting, and shares many characteristics of videotex systems.

In terms of its unique characteristics, Cyclops has three main educational strengths which make it a powerful technology in distance education. These are: a writing and drawing facility; the interactiveness of the system; and the ease of preparation of teaching material.

1. Provision of a Writing and Drawing facility. The provision of a writing and drawing facility is a major advantage of Cyclops teleconferencing. Writing on the screen is controlled by the Cyclops terminal. When the terminal is switched on, the user accesses a menu of commands by pressing the light pen against the screen. The screen converts from grey to white and the four commands are automatically displayed at the bottom and remain there until the system is switched off. Each command is chosen by pressing the light pen against it. The choice of command is registered and is made apparent to the user by the background changing from white to black; so the user is always aware of which mode the system is in. The DRAW command allows the pen to be used for line-drawings, free-hand sketches and writing. The pen leaves a black trail on the screen about the width of a felt-tip pen. The LINE command is used for drawing and joining-up straight lines such as the axes of a graph or the lines on a musical stave. One part of the screen is touched with the light pen, leaving a small registration dot. When a second point is touched, a straight line appears between the two

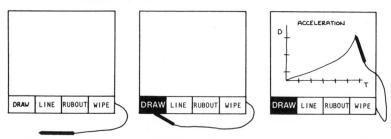

1. CYCLOPS DISPLAY SCREEN    2. TOUCHING COMMAND    3. DRAWING ON PICTURE AREA

**Figure 2**

points. Touching a third point creates another line between the second and third point , and so on. To start a new line, the LINE command is re-selected and the pen pressed on the first new line point.The RUBOUT command allows the light pen to be used for erasing unwanted parts of drawings and writing. The pen is traced over the unwanted areas, leaving a band of cleared screen. The WIPE command is used to completely clear the picture area of the screen. After using the WIPE command, the system automatically reverts to the DRAW mode.

When the terminal is used in the 'local mode', i.e. not connected over telephones to other terminals, the user has complete control over picture creation on the screen. By linking two or more terminals together, the screen becomes a communal picture area. Whatever one person puts on the screen will be seen simultaneously by everyone else, and can be added to or changed by themselves or by someone at a distant location.

Scribble-pads (digitizing tablets) can also be interfaced to the system. These are large electronic writing pads which have an area for writing on which is much the same size as the picture area on the Cyclops screen. The pad can be placed the knees or on a table. An electronic pen linked to the pad is used for writing and drawing. The four commands are displayed on another area of the pad and are chosen by pressing the pen against them. There is ink in the pen, allowing the user to see what he or she is drawing. The scribble-pad allows finer resolution of writing and drawing than the light pen (McConnell and Sharples, 1983). Diagrams drawn on paper can be brought to the tutorial and traced over on the scribble-pad, displaying them quickly on the screen.

2. Interactiveness of the System.    Another major strength of the system is its interactiveness.    Students and tutors in different locations can speak to each other and hold involved discussions.    By means of the light pens and scribble-pads they can also interact in a visual mode.    Each has equal access to the shared-screen and anyone can add to, alter or change whatever is displayed.    This can give considerable power to students in structuring the teaching and learning experience in a way that could never occur in conventional teaching.    This is particularly true in subjects which have a high dependence on visuals for explaining difficult concepts, for example biological sciences, geography, technology.

Teaching by Cyclops requires tutors to experiment with their teaching methods so as to make full use of the interactiveness of the system. This can lead to unique educational experiences.  For example biology tutors have used the screen to develop in an interactive manner complex diagrams of physiological systems, such as hormonal feedback mechanisms and mammalian nervous systems.  In one tutorial students had difficulty in understanding how nerve-cells produce a reflex in muscles.    The tutor explained the process visually by involving students in different centres in developing a series of diagrams to show how nerve-cells work.  Such an interactive visual-verbal learning process is not possible in conventional biology classes. The interactive nature of Cyclops makes learning in this way quite feasible.

Tutors of less visually oriented subjects, such as education or arts subjects, can use the screen for displaying titles and points emerging from discussions.    The system has effectively been used for cross-centre discussions and debates.    Students in different centres are given particular tasks to carry out.    The group as a whole then comes together to discuss the various outcomes. Students in different centres write their points on the screen for everyone to see, providing a verbal explanation at the same time. The tutor in her centre can underline key words for emphasis.    Words and phrases are connected by circling them and joining them up with lines.    The screen is a powerful visual statement.    Participants can focus on it during the discussions, and it can be used later as a summary of what was said.

Student comments, and data from observation studies, suggest the interactiveness afforded by the light pen can add to a tutorial in several significant ways:

     i)      in aiding clarification of difficult material:    students have commented that the pen is useful for completing formulae, graphs and drawings originated by the tutor.    A typical student commented that "It allowed one to clarify points that were difficult and confusing to do verbally, eg. mathematical formulae;    exact graph positions";

ii)     by increasing involvement with the tutor and other remote students:  one of the greatest difficulties in teaching at a distance via any medium is to encourage students to participate actively in the learning experience. It is easy for students to become passive learners, and equally easy for tutors to monopolise use of the medium.    The light pen provides another means of involving students.  As one student put it" ... it seemed to make the contact with the tutor and other remote students more personal."   This benefit is perceived by tutors also:   "...interaction improved possibly because of ability to modify visuals.";

iii)     by promoting thinking, forcing students to think about what they are writing or drawing on the screen:  "It made me think about the diagrams which I was asked to add to" (student quote.). This last point can be especially important when a student is drawing a complex diagram or completing a mathematical equation.   Such activity has important implications for cognitive learning.

Compared with slow-scan or full motion video teleconferencing (which are one-way), Cyclops is potentially more powerful. Participants can modify shared images.  The ability to contribute from any centre in this way makes for greater involvement of students, and hopefully greater learning gains.


3.     Ease of Preparation of Teaching Material.   Preparation of teaching material for Cyclops tutorials is easy, by comparison with TV and video production.  It is also much cheaper.  There are two main ways of preparing teaching material:

i)     Mini Studio:  Simple line diagrams and drawings can be prepared immediately prior to a tutorial using the scribble-pad and light pen, annotated from a keyboard and stored on cassette.  This mini-studio can be set up at any Cyclops site by connecting a portable interface box to the standard set of equipment. On playback, pictures prepared on the mini-studio appear on the Cyclops screen at the speed at which they were originally prepared.

ii)     Main Studio:  More sophisticated pictures containing complex line and block diagrams are prepared in the main Cyclops studio.   Alphamosaic pictures similar to videotex, alphageometric diagrams of the kind used in computer graphics and alphaphotographic pictures can all be created in what is basically a "user friendly" graphics studio.    Users require no knowledge of computing (see Woodman, 1982, for details).  A large number of pictures can be prepared for each tutorial in this way. They are stored on ordinary audio-cassettes either as single frames (or "picture jingles") to be played during the tutorial (in the way a D.J. plays a sound jingle on radio); or as a stream of frames on the same cassette, to be accessed linearly. Pictures prepared in the main studio can be recorded so that on playback they appear as fast or as slow as the tutor wishes. Each tutor can develop a library of pictorial information relevant to his/her particular subject area. Diagrams which are frequently referred to in their teaching can be stored on cassettes and quickly displayed on everyone's screen. They can then be altered or amended by any participant without affecting the original recording, which can be re-played on to the screen at any time.

There are various ways in which graphics can be produced and recorded on to cassette for re-playing during a tutorial. For example, diagrams, maps, instructions, and other much referred to material can be stored for replay as complete frames. This is particularly useful in subjects where information is often provided in graphical form, for example in economics, geography and statistics; or where complex diagrams are needed, for example in biology, technology and so on.

A diagram or chart can be recorded so that it is revealed section-by-section on the screen, with pauses between each section to allow the tutor to discuss each part as it is shown. Difficult concepts can be taught in this way, allowing the tutor to explain the concept by gradually 'unfolding' a pictorial representation of the information by building one frame on top of another, until the topic is fully explained. Students can then discuss the concept or carry out calculations or other work designed to reinforce the concept, after which the tutor can replay the original sequence of diagrams to further reinforce student learning or clear up any problems in comprehension.

Material which is built up bit-by-bit might also be stopped to allow the tutor or students to add to the information on the screen before the next sub-frame is played from the cassette. For example, an incomplete equation could be played on to the screen with enough room below it for students in the various study centres to write their completed version. This could be followed by the "correct" completed version being played on to the screen from the cassette. Using the frames interactively in this way ensures that everyone is involved in the tutorial.

Large numbers of Cyclops pictures can be stored on a cassette and used as an easily accessed data-base, in the manner of videotex systems. Cassette tapes holding dozens of frames have been prepared in this way for Cyclops tutorials.

Analysis of a tutorial in which cassette pictures were used in this way will illustrate this kind of teaching session. The tutorial was the last of a series of seven, given at the end of the academic year prior to exams. It was a revision tutorial, designed to cover those parts of the course that the students had found most difficult, as well as to provide a comprehensive overview of the course content. Two tutors specialising in different areas of electronics ran the session. Five Cyclops centres were linked together during the one and a half hour tutorial.

A data base of Cyclops pictures was recorded on to cassette tape. The beginning of each frame had been previously noted on the cassette counter, so that it could be accessed quickly when needed. The frames were arranged in a "branching-tree" format, from the general to the specific. After the customary warming-up session and personal introductions, one of the tutors explained the aims of the tutorial and the format it would take. He then displayed the first frame, showing a list of the course content. Students in the different centres were asked to choose the parts of the course they wanted to discuss by placing an X with the light pen against the list. At the same time the other tutor made a note of those topics chosen.

The tutorial then moved on to discussions of the chosen areas, with each tutor leading the session in which he was expert. Analogue and digital conversions were discussed, with reference to frames summarising these topics. A detailed analysis of amplifiers was provided, with the tutor giving a mini-lecture based on four frames of drawings and typed summaries. Students were given opportunities to use the information on the frames to solve problems or answer questions posed by the tutors. On one frame, a diagram of a transistor amplifier was displayed on the left hand side of the screen. The students were asked to explain their understanding of the electronics by writing with the light pen on the right-hand side. After each explanation, the RUBOUT mode was selected and the pen used to erase the student's answer, leaving the area clear for re-use by another student. Finally, the tutor played his answer on to the right-hand side.

Throughout the tutorial both tutors also used the light pen for free hand sketches to explain points not recorded on cassette. Occasionally, students requested the course content list again to choose additional areas for discussion and analysis. A great deal of material was covered in the tutorial with students benefitting from pictorial explanations of course content. The material stored on the cassette was also easy to copy into notebooks for later reference.

Cassette pictures enable tutors to show more elaborate diagrams than is possible using the light pen or scribble-pad. Their use can reduce some of the managerial aspects of Cyclops tutorials, allowing tutors to talk with students as the images appear on the screen. This is an important attribute in a situation where the tutor is both teacher of students in several different, distant locations and manager of a complex group experience.

These are the three main educational strengths of Cyclops. To these can be added the user friendly nature of the technology; the simplicity of the system (no intervening cameras, studio lighting, props or technicians); and the low cost of running the system, by comparison with other media such as video or CAL. All of this makes Cyclops an attractive communications medium with powerful educational potential.

## Disadvantages of Cyclops

With practice, tutors and students soon adapt to this style of tutoring and learn how to get the most out of the system. However, in common with other teleconferencing technologies, there are several aspects of Cyclops teleconferencing which might initially prove constraining to participants, and therefore be thought of as disadvantages.

1. **Training in the use of Cyclops.** To use Cyclops effectively, some training is required. Students are sent a copy of the "Distance Teaching by Cyclops" handbook (McConnell & Sharples, 1982) and are given the opportunity to take part in a Cyclops link-up before their first Cyclops tutorial. Tutors receive an expanded version of the handbook, attend a days briefing and training and review their first few Cyclops tutorials with a colleague.

2. **Increased Management and Advance Preparation.** Teaching by Cyclops requires good management of the learning experience. A tutor may be linked to up to seven different Cyclops sites, each with three of four students in them. The tutor has to know who is present at each site, and has to facilitate verbal and visual interaction. Before the tutorial, advance planning is generally needed. This might include mailing circulars to participants, outlining the tutorial content and telling them what books or equipment (such as calculators) to bring with them. Cassette diagrams may have to be prepared. Activities for students to follow-up after the tutorial will have to be formulated.

During the tutorial, the tutor is both teacher and manager. Some of the points of management which they will have to bear in mind are:

- structuring and planning the learning experience; it helps to put a plan of the tutorial on the screen at the beginning for every one to see;

- thinking in "screen-size" chunks; because the screen cannot be scrolled back and forth, the tutor has to think in "screen size" chunks so that the screen doesn't have to be wiped in the middle of writing or drawing something.

- allowing students time to copy down information; because the tutor cannot see when students have finished taking notes as she would in a face-to-face session, she therefore has to estimate when they are finished;

- keeping something on the screen at all times, even if it is just a title or reference; this helps focus students' attention and keeps them involved;

- using time effectively by varying tutorial activities; structuring pauses for study centre based activities; discussions; reading, and so on;

- involving every student, by keeping a note of student talk and ticking beside each person's name when they have participated.

This may seem like a daunting set of tasks. However, we have found that tutors soon become accustomed to dealing with these points of planning and management after their first few tutorials.

3. Lack of visual cues. In Cyclops tutorials, there are no visual cues to monitor student reactions. The lack of visual cues such as heads nodding in agreement, smiles, body-postures and so on, used in face-to-face teaching for monitoring progress, makes the role of verbal cues more important. Participants have to verbalise their reactions much more and answer "yes" or "no" when necessary instead of nodding or shaking their head. This can become somewhat tedious. Tutors have to be aware that many students may be reluctant to constantly verbalise their reactions in this way. For some tutors, this is one of the most difficult aspects of running a Cyclops tutorial.

4. Attendance at Study Centres. At this present stage of development, students have to attend a study centre for a Cyclops tutorial - as they would for a normal face-to-face tutorial. However, Cyclops has been used at the O.U. for courses where it would otherwise be impossible to provide local tutorials. Secondly, in the future, it should be feasible for students to use Cyclops at home.

These are four main drawbacks to Cyclops tutorials. They are not insurmountable and in the main they diminish in importance with practice, but they do exist and have to be considered, especially by those using the system for the first time.

## Costs

Estimating the cost of Cyclops for distance teaching is difficult at this stage. Developments in microprocessor controlled systems are occurring at a rapid pace, so that the Cyclops of today may be quite different to what will be available in the near future. For example, at current prices the Cyclops terminal costs about £1,200. The proposed development of a Cyclops chip or ROM which could be added to a small micro-computer (e.g. the BBC micro) would reduce the cost to about £50 (plus about £450 for the micro). To this should be added the cost of a standard TV set and a cassette recorder (for pre-prepared cassette diagrams). The optional scribble-pad costs about £500. The light pen costs about £50.

Running a Cyclops network would involve the cost of the Cyclops equipment in each centre, installation of telephone equipment (including conference bridges) and annual rental of some equipment. The telephone cost of a 60 minute session between two centres is about £14 (cheap rate long distance telephone charges). With four students participating, the cost per student contact hour is £3.45. Linking eight centres together costs about £56, averaging £3.45 per student when 16 students participate (say two in each centre). To this of course must be added the cost of the tutor. However, there should be some savings in tutors' travel costs. Table 1 (over) summarises these costs.

The Cyclops Studio, in which cassette pictures are produced, costs £14,000. The studio consists of a TV camera, mini-computer, disc-drives, digitising pad and associated monitors and tape-recorders. The cost of producing cassette pictures varies according to the complexity of the pictures. In arriving at an estimation of the cost, the time taken by the teacher to produce outline drawings of the pictures and the time taken by the producer to convert them into Cyclops pictures has to be considered. Teachers at the Open University have taken 3-4 hours to prepare a series of outline drawings for a 1 hour tutorial. These have been converted into Cyclops pictures by a trained studio producer in about 5 hours.

However, there is a new Mark II Cyclops coming on the market from Aregon International, the manufacturers, during 1983, and other technical developments which will reduce costs further are quite feasible, so great caution is needed in estimating costs of future uses of Cyclops.

TABLE 1

| COSTS OF CYCLOPS TUTORIALS | POINT TO POINT CONNECTION | EIGHT CENTRE NET- WORK |
|---|---|---|
| INITIAL COSTS | £ | £ |
| Cyclops Equipment | 2600 | 10400 |
| Installation of Telecom Equipment | 516 | 2064 |
| Two Meet-me Conference Bridges (purchase) and telephone lines | Not Required | 13000 |
| | £3116 | £25464 |
| ANNUAL COSTS | | |
| Rental of Telecom equipment at | | |
| a) Sites | 901 | 3604 |
| b) Bridging Centre | N/A | 1545 |
| | £901 | £5149 |
| COSTS PER 60 MINUTE SESSION | £14 | £56 |

Other Applications

Besides its use for distance tutoring in the East Midland Region of the Open University, Cyclops is being used to train British Telecom engineers throughout Britain and will shortly be applied to the education of university students throughout Indonesia, using a domestic satellite to link together twelve centres scattered over several thousands of miles.

However, as well as its telewriting and audiographics uses Cyclops has several other applications:

- as an audio-visual aid: Cyclops pictures stored on cassette can be replayed as visual aids in live, face-to-face teaching;

- as a self-instructional system: by synchronising a voice-track with a Cyclops graphics track on a stereo audio tape, a self instructional tape can be produced. This tape could be sent to students to be used at their own convenience. Teachers could design their own tapes for use in their school. A small pilot study into this use of Cyclops has already been undertaken (see Bates et al., 1982);

- as a videotex terminal: Cyclops can be used to link into conventional videotex systems such as Prestel;

- as a computer graphics terminal.

## The Future

The many applications of Cyclops make it a versatile technology for distance education. Two developments are in progress which will make it more accessible in education. The first is the reduction of the terminal to a "chip" or ROM, which could be added to a standard micro-computer, such as the BBC micro (which is widely available in schools and colleges). This will reduce costs from the present £1,200 to about £50 plus the cost of the microcomputer. The second development is the production of a modem which can deal with speech and data. This will reduce the numbers of telephones needed in each location to one, so halving rental and delivery costs, and making Cyclops potentially suitable for use in students' homes.

Other more long-term technical developments will increase the application of Cyclops in distance education. For example, the incorporation of a full videotex system into Cyclops tutorials would allow random access of pictures rather than the present linear-access on cassette tapes. This would speed up access and display times, and increase the data base (Bacsich, 1982).

With these developments, Cyclops will be a cheap and effective way of teaching the distant student. It will be of particular benefit in situations where costs prohibit teachers and other experts from travelling to give face-to-face teaching. Thus it could be used for teaching homebound persons; those in hospitals; or those who are geographically remote. Indeed, local and national Cyclops networks, using public telephone lines, could tap the expertise of teachers in their everyday workplace for enhancing the education of the nation. The technology exists. The potential is tremendous.

Whether or not such developments do occur depends on commercial considerations. What is clear is that something very similar to Cyclops will almost certainly be available within the next few years for distance education, whatever the future of Cyclops itself.

## References

BACSICH, P. (1982) Audio-videotex Teleconferencing. Paper presented at Viewdata 82 Conference, London October 1982. (Available from the author at the Open University, UK)

BATES, A.W., et al (1982) Cyclops in schools: A Small Pilot Study. A Report for the Microelectronics in Education Programme. I.E.T. Paper on Broadcasting No. 200, The Open University, UK.

BORDEWIJK, J.L. et al (1982) Vidibord Technical University of Delft, Holland (mimeo).

FRANCIS, A. (1981) "CYCLOPS - Graphics for Videotex" International Videotex and Teletex News, 1982 As reported in issue number 36 (December)

LIDDEL, D.C. and PINCHES, C.A. (1978) The Production of Programme Material for the CYCLOPS System. Institution of Electronic and Radio Engineers (September)

LIDDEL, D.C. and PINCHES, C.A. (1978) Cyclops - An audio-visual Cassette Television System. Institution of Electronics and Radio Engineers (September 1978)

McCONNELL, D. and SHARPLES, M. (1982) Distance Teaching by CYCLOPS: Tutor and Student Handbooks. The Open University, East Midlands Region.

McCONNELL, D and SHARPLES, M. (1983) Report to British

Telecom on CYCLOPS Human Factors. Institute of Educational Technology, The Open University, U.K.


MONSON, M.K. (1980) "A Telewriting System for Teaching and Training: Some Principles and Applications", in PARKER, L.A. & OLGREN, C.H.: Teleconferencing and Interaction Media. University of Wisconsin, Madison, Wisconsin.

RAHUEL, J.C., et al (1980) Télécriture et Audiographie Preprints of contributed papers at the International Conference on New Systems and Services in Telecommunications, Liege University.


SCHRIJVER, ir F.J. (1982) Vidibord: A Description of the Dutch Videowriting System. Netherlands Administration (mimeo).

VIALARON, M. and GIRARD,T. (1980) La Téléconference Audiographique: Un Moyen de Communication de Groups. Preprints of contributed papers at the International Conference on New Systems and Services in Telecommunications, Liege University.


WOODMAN, M. (1982) "The Cyclops Studio - A Computer Graphics and Videotex System for Novice and Expert" IUCC Bulletin, Vol. 4, pp 11 - 15

ACKNOWLEDGEMENTS

The development of Cyclops for distance teaching has been a team effort. Thanks are due to Mike Sharples and Caroline Reed, Cyclops Evaluation Group; staff and students of the Open University, East Midlands Region (especially Dr. D. Elliott and Dr. A. Howe); and colleagues at British Telecom Research Labs, Martlesham.

# 13.  COMPUTERS IN ACADEMIC ADMINISTRATION

Zvi Friedman
Senior Systems Analyst, Management Services Division, Open
University

There can be few distance teaching administrations in the developed
countries in which the computer does not play a significant role.
For most of these institutions it is the traditional large mainframe
computer with its attendant department of systems analysts and
programmers which provides a centralised data processing service to
the whole administration. And, of all areas of administration, it is
academic administration which depends most on the computer.

## Academic Administration

The general emphasis of this book is naturally on the teaching systems
of distance education. For the administrator, the support of teaching
falls within the area of academic administration, that bundle of
functions concerned with the admission and support of students, and
the administration of the courses that they follow.

For the distance teaching institution, the functions of academic
administration afford a special place to the computer. At the root
of academic administration is the maintenance of records of enrolled
students, and the use of those records as a base for the institution's
relationship with its students. Talking about the use of computers
in the context of academic administration within conventional higher
education, Wise (1979) comments:

> "As an institution grows in size and complexity, routine
> information processing seems to grow exponentially. Four years
> of college can generate a sizable amount of information in
> each student's file, and each student also generates a large
> number of financial transactions. The volume of information
> to be handled appears to grow faster in an educational enterprise
> than it does in a business or industry as size increases."

Certainly the Open University's experience, although in the context of distance teaching, supports Wise's observation. Administrative data processing at the Open University, for example, regularly consumes 5% of total recurrent expenditure, and with a staff of 150 the data processing department is larger than some faculties. Yet we run thus fast in order to stay where we got to some years ago.

Student records. As a sophisticated filing cabinet the computer has an obvious role as a tool for record keeping, and as such has been used within colleges and universities since the early 1960s. Lockwood (1972) describes a terminal-based system operational at Yale University soon after 1964. For the large educational institution the ability of the computer to manipulate large files of enrolled students in an environment of complex and possibly closely integrated systems, is especially valuable. Around this student record file many procedures will cluster: procedures to extract students behind in their fee payments, procedures to output course and class lists to assist the administration of teaching, procedures to print lists for the mailing of study materials, and so on. Of particular importance is the machine's powers of analysis and tabulation, providing insights into the nature of large populations impracticable by manual means.

The chief duty of the computer in this student record aspect of academic administration is to ensure that the central student record at all times reflects the state of the student's relationship with the institution, carrying the current state of financial information, academic progress, past, present and possibly future courses, and, of course, such mundane but essential data as the student's current address (often a highly mobile item of data).

Interaction with the computer. In the face to face situation, most of the communication of administrative data occurs by direct interaction between the student and administrators. Teaching at a distance implies less direct communication, and thus the storage and transmission of information by more mechanised means. For the distance teaching institution this will often demand the processing of high volumes of data, representing many students and many transactions between them and the institution. It is important that these transactions are applied with maximum speed and minimum loss of information. At the Open University the two most common transactions affecting student records are changes of address and changes of current course. Now since a very high proportion of our student systems regularly select cohorts of students on the basis of their course and then proceed to mail letters or study materials to them, it is clearly very significant that such changes should be applied without undue delay. Similarly, when the student mails an assignment for marking, it is important to progress and motivation that it is returned as rapidly as possible.

The nature of the student's interaction with the administrative computer is highly significant. So too is the nature of the administrator's interaction with the computer. The establishment of the large distance teaching universities coincided in the evolution of data processing with the general movement from batch processing methods to online or demand processing, a movement which advanced the course of keeping records more up to date. The Open University started with entirely batch systems for its administration, but by 1972 had made the decision to move to online working, using a large student database supported by a network of terminals at key administrative offices (for a discussion of this evolution see Friedman, 1982). Thus we (eventually) put our administrators online, and greatly reduced the delay caused by transactions waiting in batches for their turn to update the main file.

The Online Student. This was a significant move in reducing systemic delay, but it has not got to the heart of the problem, which is, of course, the fact that most transactions between the institution and its students are sandwiched between two mailings. Now, a decade on from that 1972 decision, we are approaching the feasibility of providing our students with the same direct communication with the computer as our administrators have exercised for some years. The tumbling cost of electronics, the almost universal penetration of the television and telephone, and the relaxation in the United Kingdom of restrictive state monopolies over use of the telephone system, all suggest that very soon it will be feasible for the Open University to provide its students with adaptors to convert their television and telephone into a computer terminal which can talk directly to the administrative computer.

The costs of such a facility need not be very great. Just now, for example, owners of a number of types of common microcomputers can buy a British Telecom package to receive its Prestel viewdata service for an initial charge from about £50, plus annual rental charges of about the same amount. It should be said that this is a very basic system using a simple acoustic coupling between the microcomputer and the telephone, and average costs are likely to be rather more. Without your own microcomputer the cost rises to about £150-£200, but there can be no doubt that this cost will soon begin the familiar descent as the domestic viewdata terminal, aided by the banks, building societies, stock brokers and others, becomes a familiar piece of household equipment.

The implications of putting our students online are far reaching. We could allow students to maintain their own basic data. When they move house, they can update their own address (and do it exactly when they want it to change, rather than depending on chance factors to apply the address change not too soon and not too late). Students can input their own course requests for the next session, or tell us which summer school they wish to attend by putting their preferences directly into the appropriate system (naturally, we would protect academic and assessment data ). The Open University employs some hundreds of staff to process many thousands of transactions a week, and to generate and mail equally large numbers of letters and other administrative and informational materials. A large proportion of this activity could be replaced by a viewdata database accessed by the student in his home.

There are too very significant implications for teaching, discussed in other chapters of this volume. With the right equipment, the online student might benefit from online objective testing, or tutorial CAL, or at least be spared the journey to the study centre to use the terminal. The prospect of the online student gives us, at the Open University as elsewhere, some very fundamental issues to examine, issues close to the heart of distance teaching. The fundamental problem of distance teaching is just that - distance - and the consequential loss of the immediacy of face to face communication. However close our administrators are to the computer, we still have the problem that a student communication system based on mailing is highly constrained. A system of communication based on a network of thousands of terminals may seem to some to be a poor substitute for face to face interaction, but just as the structured response is at the heart of computer assisted instruction or assessment, there seems no reason to deny similar degrees of structuring to academic administration.

Extrapolating from the point about structuring responses to student academic input made by Ehin (1973), where it is possible to store a highly structured response, for administrative purposes just as much as for academic ones, then the computer should be used. People, administrators as much as tutors, are most productively used when responses are not predictable, or where subjective factors intervene.

There can be little doubt that over the next very few years, distance teaching administrations will meet strong pressure to put their students online. For large and complex administrations like the Open University, such pressure will present a major challenge to their ability to make adequate adjustment.

## Support for Teaching

The structured response is central to that other function of academic administration, the support of teaching and assessment. From the administrator's perspective, however, using the computer to support teaching begins with relatively uncomplicated functions such as allocation to the face to face components of courses. We have summer schools and weekend schools at the Open University; students of the Finnish Institute of Marketing attend twice yearly classroom sessions at the Institute's headquarters in Helsinki and at a branch further to the north. Then there is the function of materials distribution. Study materials are mailed to Open University students on a regular schedule. The Finnish Institute of Marketing neatly combines the two above functions by giving each student the next package of study materials at each classroom session.

Objective Testing. The computer is an ideal tool for administering tests based on objective testing techniques, where responses to questions (or "items" in this context), are selected from a limited number of options, and the overall result is arrived at often after a good deal of calculation. It is not surprising, then, to find that a major application of computers in support of teaching is in the administration of such testing, which can be applied to both formative and summative purposes. For some years the system operated by Hermods Skola in Sweden has provided a model for other institutions. The Hermods CADE system offers full diagnostic comment for the student, and, in implementations such as at the Finnish Institute of Marketing, many of the problems of control were solved by constraints such as fixing the number of items at 21 for each test or assignment. The Open University in its computer marked assignment (CMA) system, developed around 1971, went for maximum flexibility, with a very wide range of scoring options, but gave the student no more than a single alphabetic grade as a result. Belatedly, the University is now redeveloping the system with full diagnotics and with fewer scoring options. We found that of the thirteen scoring options available to users of the systems, two multiple choice options accounted for over 90% of general usage.

Computerised objective testing poses a number of operational problems, one of which is getting the student's responses into the computer. Most implementations in distance teaching are, as yet, offline, and are dependent on mailed input and response. There is the problem of minimising turnaround time. The critical time seems to be ten days. Less than that, and your system is doing well; exceed it, and people begin to ask if the whole thing is worth while. As with the student record update problem discussed earlier, delay is built into the system; two mailings and a batch process in the middle. Whether you input students' responses on a document reader or use key to disk, or even punched cards, is of little consequence to this critical factor.

Another technical problem is the control of printed output for sending to the student, which could be a few lines or several pages. With low course numbers, this can be controlled manually, as at the Finnish Institute of Marketing, but this option is less practicable with course populations of several thousands. Online systems would not have this problem, since the student user communicates with the computer through the display screen. One might speculate, though, whether the online student in his own home would require a printout of the results. Unlike terminals, adequate printers seem likely to remain relatively expensive.

Item Analysis and Item Banking. Ultimately the validity of an objective testing system depends on the quality of the items which comprise the tests or assignments. The Open University systematically analyses samples of CMA returns to provide feedback on item quality. This consists of a standard set of statistical tests of consistency and discrimination designed to identify untrustworthy items, which require improvement or elimination. Objective testing via the computer is doubtless a powerful academic tool, but its use does set the academic serious problems in the regular production of good test items. For some years now, we have talked about maintaining proven items along with their statistical indicators in an item bank, that is a computerised file of objective test items, and its use to aid, or even automate, the construction of objective assignments. Systems of item banking have been around since the early 1970s, and a substantial corpus of literature exists on the subject. However, if one were to generalise, it is probably the case that academic users have rarely found such systems to be satisfactory, and that the major reasons for this dissatisfaction have been the excessive demands on computing resources coupled with a neglect of well-documented and easy to use operational procedures.

A number of problems inherent in the use of computerised objective testing are less to do with the computer than with the academic's traditional image of his role. For example, the parameters which instruct the computer how to score a particular set of student assignments naturally have to be stored on the computer by the time that the assignments begin to arrive, and, naturally again, they have to be correct otherwise some thousands of assignments will be wrongly scored, and probably sent off to students before the error is detected. Originally, the Open University's Computer Marked Assignment system had no facilities for dealing with the results of errors in scoring parameters, or with the late receipt of scoring parameters. It simply had not occurred to us that academics would get the parameters wrong, or fail to provide them to schedule. We soon ran into serious operational problems, and were forced to correct these omissions, but I'm not sure that we have ever satisfactorily resolved the root problem, which seems to be one of demanding of academics an operational responsibility which they might feel to be incompatible with their traditions. The distance teaching institution may well have amplified this problem.

<u>Subjective Marking.</u> It seems unlikely that the computer will entirely replace traditional manual methods of marking. However, with minimal contact between tutor and student, assessment by performance allied to personal contact is replaced by assessment by performance alone. For this reason, among others, the distance teaching institution will often go to considerable trouble to achieve a consistent standard of marking. Many institutions, Open University and the Finnish Institute of Marketing among them, have computer procedures for the analysis and adjustment of scores derived subjectively. At the Open University statistical significance testing is applied to grades given by tutors to students' assignments. (Statistically minded readers might like to know that we started by using Chi-squared before moving to the Kolmogorov-Smirnov test, which is reputedly more sensitive to small populations.) This facility is informational only; it would be possible to go on to apply automatic adjustment, but we have never done so, preferring to leave any action on deviant marking to the judgement of other humans, in this case the full-time staff tutors. We do, however, have a facililty for the automatic standardisation of examination scores. This is available to equalise the distributions of scores between alternative papers set for the same examination, where there is statistical evidence to suggest that one was more difficult than the other.

<u>Student Progress.</u> A high level of student dropout is without doubt the severest threat to the viability of distance teaching. So far, it seems that the computer's impact on this problem is very limited. At the Open University we do little more than hope to detect students in difficulty by circulating their tutors with regular lists of assessment results. The Finnish Institute of Marketing's computer outputs a fortnightly exception list for each course secretary, and also a less frequent, but available on demand, progress report on each student. Lampikoski (1982) discusses this application, and others in academic administration, in a contribution to the sparce literature on the subject.

Using the computer to monitor student progress presents considerable problems with offline methods of working. The online student could have immediate access to a corpus of information structured to facilitate problem solving, but this still requires the student to take the initiative in seeking help, even were we to provide more powerful tools for this purpose. If there <u>is</u> a satisfactory solution to the problem of detecting faltering students before it is too late, so as to avert dropout, and assuming that the close and frequent contact between student and tutor which can exist in face to face teaching (although it often doesn't ) is infeasible, then that solution must lie in developing online electronic substitutes for direct contact. It is possible to envisage highly developed teaching and administrative links via a large terminal network, where all contacts between students and the institution are maintained by a student progress system which reports symptoms of faltering, such as reduced frequency of contact, or repeated difficulty with assignments. All the components of such a system are available but the cost of operating it must for some time leave it in the realm of futurology.

In sensitive areas of human behaviour technology has severe limitations. However sophisticated our computer systems may become, a small number of students will run into difficulties which only other people can remedy. When the need is to talk over problems with other people, it is important that the computer does not stand in the way. In other words, in such situations, there must always be a way round the system.

## Computers Big and Small

I have said little about computer technology in this chapter. The chief reason is that, given adequate resources of finance and skilled manpower, the range of current computer products is such that rarely will the technology impose constraints on the administrator. Besides, even such recent and able treatments of the subjects as Gwynn (1979) now show signs of dating. Today, from the stand-alone microcomputer through to national and international networks of minis and mainframes, the technology is there to fit applications of all shapes and sizes. Never before has the system developer had so wide a choice of solutions once he has defined the problem.

The impact of the micro has yet to be felt in the large centralised data processing departments of our institutions. The microcomputer promises real devolution to the user departments, in place of the largely illusory devolution provided by the mainframe based terminal network. Movement away from the inefficiencies of large machines promises a healthier future for administrative computing. In many applications the micro offers an alternative to the tyrannical rule of the mainframe, and its ever increasing demands for staff and resources to maintain systems that have become too big to be manageable, too essential to be done away with, and too costly to replace.

Still looking for trends, I see the labels "academic" and "administrative" becoming increasingly less useful within the context of distance education. Time was when administrators used the institution's computer when it wasn't busy with its important work, i.e., its academic work. Many factors have changed this, and not only in distance teaching. Now we are all administrators.

## References

EHIN, C. (1973) "Suggested Computer Applications in Correspondence Education", Educational Technology, October 1983.

FRIEDMAN, H.Z. (1982) "The Contribution of Data Processing to Student Administration at the Open University", in DANIEL, J. et al (eds.) Learning at a Distance: A World Perspective, Edmonton: Athabasca University/ICCE.

GWYNN, J.W. (1979) "The new technology means power to the people ", New Directions for Educational Research, Number 22.

LAMPIKOSKI, K. (1982) "Towards the Integrated Use of the Computer in Distance Education", in DANIEL, J. et al (eds.) Learning at a Distance: A World Perspective, Edmonton: Athabasca University/ICCE.

LOCKWOOD, G. (1972) "The Information Systems for Universities", in University Planning and Management Techniques, Paris: OECD.

WISE, F.H. (1979) "Implications of computers for the administration and management of higher education, New Directions for Educational Research, Number 22.

## 14. TELETEXT SYSTEMS

Peter Zorkoczy
Senior Lecturer in Electronics, Faculty of Technology, Open University.

### The Technology

Teletext is an electronic data distribution method, using broadcast and/or cable as the transmission media. The data are organized into pages, which may contain text and graphic symbols.

The first operational teletext systems, CEEFAX and ORACLE in Britain, employ television broadcasting as the transmission channel (see Money, 1979). More recently, VHF radio broadcasts, and also cable networks, have been exploited (see Smith and Zorkoczy, 1982).

A computer terminal, and appropriate software, is used to create the pages. The computer-stored versions of the pages are then transmitted, one after the other, via the chosen medium, in an electronically coded form. The receiver usually takes the form of a broadcast receiver which incorporates decoding and data storage facilities to display the pages of teletext information, as an alternative to the standard broadcasts. Each page is identified by a numerical reference, and the user selects a page of interest from the transmitted stream of pages by means of a simple keypad. A brief index to the contents of each page, or sequence of pages, is usually contained among the transmitted pages. Once 'captured' a page is held in the receiver's local electronic memory and thus can be displayed for as long as is required. As an option, the contents of the page may be printed out, or recorded on magnetic tape or disc for future reference. Figure 1 (over) shows the main components of a teletext system.

The amount of detailed information (the number of text characters, the fineness of graphics) contained in a page is determined by technical and economic constraints. Thus, the CEEFAX and ORACLE systems employ a 'mosaic' layout of the page, with 24 lines and 40 columns, giving 960 character positions. Each position can contain an alphanumeric character, or a graphics 'character' in one of 7

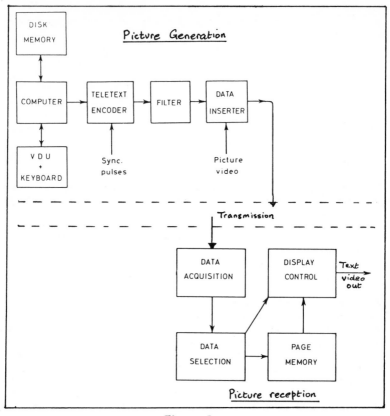

**Figure One**

colours. The graphics characters are made up of all possible combinations of 2 x 3 grid elements each of which may be dark or light. Thus the maximum graphics resolution is 72 x 80 picture elements, or 5760 elements per page.

In addition to constraints on the amount of detail contained in each page, the rate of transmission of pages and the number of pages that may be conveniently transmitted are also limited. Thus, on the current CEEFAX and ORACLE systems, pages are sent at a rate of approximately 4 per second. As the sequence of pages is cyclically repeated (in order to make any page available without an unreasonable

166

waiting time) the total number of pages is limited to about 100 per TV channel. There are several proposed ways of overcoming these limitations, and these will be reviewed below.

## Educational advantages and disadvantages

It is fair to say that so far the educational impact of teletext has been minimal. Applications have been largely on an experimental basis. For example, in Britain the BBC (the operators of CEEFAX) and IBA (the operators of ORACLE) supported a study by Brighton Polytechnic of the transmission of computer programs for educational microcomputers. In this type of application, known as telesoftware, programs can be made available to very large numbers of users at very low transmission costs. The assumption is that, at the receiving end, there is a teletext decoder which directs the character-coded programs straight into magnetic tape or disc storage. Also, there is a need for agreed technical standards which govern the various stages of transmission and data conversion. The Brighton pilot project involves a network of nine schools and distributes software from various sources, including the teachers themselves. A report on this project is expected during 1983. Regular telesoftware services started in Britain in the autumn of 1983.

The material transmitted need not be computer software. It can take the form of general or specialised educational reference information, subtitling on broadcast programmes for the hard of hearing, or, as in the case of the 'Think Shop' experiment in Los Angeles, classroom material for pupils and teachers. In the 'Think Shop' experiment, conducted by the public TV station KCET, a 50 page teletext magazine was transmitted, for 4 hours a day. The activities presented on the pages involved the students in reading and responding to questions in an interactive way. Although teletext is essentially a one-way medium, a degree of interaction may be achieved in one of two ways:

- through the 'prompt and reveal' facility. This is provided by coding a page in a way which keeps some portion of it in an initially non-displayed form (through the use of special character codes). The hidden portion is revealed when the recipient presses the 'reveal' key on the keypad;

- by additional 'intelligence' in the receiving terminal which in response to a multiple-choice answer by the recipient automatically selects the next page to be displayed. This pre-programmed selection will contain the information appropriate to the choice made. To make the waiting time acceptable to users pages must be transmitted at a faster rate than is common in current teletext systems. For this reason, only the first of these methods of 'pseudo-interaction' was utilised in the 'Think Shop' experiments.

The conclusions from that experiment - see KCET (1982) - emphasized the role of teletext in improving the reading skills of school children, in particular of inner-city pupils, many of whom used English as a second language. The report also suggests the use of teletext pages as source material in current-affairs classes of high schools.

The Open University's 'Radiotext' project provides an example of the use of teletext in distance education. Figure 2 shows the main components of the system.

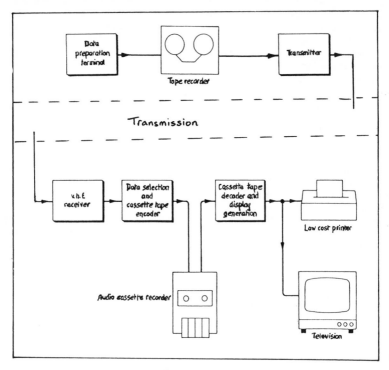

**Figure Two**

The material transmitted (which may be course-specific correspondence texts, "electronic newletters", indeed most items that the University currently mails to its students) is automatically recorded by users on a low-cost audio cassette recorder at high data rates. An overnight transmission pattern was envisaged, enabling the use of VHF broadcast transmitters which are not otherwise utilised at that time. The student can replay the recorded data, in teletext form, on the television screen, or print it out as hard copy. In this mode, the teletext is seen as a <u>bulk text-and-graphics delivery facility,</u> offering a low-cost, <u>instantaneous</u> alternative to conventional mail. This project is still at the pilot stage.

On the basis of these, and a small number of other educational trials of teletext, one can summarise its main advantages, for both the formal and informal sectors of education:

- virtually instantaneous delivery of text and graphics, (but specified pages may involve some waiting time);

- very low cost transmission medium, relying on modified, but existing mass-produced equipment;

- direct compatibility with computing facilities available in schools and homes (via a mass-producible adaptor). Thus, even though teletext is not an interactive medium, as such, the software which it carries may be down-loaded, and used interactively, by individuals or small groups.

Some of the educational disadvantages of teletext have also emerged from the earlier examples:

- at present, it uses a one-way transmission medium, thus restricting the degree of direct interaction;

- the number of pages, and the amount of information per page, as used in current systems, are very limited;

- the television screen is not a particularly suitable medium for text-based learning (e.g. due to problems with resolution, flicker, and lack of portability).

Among other significant, but not inherent, disadvantages the control exercised by non-educational authorities over the medium must be mentioned. In Britain, for example, the BBC and the commercial broadcasting network are in full operational and editorial control of teletext, and the situation is similar in other countries which operate broadcast teletext services. This is very important while the number of pages is so restricted.

Teletext in its present form is restricted to a static visual presentation but can, in principle, be extended to deal with dynamic images, accompanied by sound, which are more suitable in an educational setting. That development, however, removes the cost advantages of teletext, since teletext is currently an add-on facility to TV and radio thus making 'marginal' use of the existing bandwidths. It would require dedicated educational broadcast or cable channels for teletext to be used with dynamic images accompanied by sound.

## Availability

In Britain, teletext is being increasingly used, albeit for overwhelmingly non-educational purposes. At the end of 1982 there were 800,000 teletext sets in the U.K, representing a 3.9% penetration of all homes. About 16% of all TV sets sold in Britain are capable of receiving teletext broadcast on TV channels. These trends imply that about 1.5 million teletext receivers will be in use by the end of 1983.

However, teletext adaptors need not be built into TV sets. They are also being marketed as add-ons to microcomputer systems. It is, therefore, likely that the hardware facilities at least will become accessible to large numbers of institutional and domestic users in the next few years if home owners choose to replace their existing TV receivers or expand their personal computer systems, or if schools decide to get suitable receivers or computer accessories.

Apart from Britain, only a handful of countries (e.g. Australia, Austria, Belgium, Finland, Holland, Sweden) operate regular teletext services, with around 100,000 users in each case (at the end of 1982). In the United States, there are advanced plans for large-scale introduction of teletext via broadcast and cable.

The availability of Radiotext is currently limited by the lack of mass-produced adaptors, and by the broadcasting organizations hesitating about technical standards and the use of VHF channels for this purpose.

## Ease of use

Teletext is quite simple to use, in its present state of development. The main control device is a simple keypad, usually doubling as the remote controller. It is provided with keys to control local-memory dependent features, like the reveal facility, channel identification, time-of-the-day clock display, etc. With built-in decoders there are no problems of interconnections other than to a suitable aerial. When using separate decoders, or teletext interfaces in computers, the connections are made via standard sockets and plugs.

The visual problems of reading text for extended periods of time from consumer-grade colour television sets have already been noted. These problems are alleviated somewhat in sets with built-in teletext decoders which connect directly to the (RGB) driving circuits of the TV set. With external or computer-based decoders the use of TV monitors is recommended.

## Costs

In Britain, built-in teletext decoders add about £100-£150 to the retail price of a remote-controlled colour TV set. Microcomputer add-on versions are in the £100-£200 range. The cost of a Radiotext adaptor has been estimated as £50, in commercial quantities. Optional extras, such as a printer or audio cassette recorder will, therefore, dominate the cost of a teletext facility.

For the originators of the teletext pages access to a computer-based page editing terminal is immensely helpful. The preparation time for educational teletext material is about the same as for CAL, particularly if an interactive or pseudo-interactive mode of usage is employed.

The low cost of transmission is perhaps the biggest attraction of teletext. The teletext signal travels 'piggyback' on the TV signal, or it may be broadcast on VHF radio when the transmitter would not otherwise be used. This makes the cost of transmission per user negligibly small.

## Crystal gazing

There is one major technical development which is likely to boost the use of teletext in a wide range of applications, including education: an increase in available transmission channels, due to satellite broadcasting and broad-band cabling. This will make it possible to dedicate complete channels to teletext, rather than just a small fraction as at present. The effect of this will be either an increase in the number of pages per channel, or a reduction in the average waiting time for a specific page, or some combination of both. More widespread availability of two-way cable would make teletext into a truly interactive medium. This, in turn, would enhance its usefulness for educational applications, both in the formal and informal sectors.

Another planned technical development for teletext is also likely to make it more attractive to education: the improvement of the quality of display, particularly in relation to graphics. High-resolution TV, projected for the 1990's, will give roughly a four-fold increase in the number of picture points. More sophisticated digital transmission, and processing circuits built into TV sets, will be used to generate more complex graphics while, at the same time, needing a smaller amount of externally supplied data. (This trend is already evident in the Canadian 'Telidon' and Japanese 'Captains' systems.)

These technical developments will offer a more attractive medium to education, and at the same time offer more of a challenge and opportunity for the educational technologist: to make best use of a new mass-communication medium.

References

KCET (1982) Educational Teletext Report, KCET, 4401, Sunset Blvd., Los Angeles, CA90027, USA (Cost $25)

MONEY, S. (1979) Teletext and Viewdata London: Newnes Technical Books (Butterworths)

SMITH, P. and ZORKOCZY, P. (1982) "Radiotext", in Proceedings of InternationalConference on Computer Communication, London: Also available as Report No. 30 (August 1982), Faculty of Technology from the author.

For a broad view of teletext developments and potential application in the USA see:

TYDEMAN, J. et. al. (1982) Teletext and Videotext in the United States. London: McGraw-Hill

# 15.  VIEWDATA SYSTEMS

Paul Bacsich
Senior Project Manager, Information Technology, Faculty of Technology, Open University.

## The Technology

Viewdata is a system which allows a user to access information stored in a remote computer via the public telephone service.  This information can be displayed on a domestic television set.  Thus viewdata is a type of interactive computer system.  It is hard to give a precise definition, but viewdata systems normally exhibit most of the features listed below:

- terminal has two-way data link to computer;
- terminal is low cost;
- terminal has characters and graphics capability;
- terminal display is a domestic colour television tube;
- computer devotes limited power to each transaction;
- system has fast response;
- system is standardised by telecommunications authorities;
- system has a simple user interface;
- user interface places a heavy emphasis on menu selection by numbers;
- unit of response to a command is a screen (called a page);
- commands are expressed by menu selection and form-filling.

Viewdata systems have various names depending on the country, for instance Prestel in Britain, Telidon in Canada and Teletel in France. Perhaps as a result of this, the first point of confusion about viewdata is its name.  In Britain we talk about 'viewdata'; elsewhere people call it 'videotex'.  Some people still call it 'interactive videotex' (i.e. viewdata down phone lines), to distinguish it from 'broadcast videotex', which most people call 'teletext'.  And of course 'teletext' is quite different from 'teletex', a new form of telex-style electronic mail.  (There is even a 'Videotext', the German name for their teletext service!)

Confused? So are we all! But to keep matters under control I shall always talk about 'viewdata'. If after this chapter you want to read a whole book about viewdata, I recommend Mayne (1982).

The inventor of viewdata was Sam Fedida, then of the British Post Office Research Laboratories. Following a limited trial in 1975, a small public service started in 1979. This service has now increased to one supporting about 30,000 terminals. After a vain attempt to patent the name 'viewdata', the Post Office (now British Telecom) coined the name 'Prestel' for it.

Public viewdata systems spread rapidly to other countries, notably France, Germany, Canada and Japan, each one adding some new facility, until the original very simple Prestel system began to look rather forlorn beside its younger brothers. As well as the move overseas, many organisations in Britain began to set up their own systems. The Open University was one of these and its own 'Optel' system has been running since June 1979. (Usually you can identify a system as a viewdata system by looking for the '-tel' at the end of its name!)

The main point of contact between viewdata and teletext systems is the terminal. For example, in Britain both the teletext and viewdata displays have the same 8 colours, the same 24 rows of 40 characters and the same characters plus mosaic shapes. Internally, the terminals share a number of common components, but it is now relatively rare for a terminal to operate in both viewdata and teletext mode.

But this still suggests that there is one agreed standard for viewdata terminals. Far from it Indeed, each major viewdata country has proclaimed its own version of the viewdata terminal standard. These differ mainly in the degree of accuracy with which they can represent graphic images.

On the European side of the Atlantic, the French and British favour similar but different flavours of the 'alpha-mosaic' type of terminal with 24 rows of 40 characters and 72 by 80 graphic elements. (The Germans favour a compromise system embracing both the French and the British scheme.) On the North American side, the Canadians followed by the United States favour the 'alpha-geometric' type of terminal: this has 20 (not 24) rows of 40 characters and about 240 by 320 graphic elements. Images are created by specifying points, lines and rectangles (hence the name 'alpha-geometric') and with 240 by 320 graphic elements one can produce reasonable diagrams, but not photographs. (The Cyclops terminal is an alpha-geometric terminal.) There are yet other flavours of terminal: the Japanese have plumped for a facsimile type of terminal to cope with their character set, and there are also laboratory prototypes of 'alpha-photographic' terminals which do a fair job of reproducing photographic-quality images. A reasonably non-partisan treatment of the standards issues can be found in Heys (1981).

As well as the resolution axis, one can also classify viewdata systems by the degree of interactivity they allow. Although there is a continuum, three points on the axis stand out. The first is often called 'Prestel look-alike'. A user can retrieve pages by typing in a numeric code. He can also move from page to page by following links (e.g. references in a paper): these are called 'filials' by viewdata people. Finally, he has the facility to fill in 'forms' on the screen so that the system operators can gather information: these are usually called 'response frames'. (He does this by answering a number of questions posed to him on the screen.)

The second point is called 'gateway-compatible', for reasons that will appear later. The user still has the same commands as before, but there is more going on behind the scenes. I will take some examples from Computer-Assisted Learning. If a user requests a page number, the contents of that page may be put together on the spot from dynamically varying information, e.g. the current number of correct answers in some module of a CAL tutorial. If he types a filial number, then as well as the link being followed, some 'side-effect' may occur; for example the incrementing of a score variable. If he fills in a response frame, the system may take some immediate action on the data, e.g. run a simulation on the parameters he has entered.

The third point is the end of the axis, where any general dialogue is allowed. Indeed, since an alpha-geometric terminal is essentially a computer graphics terminal and many newer alpha-mosaic terminals can display 80-character lines, it becomes impossible to distinguish this point from general interactive computing. For that reason, I shall confine attention to the first two points on the 'interactivity' axis.

## Organisation for distance education

As in the Open University, a viewdata system organised for distance education will normally reside on a medium to large central computer at a major site of the institution. (Exceptionally, one may use pages on a public system such as Prestel, but the limited facilities and high recurrent costs of such a system make this option unattractive unless subsidised; as it is for example in Canada where a public service with full cost-recovery has not yet really started.)

The viewdata terminals will be spread round the country in locations near to the students: preferably their homes or workplaces, less satisfactorily study or resource centres. Since most terminals are remote from the computer, a direct phone call to the computer will be long-distance and thus expensive, even in the evening. Hence one has to deploy the usual general armoury of cost-reduction techniques for data communications networks, such as using rented phone lines and communications multiplexers.

There is also a specialised network solution: following the example of Germany, most countries have a 'viewdata gateway' network which allows a terminal to access a computer by going via the public viewdata network. Apart from the usual network cost, this gateway network imposes a set of rules on the user interface of the computer system which can be summarised by saying that the system has to "behave rather like Prestel". This is the origin of the phrase 'gateway-compatible'. A brief description of Gateway can be found in Prestel (1982).

## Educational advantages and disadvantages

I shall now part company with the less sophisticated of the viewdata enthusiasts and state that:

> the educational advantages of viewdata are just those of any simple to use generalist mainframe-based computer system using relatively cheap terminals.

Of course there are not many styles of such systems that have gained wide acceptance: indeed, apart from viewdata, only the electronic mail style has become reasonably general. (Interestingly enough, on microcomputers there are more candidates, e.g. the UCSD Pascal system.)

Of the two levels of genuine viewdata system I referred to earlier, the 'Prestel look-alike' offers of course the least scope. It is too restrictive to allow a reasonable CAL system, mainly because there are no internal variables in which to store knowledge of student progress. The only way of doing so is to use a large number of individually created pages and even a simple game on Prestel will require upwards of 50 pages. Many applications of viewdata in education exploit merely the fact that viewdata provides an easy to use information retrieval system - see Brown (1982) for a description of educational use on Prestel. The Open University's Optel private viewdata system has a similar justification - see Bacsich (1981).

One of viewdata's main alleged uses in education is that of 'telesoftware': the distribution by electronic means of computer software to microcomputers. Now certainly the viewdata people exploited this application first (see Knowles, 1982); but as Peter Zorkoczy has pointed out in the previous chapter, telesoftware can be sent by other means than viewdata. Indeed, in the computer world telesoftware is merely one application of file transfer over data networks. It is largely because British data networks are so underdeveloped (perhaps our data network experts are more prone to theorising about standards than producing practical systems) that it was left to the British viewdata people to produce a workable system (but not alas, an elegant one).

The 'gateway-compatible' style of viewdata system is certainly rich enough to allow the development of the whole educational computing gamut, including CAL, information retrieval, messaging, and conferencing systems. However, this has yet to happen to any significant extent: almost all 'gateway-compatible' systems still deal with travel reservation, home banking and specialist information retrieval systems. One notable exception is the Hatfield gateway system (Aston, 1982).

Availability

At the end of 1982 the number of viewdata terminals in the major viewdata countries was reported by IVTN (1982) as follows:

Table 1    Installed videotex terminals at end of 1982

| Britain | 20,000 |
|---|---|
| France | 3,700 |
| Germany | 7,700 |
| Canada | 3,000 |
| United States | 2,000 |
| Japan | 2,000 |

In Britain there are very few viewdata terminals in schools, colleges or public libraries, and only about 1,000 in homes.

Major boosts to the French figures are expected in 1983 as part of the French Government policy of promoting viewdata for telephone directory enquiries applications. In Britain a doubling of the above figure of 20,000 is expected as a result of the Micronet telesoftware scheme (see later) and the sales push into the residential market.

Longer term forecasts are as diverse as there are forecasters, and are tied up with questions of commercial secrecy and national pride. A lucid description of scenarios is contained in Campbell and Thomas

(1981). Historically, forecasts by British Telecom have been wildly over-optimistic; now they seem pessimistic. A middle of the road forecast for Britain would be to predict a doubling of the number of viewdata terminals each year for the next five years. A worldwide "commercial" forecast can be found in Chapman (1981).

Some (but not that much) of the obscurity arises from the problem of defining just what a viewdata terminal is (ignoring for the moment the various national varieties of viewdata). In Britain there are four options at present:

- a terminal (including display) which can work only as a viewdata terminal;

- an adaptor (only for viewdata) requiring a separate (standard) television set for display;

- a computer terminal which can work as a viewdata terminal as well;

- a microcomputer with additional hardware and software rendering it capable of working as a viewdata terminal.

This definition problem leads to two questions:

1) In the long term all schools and colleges, and most homes, will have microcomputers. But will they buy the additional equipment to enable them to act as viewdata terminals?

2) In the long term all public libraries, most colleges, and many schools and homes will have computer terminals. Will these be able (without further expenditure) to act as viewdata terminals?

The answer to both these questions lies partly in the hands of viewdata implementors. If they design elegant, cost-effective, easy to use systems then homes and businesses will make the investment in viewdata capability. On this scenario, Chapman (1981) forecasts 80% of British homes having viewdata access by 1990.

Ease of use

Viewdata is undoubtedly in theory easy to use, and particularly suitable for unsophisticated computer users. In its simplest form, such as early versions of Prestel, the user only has to master a 12-key pad consisting of the digits 0 to 9 plus two special symbols. (The pad is actually the same as that used for keypad telephones, but this has not up till now been of much relevance in Britain)

The user has just to follow the menu choices given, fill in self-explanatory screens, and remember a few special commands (normally engraved on the pad or screen casing).

Much of this holds good in practice, provided that the information providers (those who put the information on the viewdata system) put sufficient knowledge and effort into creating self-explanatory and consistent menus and screens. The poor reputation of Prestel, as for example documented in the Consumer's Association Report (1982), has come about largely because this was not forthcoming.

In some cases the knowledge itself was scanty, for example in the area of text legibility for colour displays (see Champness and Foster, 1982). In other areas the knowledge was there but implementors were unwilling to change their systems, for the usual mix of reasons (including national pride). The classic example is that of keywords. For several years it has been clear that allowing viewdata users the ability to type in names as well as numbers would in many cases make the system easier to use both for users and information providers. Indeed this was one of the early motivations behind the development of Optel (Bacsich, 1981). Yet British Telecom steadfastly refused to change Prestel to allow this, flying in the face of increasingly overwhelming evidence (Scott Maynes, 1982; and Bochmann, Gecsei, Lin, 1982).

The good news is that the adverse reaction to Prestel should be construed merely as a criticism of Prestel, not as one of viewdata. Many private viewdata systems now allow users to type in text or numbers as appropriate to the context, and certainly CAL systems will want to make use of this.

Modern viewdata terminals have keyboards very similar to "normal" computer terminals and have benefited from the same ergonomic developments. Although there is little experimental evidence as yet, the new generation of gateway-compatible viewdata systems should be considerably easier to use than equivalent command-oriented systems.

Since viewdata systems normally use colour terminals, one has to bear in mind the usual guidelines for these. In particular, domestic-quality colour TV sets are not suitable for prolonged regular use by users (e.g. by order-entry clerks.) However, in education this is unlikely to be a restriction.

Costs
The cost of using viewdata falls into four categories:

(i)     cost of the terminal

(ii)    cost of the communications link

(iii)   cost of the computer service

(iv)    cost of the courseware used

I shall take these in turn, using Britain as my example.

A viewdata terminal costs between £500 and £1500 depending on facilities. The more expensive kinds are normally only used by information providers. A viewdata adaptor (i.e. without its own display) costs between £100 and £200, but usually the keyboard will be unsuitable for "professional" use. Increasingly the most popular solution is to procure appropriate hardware and software to turn one's microcomputer into a viewdata terminal: this again will cost between £100 and £200, and cheaper than this if one takes a "package deal" such as the one offered by Micronet in Britain (see Micronet, 1982).

The cost of the communications link can vary enormously. At one extreme, a user may have to make a long-distance telephone call to the viewdata computer (currently £3.70 per hour in the evenings, when presumably most distance education would take place). At the other extreme, a large organisation such as the Open University will normally have invested heavily in its own private data network serving its offices, so that the link is free to the user. The typical solution is a compromise between the two. A user (e.g. at home) will make a telephone call to an access point, and the call will then be routed by a public data network to the viewdata computer. For example in Britain we have the Packet Switch Stream (PSS) public data network, typically costing £1 per hour to use, but the access points are fairly few and the service is not easy to use for viewdata. An alternative approach is to use the Prestel Gateway network, where the access points are the local Prestel nodes; British Telecom have promised to raise the coverage of these nodes to service some 92% of telephones by a local call by the end of 1984. The cost to the user should be similar to that of PSS, but the cost of connecting one's viewdata computer to Gateway is rather high (see Prestel, 1982, for more details). In many other countries such as Germany, the public data networks are cheaper and more oriented towards viewdata.

The cost of the computer service can be dealt with in several ways. Many educational applications of viewdata are likely to run on the organisation's own computer, and the cost of this is not likely to be passed on to the user. If an application uses the public viewdata service, costs could be quite high; for example Prestel charges £3.00 per hour for daytime use. Evening use is free at the moment, reflecting the business orientation of the service. Indeed, many computer bureau services charge much less in the evening than in the day, and so at the moment distance teaching could benefit from some attractive tariffs; but as use builds up, this will change, as it will with Prestel. It is important to remember that there are other evening uses besides education: not just home banking and the like, but such systems as those used by firms for communicating with their field sales forces. The old story of education getting squeezed out of a medium once it becomes attractive could be repeated here as well.

In the cost of the computer service one has to include the cost of the software required as part of that service. A current problem is that viewdata is a relatively new type of computer application and one relatively unpopular with computer scientists and "serious" computer implementors (perhaps because they feel that it is too simple-minded); consequently many otherwise reasonable computers are without an available viewdata system. The situation has been made worse by the belief that viewdata requires some special kind of computer oriented solely towards high-speed transaction processing. (The belief probably arose from the natural orientation of telecommunications authorities towards such computers.) In fact any minicomputer or mainframe computer capable of running a time-sharing computer service (e.g. of the sort normally found in education) is capable of running an adequate viewdata service. Sadly, virtually no viewdata systems have been designed to be portable across many computer types: only the Open University's Optel system has made an attempt to overcome the problem (see Bacsich, 1981).

The final cost is the courseware cost. If one first concentrates on CAL systems, it is impossible to give any experimental evidence for the authoring costs associated with viewdata. They will probably be much the same as for other CAL systems, possibly slightly higher because of the need for greater care with the user interface. Most information on authoring costs comes from work on providing databases for viewdata (and Prestel in particular), and does not seem directly relevant to CAL. However, for those interested in providing educational databases the following crude thoughts may be useful.

In the more straightforward kind of viewdata system one has to enter the items of information and also the links between them; whereas in an electronic mail or bibliographic retrieval system one has just to enter the items of information, the system providing the links automatically. So information provision for viewdata takes about one and a half times as long as for "similar" systems (links are quicker to input than data, so it is not as bad as two times as long).

Consequently, if you wish to make serious use of databases, you would be well advised to develop your viewdata system so as to provide 'gateway-compatible' access to your mail or bibliographic system.

## Institutions who could use viewdata

Any distance teaching organisation currently planning its media portfolio should be considering the role of a centralised computer resource in its teaching and administration. (Indeed, the long term cost-benefits of home terminals in distance education may have as much to do with economising on administration as with direct teaching applications.) Viewdata systems can provide a cost-effective use of that resource, especially in those countries with a strong tradition of viewdata leading to cheap terminals and generally available data networks.

A distance teaching organisation which is a consortium rather than one organisation may have difficulty in coping with the administration of any centralised computer resource such as viewdata. Indeed, recent British experience suggests that such organisations have difficulty perceiving even the need for a centralised resource, believing instead in carrying out the teaching functions purely on microcomputers. But microcomputers need software, teaching needs coordination, and students need administration, all of which points to the need for centralised computing resource. (Few organisations, and none in education, have as yet the technical capability to handle a distributed microcomputer network.)

## The next ten years

As home terminals proliferate, organisations such as the Open University will begin to find it cost-effective to link these terminals in to their central computer systems. As pointed out previously, the primary justification may be administrative, but will be closely followed by applications such as telesoftware and computer-assisted feedback systems (moving towards true CAL). A minority of students, but an increasing one, will use their terminals to access the main computer for systems unavailable on their home or local microcomputers, e.g. new artificial intelligence languages or large database systems. The same home viewdata terminals will undoubtedly be capable of telewriting activities (e.g. Cyclops) at least in some countries.

As home terminal users increasingly demand facilities similar to those they have at work, the limited speed of the national communications network will begin to be a restriction within about five years time. Some alleviation will be possible by using cable TV networks (provided these are allowed to be connected to public data networks; by no means a foregone conclusion). Some increase in speed will come from developments in modems (the boxes that couple the terminal to the phone line). However, the major advance, probably not occurring on any scale till the end of the ten year period, will be the advent of the Integrated Service Digital Network (ISDN) which will bring reasonably high speed data links into people's homes. These links will allow viewdata, telewriting, facsimile and still colour picture transmission. (But they will be far short of the bandwidth required for naturalistic two-way moving video.)

A by-product of the ISDN should be a country-wide "intelligent" data network with reasonable transmission costs, permitting the widespread use of most of the viewdata and related computer techniques currently being developed. Indeed, the present distinctions between viewdata, computer, telewriting, and facsimile terminals will probably have vanished. Whether this means that viewdata has "won" or "lost" depends on your point of view.

References

ASTON, M. (1982) "Telesoftware and microcomputer information retrieval experiences with Prestel gateway", Viewdata 82 Proceedings, Online Publications Ltd

BACSICH, P. (1981) "The Open University Viewdata System", Viewdata 81 Proceedings, Online Publications Ltd

BOCHMAN, G., GECSEI, J., LIN, E. (1982) "Keyword access in Telidon: an experiment", Videotex 82 Proceedings, Online Publications Ltd

BROWN, M. (1982) "Videotex development work in education and training", Viewdata 82 Proceedings, Online Publications Ltd

CAMPBELL, J., THOMAS, H. (1981) "The videotex marketplace - a theory of evolution", Telecommunications Policy vol.5 no 2.

CHAMPNESS, B., FOSTER, J. (1982) "Attractiveness and readability of text and tables",Videotex 82 Proceedings, Online Publications Ltd

CHAPMAN, T. (1981) "Videotex applications: an international review of current and potential market penetration", Viewdata 81 Proceedings, Online Publications Ltd

HEYS, F. (1981) "International videotex standards - how will they affect the user?", Viewdata 81 Proceedings, Online Publications Ltd

IVTN (1982) International Videotex Teletext News, No 36. Washington: Arlen Communications.

KNOWLES, C. (1982) "An operational telesoftware service", Viewdata 82 Proceedings, Online Publications Ltd

MAYNE, A. (1982) The Videotex Revolution, London: October Press.

MICRONET (1982) Micronet 800: it brings your micro to life, Peterborough: Micronet.

PRESTEL (1982) Welcome to Gateway. London: Prestel.

SCOTT MAYNES, E. (1982) Prestel in use: a consumer view. London: National Consumer Council.

## 16.  TUTORS AND MEDIA

Rudi Dallos
Staff Tutor, South-West Region, Open University

### Introduction

Earlier in this book, various aspects of course design have been discussed.  In this chapter a central theme is that course design should necessarily be such that the main teaching components - textual materials, the media and tutorial provision - are employed in an integrated, 'holistic' way.  In this way the course team, having decided upon the course content, must decide upon the most effective ways of employing the above components.  Within such an integrated framework the potential contributions of each component are not considered in isolation from the others but, where possible, attempts are made to employ them in complementary combinations.

Figure 1:     Scheme of tutor/media/text interaction

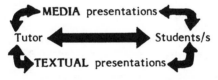

The three components tutor, media and text can be seen as a system organised around the tutor-student relationship.  The model of learning employed here is that of the student operating within a learning system.  In other words learning is not a passive process characterised by a banking model wherein the student 'receives' knowledge (Freire 1968).  Instead the tutor and student can be seen to represent the central human component and hence constitute the core of the learning 'system'.    There has been a growing discontent with explanations of human action, including, of course, learning, in terms of mechanistic and positivist explanations (Harre and Secord 1972). Instead a model of human action is proposed in which people are seen as active agents who plan and monitor their own actions and the effects these have on others.  A student in this way can be seen as taking charge of, and monitoring, his or her own learning process.

This represents a vivid contrast to early behaviourist models of learning upon which much of the early educational technology innovations were founded.

This model of the learner as an active agent of course has been advocated vociferously by a number of educationalists including Jerome Bruner (1966). The idea of active learning extends further than a concern that the learner responds physically or answers questions. Instead learning is seen as inevitably taking place within a social context. This context centres around the tutor-student relationship but of course includes friends, family and others with whom students may discuss and test various aspects of their studies. Within this central tutor-student relationship learning can be seen to emerge as part of an interactional process involving negotiation and mutual construction of understanding (Bruner, 1971; Pearce and Cronen, 1980). Obviously the nature and importance of this relationship to the student's understanding varies according to the subject. In a science or technology course a presentation of a technique may seem straightforward and unambiguous. Yet the tutor and student may together formulate an idea as to, say, the value and elegance of the technique which may be vital to the student's subsequent retention and overall understanding of the subject area. In the social sciences the range of possible interpretations is much wider. In a television documentary-style format for example, a range of interpretations or meanings may be imposed on the subject matter. One of the vital functions of the tutor in such presentations may be to discover with the student the different implicit interpretations that they may be imposing on the material. This, of course, is also the case with textual materials. Stuart Hall (1981) though has alerted us to the strong tendency for media audiences to regard the products as 'slices of reality' rather than constructions involving elements of selectivity, sequencing of events, and personal emphasis.

## The constraints imposed by distance teaching

It is something of a joke in many conventional (non-distance) educational institutions that some teaching resembles a sort of audio-visual road-show. During a tutorial or lecture an array of visual and auditory materials may be shown. The lecturer may employ these to illustrate teaching points or even as the basis of the presentation with a following discussion. The provision for a large amount of face-to-face tutor-student contact permits such fully integrated multi-media presentations. Of course, the type of media used varies from one discipline to another, but in conventional teaching there is enormous potential for using more than the mere spoken word.

In distance educational institutions, such as the Open University, this amount of opportunity for <u>integrated</u> multi-media teaching is not available. Typically on most courses students may see their tutors at most half a dozen or so times during a full-credit course and less on a half-credit one. Students and tutors are therefore much more critical and selective about the use of audio-visual materials during a tutorial unless it is seen to be of absolutely central relevance to the course. This may be the case for example in Arts courses where paintings may be shown, or music listened to. Invariably one of the important criteria employed by students and tutors is whether the media-based activity could be accomplished reasonably well by the student alone or in a self-help group setting with other students. In other words, there is usually a strong impetus on the tutor to <u>talk</u> with the students rather than employ any media presentations. This is not unreasonable, since students may want to raise specific points which are troubling them, discuss their continuous assessment assignments, prepare for their exams and so on. We may well ask then if the tutor's involvement with media aspects of a course is significant enough to be worth considering?

## Course Design

In order to answer this question it is necessary to think of current trends in course design and even to imagine the future, a significant feature of which will be the wide availability and use of video facilities. I have already suggested that for students and tutors to make serious use of media presentations the various media components must be fully integrated into a course. This requires a consideration of the teaching objectives of a course at its inception and subsequently a thorough analysis of what is best done by an emphasis on the written text, the media components available and how these can best be integrated. It then becomes possible to improve the relevance and contribution of the media components to the course as a whole. More especially the media components can be employed in a much more direct way with implications for the tutors' involvement. Not only are the students and tutors therefore better motivated to employ the media but specific functions involving the tutor can be delineated. For example, assignments may be set requiring a viewing of a broadcast or video/audio cassette, tutors may be guided to include discussions of media components in tutorials, and project work involving the use and evaluation of media components can be employed (as for example in the Open University Social Foundation Course D102, 'Making Sense of Society'). So the contribution that the media make to a course is a "chicken and egg" situation in that students will not make use of the media unless they are seen as significant components, while course teams are reluctant to make extensive use of the media since students often use media less than is considered desirable (Stevenson, 1981).

## The role of the tutor in distance teaching

Before considering the role of the tutor in relation to the media it is essential to consider the role more widely in the context of distance teaching. In reality this essentially consists largely of the role of the tutor in relation to written textual materials. There is not space to go into the tutor role in great detail. It is set out formally in the Open University publication 'Teaching for the Open University, 1982'. The brief summary here is based upon the author's observations, and publications such as Murgatroyd's (1980) describing what occurs in tutorials, for example. The purpose of this summary is to point to some of the similarities and differences between the tutors' functions in relation to written materials and media presentations.

## Academic

- learning skills - the tutor must encourage students to learn to learn (see Bateson, 1972). This involves students in reading 'actively', in setting their own personal goals, in asking questions, and in relating the information they are encountering to their own experience and existing framework of understanding.

- communication skills - students must be taught the appropriate formats and conventions for communicating their understanding.

- academic skills - this is of course the most nebulous and difficult area of skills to teach. The student must acquire the ability to examine evidence critically, be rigorous in the analysis of problems, and formulate alternative explanations and hypotheses. In turn, these analytical abilities must be integrated with the abilities to synthesise and present their understanding in a logically, consistent, well-planned way.

- academic knowledge and experience - a tutor serves an important function of giving life, or sense of personal meaning, to the material. The material is interpreted with the student within the tutor's (and the student's) overall conceptual framework. In this sense, the tutor's 'biases' are important and form the basis for a personal context for the student's learning.

## Motivational

-   encouragement and support - this is perhaps more central
    to the tutor-counsellor role which deals with the early
    stages of a student's career. Generally, however, this
    remains a consistently important function since students
    have so little contact and feedback from their subject
    tutors.

-   stimulation/inspiration - as in any educational setting, the
    tutor can bring a subject alive and inspire interest.
    Alternatively, his or her lack of interest in an area may
    likewise kill interest even if the materials are excellent.

## Tutor-student relationship

-   reciprocity - the tutor-student relationship involves mutual
    understanding and acceptance. The tutor and student
    learn from each other. As Bateson (1972) explains: the
    student learns to learn from the tutor and the tutor learns
    how to teach the student More specifically, tutor and
    students acquire a joint framework of understanding.

-   flexibility - the tutor has to be able to adapt the teaching
    to the needs, abilities and existing understandings of the
    student. Even if the teaching method is of a 'chalk and
    talk' format, the tutor must employ feedback and personal
    knowledge of the student. In a distance education context,
    this will be based upon marking of set work, contact at
    tutorials, telephone conversations and possibly even social
    contact.

To summarise, the importance of the tutor-student relationship must
be emphasised. Together a shared conceptual framework and
understanding develops. Of course this does not imply that the tutor
does not often operate didactically. The important point is that as
Figure 1 earlier indicated, the tutor-student relationship is the
framework within which the media and text materials are translated.

## The media and the function of the tutor

The functions constituting the tutor role outlined so far apply also
to the specific role in relation to the media. In fact, as was
suggested at the outset, it is very difficult and inappropriate to
consider the components "tutor-media-text" in isolation. However,
it is possible to point towards some of the features of the tutor's
function in relation to the media which are in some ways different
to that for written materials.

In order to do this, it is useful to split the media into four categories.

|          | Cassettes       | Broadcasts  |
|----------|-----------------|-------------|
| Visual   | video-cassettes | television  |
| Auditory | audio-cassettes | radio       |

Firstly a broadcast format delineates different possibilities to a cassette format for the tutor function. Primarily opportunities to employ a broadcast in an ongoing tutorial situation are constrained by broadcast times. Even it is is possible to synchronise the tutorial to a broadcast the tutor cannot manage the presentation of the material by, for example, pausing the programme to raise and discuss questions or to repeat sections which students found difficult or ambiguous. Analysis and discussion of the programme is therefore impressionistic in that it is limited to what the tutor and students can remember or managed to note down during the presentation (transcripts can be used but may be cumbersome). There is therefore much less potential for the tutor to manage the learning experience and integrate it into the wider course framework than with a cassette format. It is not untypical in my experience to note that the major response of a tutor to a television programme is to consider whether it was good, or bad, interesting or not. In part this may be a function of the 'entertainment set' that a broadcast format is likely to elicit and to which tutors are perhaps not immune. So, use in tutorials or associated discussion of broadcast programmes is typically minimal.

The second categorisation is concerned with whether the presentation is within an auditory or visual format. Sometimes the basis for the choice is clear as in the Sciences when a technique is being demonstrated, or in Arts when the subject matter is visual such as paintings, or auditory, for example, music. However, in many areas, particularly in the Social Sciences and Education, the implications of the choice of auditory or visual modes are important for the tutor functions. For example, it has been noted that there is a strong tendency for audiences, including students, to accept visual documentary-type presentations as a 'slice of reality' (Hall 1973, 1981). The tutor here has an important function in educating students to consider such presentations critically as impressions and 'constructions', rather than 'reality'. The Open University has produced a video/text package (Open University, 1981) specifically to teach students, with the assistance of their tutor counsellors, how to learn from television. It is suggested here that the increasing use of video-cassettes is one of the most exciting and interesting areas of development of the tutor function in distance education. We are only just beginning to explore the potentials of video-replay facilities for the above. An example is available in the new Social Psychology course, D307. As part of the first project, dealing with the application of a theoretical framework (systems/interactional theory) to the observation and analysis of family dynamics, students are sent a video/text package. This contains material illustrating family dynamics which the students are shown how to analyse with the help of the video itself and a written commentary. The package can be employed in a tutorial format wherein a tutor may discuss the analysis and possibly offer alternatives to those presented by the authors. Most importantly the package provides an opportunity not only to acquire a theoretical understanding but to practice analysis of realistic material. Subsequently students apply their skills to the analysis of real-life situations. One important implication of such a package is that since the material is so rich and complex an unambiguous analysis is not possible. Hence the tutor's function expands to include that of a research supervisor.

It is possible now to summarise some of the aspects of the tutor functions which are significant to media presentations:

Academic. As has been emphasised, one of the major difficulties with a broadcast format (and this could carry over into future use of video) is the tendency towards passive viewing. In part this problem can be seen to derive from the fact that most students have had the experience of being only 'consumers' rather than 'producers' of media presentations. In contrast most of us have considerable experience of producing written materials, but creation of media products is mainly restricted to professionals. This represents a formidable problem in that students do not have the accumulation of prior, as well as current, experience to use the media critically and regard it analytically.

Likewise tutors are not typically experienced in production of media materials and may therefore find it more difficult to prepare students to use the media most effectively.

On the other hand many of the principles of 'good' study habits and skills relevant to learning from written materials can be transferred to learning from media presentations. But it is necessary to be wary of assuming that this is sufficient. In fact our knowledge of, for example, the nature of visual learning, including the use of imagery, translation and codification of images into symbolic representations and vice versa is still exploratory (Dallos, 1980; Bandler and Grinder, 1980). Nor have tutors usually sufficient personal experience of learning from media presentations to offer much helpful guidance to students based upon their 'intuitive' theories.

Motivational. Here there is obviously a large overlap between the tutor's function in relation to written materials. In some ways the tutor input here may need to be greater, especially if the media presentations are not explicitly integrated into the course. Considerable encouragement and inspiration may be required by the tutor to persuade students to watch say a television broadcast at some 'insomniacal' period.

Tutor-student relationship. Media presentations are interpreted within the broad framework of understanding developed by the tutor and student. The importance of this varies, depending on the nature of the subject matter. However the richness of media presentations permits a more flexible and varied range of interpretations in many subject areas. In many ways therefore the personal frameworks of the students, based upon their own experiences, may play a greater part in that students may potentially have a greater input to the tutor group tutorial. Certainly this is the case in many Social Science areas in which students almost inevitably have had life experiences relevant to the realistic situations displayed. Bearing in mind the greater equality of student and tutor in terms of expertise in learning from media presentations, the ensuing relationship emphasises perhaps more sharply the mutuality of the learning process.

## Summary and Conclusions

A tentative model of the distance teaching situation has been employed which takes the student-tutor relationship to be central. This is based largely upon the author's own teaching experience and observations as a Staff Tutor with the Open University. The tutor-student relationship is seen to involve the development of a shared framework of understanding within which the written and media components are interpreted. The essential 'human' qualities of a tutor are vital not only in terms of motivating the student to make effective use of media presentations and to humanise the 'hardware' but most importantly in shaping them to the students' needs. This shaping requires that the tutor attempts to understand what the student understands and helps to fit media presentations into this shared framework of understandings. In many ways the media offer a richness and complexity of material which encourages a mutuality of learning between tutor and student. Specifically it is felt that video replay facilities offer an exciting extension of the tutor function into visual education and hence areas such as observational abilities which have previously fallen outside the range of possible course objectives, the latter having been typically restricted to symbolic and conceptual goals.

References and additional reading

BANDLER, R. & GRINDER, J. (1980) Neurolinguistic programming. Palo Alto: Science and Behaviour Books.

BRUNER, J.S. (1971) The Relevance of Education. New York: Norton.

BATESON, G (1972) Steps to an Ecology of Mind. New York: Balantine.

BRUNER, J.S. (1966) Towards a theory of instruction. Cambridge, Mass: Harvard University Press.

DALLOS, R 1981) Active learning and television. Teaching at a Distance, No. 17.

FREIRE, P. (1968) Pedagogy of the Oppressed. London: Penguin.

HALL, S. (1973) "Deviancy, politics and the media" in McINTOSH, M. and ROCK, P (eds), Deviancy and Social Control. London: Tavistock.

HALL, S. (1981) "Study Skills" in Learning from Television. MIlton Keynes: Open University.

HARRE, R. & SECORD, P.F. (1972) The Explanation of Social Behaviour. Oxford: Blackwell.

MURGATROYD, S. (1980) 'What actually happens in tutorials'. Teaching at a Distance, No. 18.

OPEN UNIVERSITY, 1982 Teaching for the Open University. Milton Keynes: Open University.

PEARCE, W.B. & CRONEN, V.E. (1980). Communication, Action and Meaning: the Creation of Social Realities. New York: Praeger.

STEVENSON, J. (1981). 'Media in the Open University: a look towards the 1980s'. Teaching at a Distance, No. 19.

## 17.  MEDIA RESOURCE CENTRES

Kenneth R. Tomlinson
Tutor Librarian, Percival Whitley College of Further Education,
Halifax, Yorkshire.

### Media Resource Centres in Distance Education

A characteristic of distance education is the recognition of the need for a base where students can come together and meet their tutors, counsellors and other students.   Whilst Richard Freeman (1982) has reminded us that personal teacher-student interaction is not a sine qua non for learning, and public libraries as "universities of the people" for generations are a monument to this, Davies (1980) and Entwistle (1977) have both stressed the psychological and motivational benefits of providing the individual learner with a base.

The Russell report (Great Britain: Department of Education and Science, 1973) estimated that by 1971 69% of the adult population in England and Wales still had no full time education after age 15. Perhaps this was one factor which led to 130,000 enquiries and 43,000 applications for the Open University's first year of courses in 1971. A further factor may have lain in the enforced withdrawal of courses for London University external degrees consequent upon the Ministry of Education's 1965 regionalisation of higher level courses which took them away from many local technical colleges.  By coincidence some of these same colleges were invited to offer accommodation as one of the Open University's 237 main study centres, almost all of which are situated in academic institutions.

One of the original reasons for establishing study centres was to provide Open University students with viewing facilities for its television programmes.   However, in 1971 the demands of the University were really in advance of the technology.  Video replay equipment in those days was based on a highly expensive 1" format, so the University transferred its foundation course programmes on to super-8mm. film cassettes.   Providing copies of even the 150 foundation course programmes on super-8mm. film to all study centres was extremely expensive, and was soon abandoned. The study centres therefore became more important as locations for face-to-face tutorials and counselling. Gradually, however, as technology has developed over the last 10 years, the need has grown for centres where students can share equipment and facilities that are too expensive to provide to individual students at home.

The need for media resource centres for distance education is not limited even in the United Kingdom to the Open University. It was a conviction that amongst the masses who had left school at 14 or 15 years old there were many who would welcome some less formal way of extending their studies that led Michael Young in 1963 to launch the National Extension College. It was a correspondence college with a difference. It secured the cooperation of BBC and ITV television as well as radio in communicating its lessons to a mass audience, starting in 1964 with "O" level English transmitted by Anglia TV (Freeman, 1982). By 1981 73 further education colleges had decided that they would save money and attract students not previously catered for by offering periodic tutorial assistance along with study centre facilities for these NEC "Flexistudy" courses. After explaining how to join the library the NEC "Students' guide" directs its readers to enquire of the host college: "Is there a resources centre?" and "Can I borrow or listen to records or tapes?"

The Open Tech was officially launched by the Manpower Services Commission in 1983 principally for the "effective updating, upgrading and retraining of technicians and supervisors", removing barriers that at present exclude some people from existing provision (Manpower Services Commission, 1982). The June 1974 Policy Statement of the Technician Education Council declared that the Council believes that personal contact between student and teacher and the opportunity of studying in a college environment with access to specialist accommodation and facilities such as the library will be a necessary part of the process leading to a T.E.C. award, and therefore a programme undertaken wholly by private study would not meet requirements (Fidgeon, 1978). TEC aims to emphasise the learning approach and motivate students better "helped by information technology" and using both new and existing materials. Learning packages may include film and the new technologies of video and computer-based systems. Financial restrictions will prohibit the duplication of effort in preparing new learning material. This suggests a desire to limit the number of colleges initiating courses. The TEC proposal is that there will be some colleges that will produce print and media resources, "exporting" them to other colleges, which will act as "importers", providing tutorial facilities for local students similar in operation to present NEC Flexistudy schemes, and in a similar way offering these students the full range of services, including the library and media resources of the "importing" college. Clearly an even greater flexibility in resource servicing arrangements will be required, with a high degree of cooperation between the networks of colleges that in some subject areas are likely to arise.

An important service offered by many "host" institutions to their "guest" distance education students is the use of their library services. In 1981 204 of 254 libraries at Open University host study centres were allowing locally resident OU students to use their libraries. Whilst OU students have limited time for additional reading it is common for them to find the need to use reference books for simplification, verification or amplification of new concepts.

Evidently not all distance learners are as well provided for as OU students. In a recent publication, ACACE (1983) describes "problems in obtaining books and the inaccessibility of public libraries" as unique to distance learning. This reinforces the idea of students benefitting from having a study base. Manchester College of Adult Education charges "independent learners" a nominal fee of £1 per term for access to the library and other college facilities. Many college libraries have opened their doors to bona fide students of other institutions, in part no doubt to justify their being granted library discount licences. It is arguable that provided libraries can continue to have adequate funding to duplicate titles as necessary, an open door policy should become the norm, and academic libraries be acknowledged as part of community provision, remaining however independent of but co-operating with public libraries.

There are then three separate functions for "study centres" - a meeting place for students and tutors, a place to share the use of equipment, and the use of library facilities. These various functions have tended to develop unevenly but in parallel. Recent developments in technology suggest that it may be time to re-examine the present role and functions of "study centres". To understand this issue more fully we need to explore the impact of technology on libraries.

Libraries and Technology

The Russian launching of an unmanned satellite, Sputnik I, in 1957 was immediately hailed as a triumph by the world's mass media; at the same time it sent shivers down the spines of the decision-making establishment in Britain and had an almost immediate effect on education and the information collection and dissemination industries. Obviously we were not producing enough technologists, technicians or craftsmen of the right calibre to apply post-war scientific discoveries. Nor were the scientists getting enough information about research and development being carried out in the rest of the world.

A National Lending Library for Science and Technology was founded in 1957, one of its first objectives being to ensure a good supply of

Russian-language scientific and technical literature for lending to centres of research, academic institutions and industry. Libraries traditionally existed at the heart of every higher education institution, serving the needs of teachers, students and research workers, for it was in print that the world's existing knowledge was recorded. Libraries were developed in the new educational institutions which in turn contributed to the mushrooming of knowledge and literature in books, reports and journals now referred to as the "information explosion". Some measure of this explosion can be deduced from the fact that whilst it took 22 years (1907-39) for one million abstracts to appear in "Chemical Abstracts", it now publishes some 400,000 abstracts annually.

The amount of printed information, it is estimated, has been doubling every 15 years. The production of new books and the stocks of libraries have continued to increase. Our national British Library has something in excess of 10 million books in its Reference division and over 2 million print volumes and 2 million documents in microform along with subscriptions to 49,000 periodicals and large numbers of reports, conference proceedings and official publications in its Lending Division. Our current dependence on print is illustrated in the following approximate statistics of library holdings: in British University and public libraries, over 40 millions each; in British polytechnics and other colleges, over 30 million volumes.

It is to products of the newer "electronics revolution" that we look for assistance in retrieving specific information from this mountain of print. Instead of the time-consuming manual consultation of abstracts in one of the few libraries that ever had comprehensive collections, it is now possible to access through a library computer terminal about 200 computerised databases whose services are marketed by a number of host organisations, such as Lockheed DIALOGUE or Derwent S.D.C. So major international bibliographical sources and other data bases are now being tapped and made available in libraries throughout the country.

The British Library Automated Information Service (BLAISE) provides computer terminal services suitable for on-line or off-line cataloguing, or the interactive retrieval of information relating to British books published since 1950. Through secondary information databases it offers abstracts of monographs, periodical articles and other media produced in Britain and abroad. These secondary databases however are not yet comprehensive in subject coverage and still refer one back to the printed literature for detailed information.

In a more fundamental way the computer questions the future of book publishing, bookselling and indeed the need for libraries. The latest printing technology creates an image resulting from computerised photo-composition. As any input is stored on digital file it constitutes a database which can be transmitted electronically through a telephone line. So the technology already exists for an author to produce, edit, store, revise and electronically publish his text direct to a customer, who can similarly print out or store that information. The customer could be a student learning at a distance.

Maurice Line (1981) has given his opinion on why he thinks many documents will continue to be published in more or less conventional form alongside new electronic media. Not least against a total transfer to electronic publishing are the problems of ready access to cumbersome equipment and the inflexibility of frames of information for scanning, skimming and comparison with alternative texts.

As for the trend towards independent study, Hill (1981) sees books playing a less important role except in the "broad purposes of education", with an increased use of microcomputer programmes in teaching. Apart from the now norm in colleges of classrooms equipped with a range of micros, a recent survey by Paul Burton (1983) has revealed that one in seven of 742 college library resource centres in the UK has already installed at least one micro. Hills acknowledges that outside the formal education setting the student has access to a wide range of knowledge-disseminating agencies, including libraries, radio and television. So perhaps print, non-print and electronically-stored information are going to continue to exist side by side and we will not after all have to convert all those millions of books in libraries to computer tapes.

Librarians in colleges continue to report an ever increasing use of literature which appears to be as directly related to quantitative provision as to size of student enrolments. There is no evidence yet that the new technology is supplanting text and library books.

The 1960's witnessed the marketing of a wide range of inexpensive audio-visual hardware and software. There was no longer any excuse for not utilising all the senses more fully in the learning process. Her Majesty's Inspectors of Education and local education authority advisers, teachers' unions, and professional bodies such as the Library Association, all encouraged college librarians to develop their libraries as multi-media resource centres, either incorporating media production facilities, or working alongside them to provide students with opportunities for multi-media study.

The most widely used audio-visual learning resource is undoubtedly the educational television and radio programmes broadcast by the B.B.C. and I.T.V. However, copyright restrictions at present prohibit the copying and use of a wide range of television programmes of high educational potential. There is an urgent need for a realistically priced licensing system. A minimum requirement of a media centre is sufficient video recorders to enable the taping on chosen format of the educational programmes that might be concurrently transmitted on different channels, with enough additional recorders for playback at the same time to groups or individual users. Previously transmitted programmes can sometimes be purchased but costs prohibit any extensive stock building in most tertiary media centres. Increasingly the Central Film Library and other agencies give their borrowers a choice of cine or video format. Inevitably teachers wish to produce their own programmes particularly to cover subjects of special local interest as well as for a variety of teaching projects such as simulation exercises. So most colleges now have video production and editing facilities.

A library based media centre can make all "in house" and commercially produced software available for class and individual study. At Percival Whitley the lower ground floor of the library houses three audio visual classrooms, two of which can also be used for production purposes, storage and replay facilities. A separate individualised video viewing room is sited off one of the libraries on the ground floor. The proximity of print and non print materials emphasises the essential complementary nature of our senses by which we learn and the media we use to communicate through them.

## The Role of Media Resource Centres in Distance Education

The availability of modern, well-equipped media resource centres will become increasingly important to distance education students if technological developments are to be exploited to the full. Already heavy use is being made of such facilities.

In Chapter 4, we saw that in 1982, the Open University made available 311 video-cassette players to its students in a variety of different locations, but almost all were in other academic institutions. Of these 311 machines, 243 were provided by the Open University, the remainder being provided by the host institutions. In 1981, 226 of the 254 OU study centres housed terminals to OU computers and an estimated 42,675 hours were clocked up by students of 41 different courses using these terminals and the computing facilities provided at Summer Schools. In Chapter 12, we saw that the Open University has developed and experimented with its Cyclops system to link geographically isolated students more closely with their tutors. Television set, telephone line and computer combine to provide an interactive system. Whilst Cyclops connects tutors with individual students, costs make its use by small groups of students more economic, so suggesting another service that is best located at remote study centres. In the future, it is likely that technologies such as

PRESTEL (or Optel) and video-disc will, like Cyclops, first be experimented with in local centres or summer schools for distance teaching purposes before spreading to home use.

## Challenges for Media Resource Centres

What we are seeing is a relatively rapid extension of the old library service within conventional educational institutions in two different but complementary directions. Firstly, the impact of technology is requiring libraries to provide materials in a variety of formats, including print, video and increasingly computers for their "own" users. This in turn requires the provision of suitable equipment, and above all, the provision of a suitable environment for studying or browsing in a multi-media manner without disturbing other users. Machines such as computer-terminals or television sets can be noisy; some equipment, such as Cyclops, requires voice communication, but not necessarily on a group basis in any individual centre. Thus the increased use of technology in media resource centres presents architectural and design challenges. These will need to be met through the construction of individual study carrels or booths, providing a clear desk-top for writing purposes, a video-monitor, a video and audio cassette player, headphones, a computer terminal and a rack for books and articles. Also required will be the provision of well-equipped, small seminar rooms, with telephone connections, video-replay facilities, a computer terminal, and comfortable chairs, for small groups interacting either with just themselves, or with other groups or tutors "at a distance".

The second development is an increasing use of media resource facilities by off-campus students, often registered with other institutions. This has of course obvious advantages. High capital equipment investment is off-set by greater use. Distance teaching costs are considerably reduced by making use of already existing facilities. Thus the installation of technology which would be hard to justify on economic grounds for any single institution becomes viable when used by students from a range of institutions.

However, no matter how sensible such developments may be in theory, there are serious practical difficulties. First of all, there is the balance of use between host institution students and students from elsewhere. This can lead to problems with access, costly booking arrangements, and at worse conflict between students and between institutions. Secondly, financial arrangements between institutions are often on an ad-hoc and informal basis. On balance, distance education institutions probably do not pay a full contribution to the costs of providing such services to their students. Because of the different vocational commitments or personal circumstances of distance students, facilities need to be provided at virtually all the times of day that the host institution is open to its other clientele. Requests to use these services are expected to increase further as the Open Tech develops, and as the OU develops its Associate and Continuing Education courses. Furthermore, many media resource centres are not open at times of most convenience to distance education students, for example on Sundays.

However, experience with computer terminals, video-cassette replay facilities, and Cyclops at the Open University indicates very clearly that the original study centre provision, consisting mainly of conventional classrooms, is totally inadequate for shared use of technological facilities. Computer terminals are often located in corridors or at the back of a classroom shared by other users; video-cassette machines are liable to be stolen from classrooms open to a variety of users and if placed in a classroom they can be inaccessible to the lone user if a tutorial is taking place in that room. Cyclops needs a quiet room, and access to two telephone lines. Above all, many students are reluctant to waste valuable study time travelling to a study centre for the use of a single piece of equipment, particularly if there are doubts about its availability or reliability, and if the environment in which it will be used is uncomfortable and threatening. A recent study also suggests that the enthusiasm of professional and technical staff in host institutions is as important as adequate physical provision and tutor guidance for achieving good use of shared learning resources.

The advantages then for distance education students of properly-equipped media resource centres with helpful full-time staff readily available on a really local basis, are obvious. These centres are likely to be in conventional educational institutions, although there are possibilities for public libraries, or the newly created Information Technology centres, or even Consumer Association or Citizen's Advice Bureaux's High Street shops. Whether though the distance education provision is for the NEC, Open Colleges, Open Tech or the Open University, it will be necessary for the maximum co-operative use to be made of already existing teaching, library and media resources.

References and Additional Reading

ADVISORY COUNCIL FOR ADULT AND CONTINUING EDUCATION (1983) Distance Learning and Adult Students. Leicester: ACACE

BROWN, S. (1983) "Learning to use video replay". Teaching at a Distance, No. 23.

BURTON, P. (1983) "Microcomputer applications in academic libraries. Boston Spa: British Library, LIR Report No. 16

DAVIES, W.J.K. (1980) Alternatives to class teaching in schools and colleges. London: Council for Educational Technology

ENTWISTLE, N. (1977) "Psychological aspects of learning at a distance", in DAVIES, T.C. (ed.) Open learning systems for mature students London: Council for Educational Technology

FIDGEON, F. (1978) 'TEC's proposals for the external student', in COFFEY, J. (ed.) Development of an Open Learning System in Further Education: a report. London: Council for Educational Technology.

FREEMAN, R. (1982) 'The contribution of broadcasting'. Programmed Learning & Educational Technology, Vol.19, No.3.

GREAT BRITAIN: DEPARTMENT OF EDUCATION & SCIENCE (1973). Adult education:a plan for development (Russell report) London: HMSO.

HILLS, P.J. (1981) 'The place of the printed word in teaching and learning' in HILLS, P. (ed.) The future of the printed word. Milton Keynes: Open University Press

LINE, M.B. (1981) 'Some questions concerning the unprinted word' in HILLS, P. (ed.) The future of the printed word. Milton Keynes: Open University Press.

MANPOWER SERVICES COMMISSION (1982) Open Tech Task Group Report. Sheffield: Manpower Services Commission.

# PART 4

# SELECTION OF TECHNOLOGY AND COURSE DESIGN

## 18.  PEDAGOGIC DIFFERENCES BETWEEN MEDIA

John Sparkes
Professor of Electronics Design and Communication, Faculty of Technology, Open University

### Introduction

The new problem for educational providers, posed by developments in educational technology, is the question of which teaching methods and channels of communication to use, in order to achieve a given set of educational aims.  This question does not simply relate to new ways of teaching traditional subjects; it relates to different kinds of audiences, different kinds of subject matter, different kinds of courses, different forms of access to education, as well as to different study patterns amongst those who want to learn.  The use of distance teaching methods to facilitate home-based, part-time study brings into consideration all those students who would not, or could not, attend full-time or evening classes, as well as the many different kinds of courses they might want to take.  Distance teaching methods, as compared with the more traditional face-to-face teaching, involves quite different costs in terms of both money and manpower for the providers, as well as quite different cost structures. Equally the costs for students in money and time are quite different. In earlier chapters the range of new methods offered by technological developments has been described; the purpose of this chapter is to begin a discussion on how to choose between them.

All the above factors have to be taken into account if successful courses are to be designed, but this chapter concentrates on the pedagogic ones, including the problem of motivation of both students and teaching staff.  Other factors, such as costs and access, are considered in the next chapter.  My main concern here, therefore, is with the provision of specific courses or materials of one kind or another, rather than with the various forms of student-centred, "open learning" systems which now exist.  I shall be discussing how best to achieve successful teaching-at-a-distance, assuming, in the main, that students are motivated to learn, have access to the courses they want, and can afford what they cost; but I shall compare such courses with the more traditional face-to-face teaching provided by colleges and universities.

Within the confines of pedagogic considerations, there are five main dimensions to the specification of courses, whether for continuing education or for other purposes, and whether for teaching at a distance or face-to-face. These are, for each course:

1. The subject matter (e.g. chemistry or electronics etc.).

2. The type of course or material (e.g. academic, practical, etc.).

3. The level (e.g. technician, undergraduate, postgraduate).

4. The method of presentation (e.g. text, face-to-face, TV).

5. Student study patterns (home based, work based, visual, verbal, solitary, slow or quick on the uptake).

Traditionally, universities for example have been pretty clear about where they stand on each of these factors.  As regards subject matter the range of academic subjects offered has a strong traditional academic core with a few more recent innovations added on.  The subject titles change only slowly, even though the content of each subject might well change considerably.  Universities have created rather strong demarcations between one subject and another so that broader areas are difficult to encompass.

Also, University courses are in the main academic; indeed the more practical subjects like medicine and engineering, in Britain at any rate, still seem to be accepted with little enthusiasm on to traditional campuses. Equally, level has been tightly controlled both by external monitoring and by strict criteria as regards student entry. Universities have, of course, concentrated on undergraduate and postgraduate levels.

Finally as regards presentation and study patterns, it is taken almost for granted that lecturing, tutorials, laboratories, libraries, student interaction and to some extent computers will be the main components of the activities by which students are expected to learn.  This presents a reasonable variety of methods and so caters quite well with variations in students' learning methods and study techniques. None of these methods, however, transfers directly into the field of distance education although a comparable variety is likely to be needed for some kinds of courses.

By and large this concentration by universities on a particular domain, within this five-dimensional field of course specification, has served its particular section of the community well. The teaching has been directed almost solely at the 18 to 25 age groups and at the academic elite amongst them. It has required them to join an academic community for 3 years or so, and has succeeded in its most cherished aim, that of "teaching students to think", even though each subject area seems to have somewhat different interpretations of what "thinking" means. It has also, inadvertently, moulded the attitudes of both staff and students so that the term 'academic' has come to refer to more than knowledge and expertise.

Nowadays Higher and Further, as well as Continuing Education, especially that part of it that involves teaching at a distance, demands a widening of the field in all directions beyond that occupied by university courses. Furthermore, the capabilities and limitations of different teaching methods, especially those using advanced technology, depend very much upon what is to be taught.

So our first task, in the next section, is to make a number of distinctions between different kinds of courses. Then I shall consider the teaching strategies appropriate to each kind of course. Finally, aspects of the problem of ensuring teaching quality are discussed. The questions of student study patterns and access are considered in detail in the next chapter.

## Specifying Courses

In this section the various dimensions of course specification referred to above are discussed in turn.

Subject Matter. Hitherto it has often been sufficient to name the subject matter of a course in a particular institution to give a fairly clear specification to a student of what to expect. The teaching style, the type of course, its level, and the need to attend college have been more or less standard. Most students have registered for the purpose of obtaining qualifications in their particular subject.

Nowadays, in distance teaching, naming the subject is only a part of the matter, even though it is a very important part. The variety of types of audience, and the greater opportunities for access they have, brings about a demand for a much wider range of subject matter, from professional courses through academic and practical courses to community interest courses. Evidently courses aimed at examinations are very different from general interest courses, and this fact is reflected in the topics offered. Thus the title or subject matter of a course needs to be accompanied by both a syllabus, to show the area covered, together with educational aims or objectives to indicate the type of course and the depth to which each topic is taught.

Types of Courses. Most universities place "teaching students to think" high on their list of educational aims. "Developing the general powers of the mind" was the Robbins Committee expression of this idea. So, much of university education is directed, in one way or another, at this rather imprecise cognitive aim. But even this has different aspects to it, ranging from intellectual skills, like analysis and design, to making rational decisions and solving problems. The teaching/strategies appropriate to each cognitive aim are not in general the same, so the methods to be used to achieve them have to be carefully chosen. So "the ability to think" is a portmanteau phrase that needs to be broken down.

Its main ingredients seem to be "understanding" and "intellectual skills". Learning to understand is concerned with conceptual development, with becoming familiar with new concepts, and the words used to refer to them, and with being able to explain events in terms of these concepts. Intellectual skills on the other hand are concerned with applying knowledge and understanding to practical problems of one kind or another. So "thinking" is being able successfully to apply one's understanding to new situations.

The implication of this is that "knowledge" (e.g. of facts or processes) is a different cognitive category from "understanding" and should be kept apart from it. Whilst it is possible to know the actions appropriate to given situations, it is not possible to know about new situations. These require thought. Understanding provides the framework or structure of knowledge, a kind of interconnected matrix of conceptual elements or pigeon holes. Knowledge is what these pigeon holes contain. Indeed it is very important to appreciate that knowledge can only be acquired if some measure of understanding already exists - even if this is only being able to understand everyday language. Specialist knowledge presupposes some specialist understanding.

There have been several taxonomies of educational aims, beginning with Bloom's classic work (1956), but for the purposes of this chapter let us distinguish between only three kinds of learning in the cognitive domain, namely knowledge, understanding and intellectual skills. These three ingredients, however, can be combined in different ways to produce different sorts of courses in the cognitive domain, all of which are of particular relevance to adult education.

There are two further kinds of educational aim which must not be forgotten, namely manual or motor skills (ranging from tennis to typing) and learning in the affective domain; that is, learning attitudes, (such as diligence, tolerance, flexibility of thought, etc.), and values (in such fields as aesthetics, politics, religion, etc.). For the moment, though, I will concentrate on courses within the cognitive domain.

A number of terms are being used nowadays to describe different kinds of course, such as awareness courses, training courses, academic courses, upgrading courses, etc. In terms of the three educational aims listed above these types of courses can be given more precise meanings. For example, training courses are concerned mainly with skills, awareness courses with knowledge, academic courses with understanding; indeed academic courses provide the understanding in specialist areas upon which professionalisms depend.

Updating courses, like awareness courses, are concerned mainly with knowledge, but they assume very different levels of prior understanding. An updating course is best thought of as a course for a specialist or professional (e.g. a doctor or engineer) whose knowledge has not kept pace with development, but whose understanding of the specialism remains. So an updating course is mainly factual but only comprehensible to the appropriate specialist. An awareness course is also factual but is intended to inform people in fields outside their specialism, and so must be in a language that is comprehensible to non-experts. Thus "assumed entry behaviour", as it is often called, is a fourth important factor to take into account in the design of a course. A better phrase would be "assumed prior understanding", but the importance of the factor is clear enough.

Assumed prior understanding also marks the difference between upgrading courses and the so-called interface courses. Both courses aim to increase the knowledge and understanding of the students but do not aim to produce skilled practitioners. But upgrading courses are intended to extend a students' understanding of their specialisms, whilst interface courses are intended to develop understanding in areas outside their specialism. For example, interface courses are for managers and supervisors who have to work intelligently with practitioners. So the two types of course, even if they are dealing with the same subject, must differ greatly because of the prior understanding in the students that can be assumed.

Table 1 summarises these distinctions between types of course. It represents a greatly simplified model of the differences between them but is nevertheless a very helpful guide.

Table 1: The cognitive content of different types of course

| Type of Course | Percentage target content | | | Assumed prior understanding in the subject being taught |
| | Knowledge | Understanding | Skills | |
| --- | --- | --- | --- | --- |
| Awareness | 100 | 0 | 0 | little |
| Updating | 100 | 0 | 0 | much |
| Practitioners | 0 | 40 | 60 | some |
| Training | 0 | 0 | 100 | little |
| Interface | 45 | 45 | 10 | little |
| Academic | 10 | 80 | 10 | some |
| Upgrading | 45 | 45 | 10 | much |

Level. The concept of level applies primarily to academic courses, and refers, essentially, to the depth of understanding being taught. Since other types of course also teach understanding it applies rather more loosely to them too.

Again, a simple model of what is meant by depth of understanding is helpful. Understanding means familiarity with the general principles and concepts of a subject. Three levels are worth distinguishing. At the most superficial level are simple generalisations about objects and events (e.g. all bodies tend to fall, all 'workers' vote socialist). There are usually exceptions to every generalisation (including this one). At a deeper level there are theories about, and explanations of, these generalisations, often in terms of abstract concepts (such as gravitation, equality, freedom, etc.). Note that explanation can take many forms: causal, historical, teleological, etc. At the deepest level lie theories about the interrelationships between abstract concepts. Thus, in general, in the academic hierachy, O-level, A-level, undergraduate level and postgraduate level refer to a progressive deepening of understanding.

## Educational Strategies and Methods

Feedback. Before considering the educational strategies appropriate to the three main ingredients of courses, namely knowledge, understanding and skills, we must first consider the concept of feedback.

The main purpose of feedback, whether in education or in engineering or elsewhere, is to remove error from the overall operation of the system, and to ensure that progress is being made in the required direction. Deviations and errors in learning can occur for a variety of reasons. For example, the teacher may make mistakes or be misleading; the transmission method (e.g. printing, telephone, computer, TV, etc.) may be faulty and noisy; students' abilities and prior understanding vary so that some may misunderstand or forget quite clear instructions and explanations. Feedback can be between student and teacher, between students themselves or between student and computers. If properly used it can correct or at least detect many of these errors. So in general feedback methods are needed in education. As we shall see, however, the form the feedback should take differs considerably.

The Teaching of Knowledge. Knowledge is easy to present but it will only be learnt by those who are motivated to learn, who have good memories (e.g. not too old,), and who have acquired sufficient prior understanding to make sense of the information being offered. Specialist knowledge in, say, medicine or engineering, requires appropriate academic courses as prerequisites. Motivation is rarely a problem in adult education. Students who undertake courses in their spare time usually want to learn. It is quite a different matter in full time secondary or tertiary education when students are expected to learn. For the latter it may be necessary to make the teaching "relevant" or "interesting". With adults it needs only to be effective, since it is already relevant and interesting.

The method of presentation should match the kind of knowledge being taught, though each method must be supported by appropriate verbal descriptions, either spoken or written. So, for example, when the information to be conveyed is known and agreed:

- use television, films, colour slides etc, for natural history, architecture, etc.

- use printed material or computers (e.g. teletext) for numerical data, lists, etc.

- use audio tapes for music, language, etc.

- use audio-vision, Cyclops, computer terminals for engineering, design, science.

These media are satisfactory for <u>awareness</u> courses, but are not sufficiently interactive for <u>updating</u> courses. Students who already possess a good deal of specialist knowledge and understanding often need to ask questions of their expert teachers, and to explain their particular problems. For example, doctors might need to describe a particular set of symptoms before expert advice on the latest diagnosis and treatment can be given:

- for such "question and answer" sessions use telephone conferences, TV or radio phone-ins, face-to-face classes, or expert (computer) systems.

- for information on request use encyclopaedia (or other forms of printed information), teletext or Dial Access.

<u>The Teaching of Understanding</u>. There are two basic strategies to use in teaching understanding: the use of <u>redundancy</u>; the use of <u>discussion</u>; or <u>both</u>. Either method achieves the all-important necessary operation of driving the new concepts and thought processes through the learner's mind several times and in different contexts. Understanding, unlike knowledge, cannot be learned by heart; it needs a much deeper mental grasp.

The use of <u>redundancy</u> simply means teaching the same <u>ideas</u> in several different ways: for example, analysing them in terms of other concepts, by analogy, by applying them in different contexts, by contrasting them with alternative ideas, by repetition but in different words, by the use of different media, etc.

The use of <u>discussion</u> involves clarifying the ideas and concepts, once they have been presented, through discussion with other students, with a tutor or teacher, with a computer programme, even with oneself (through self-assessment questions), by tackling problems and, where necessary, by reference to text books.

These strategies are not exclusive alternatives. Obviously aspects of each can be welded together in effective courses of several cost-effective kinds. The following are some examples:

(i) <u>Traditional university or college face-to-face teaching</u>: this involves lectures plus tutorials plus libraries plus student interaction (plus labs where necessary). Note that lectures are often regarded as a teaching method. They teach <u>knowledge</u> and sometimes they teach in the affective domain, but they only provide one component of a mainly-discussion based strategy for teaching understanding. Most of the learning of understanding takes place outside the lecture theatre. The lectures are mainly an explanatory statement of what has to be learned; the learning occurs in the "mulling over" that follows. Thus universities present their courses using a mixture of strategies; redundancy is provided by lectures plus libraries plus labs. Discussion is encouraged by residential accommodation and tutorials and small group teaching. The lectures play quite a small part in the learning process. The discussion strategy is applied in its purest form in good school teaching. Here the classroom is the place where learning takes place. Homework concentrates on intellectual skills. Far more time is spent in school classrooms however than is spent in university lectures.

(ii) Multimedia Teaching, as at the Open University. Difficult concepts are best taught using several media, selected as appropriate, from (i) structured teaching text; (ii) TV (preferably on cassette); (iii) audio cassettes with or without visual additions (e.g. Cyclops); (iv) home kits. This use of redundancy can be augmented in distance teaching by discussion strategies, using, where appropriate, telephone conferences, face-to-face tutorials or TVI. Just as the function of lecturing, in teaching understanding, is often misunderstood, so too if the function of small group tutoring. It is often regarded as remedial in the sense that its purpose is to correct or reveal students' misunderstandings. Tutorials, of course, achieve this to some extent but not very efficiently. Misunderstandings and errors in learning are normally very personal, so they are not well dealt with in a group if everyone's time is to be well spent. (Individual errors are best dealt with by individual attention, often quite brief, by a tutor or a fellow student.) The tutorial or teleconference, in teaching understanding, should be regarded as a way of teaching through discussion, rather than remedial.

(iii) Tutored Video Instruction (TVI). This method involves the playing of a video-taped lecture to a group of students but with many interruptions to allow discussion of the topics being presented. The taped lecture states in orderly and explanatory manner what has to be understood; much of the learning takes place during the frequent discussion sessions into which the taped lecture is broken down. The tape is a guide and a source; text books, the tutor and other students provide the discussion of the ideas in different contexts and so bring about the learning. Alternative guides to study and sources of material, such as structured text or audio tapes do not provide the same rich focus for common student experience as a video tape does. For TVI to be appropriate it is essential that distance students are able to assemble frequently in small groups with a tutor (e.g. in companies or organisations). It is not a home-based learning method

- at least not until some advances in information technology have been made to allow simultaneous viewing and interruption of TV tapes in students' homes.

Note that it is part of the strengths of the first two methods that they can be used for teaching knowledge and for demonstrating skills, as well as for teaching understanding. TVI is more limited, but for teaching understanding at a distance it is an almost ideal use of the discussion strategy.

The three methods (face-to-face teaching, multi-media teaching, and TVI) are what might be regarded as pedagogically optimal, but none of them is cheap. The first and third are expensive in manpower where large student numbers are involved, since costs increase with student numbers. The second is expensive in production so becomes cheaper per student as student numbers increase. Less expensive methods can also be fairly effective - depending a good deal on student motivation, and on subject matter. For example successful courses that teach some understanding as well as knowledge or skills can be taught by:

- highly structured teaching texts on their own;

- teaching text plus home kit (e.g. microprocessors);

- television plus radio phone-in (e.g. economics);

- audio vision or Cyclops (e.g. mathematics) on its own.

The teaching of skills. The teaching of skills consists of two parts, and, in principle is quite straightforward, although the implementation of the second part in distance teaching can be difficult.

The first part comprises instruction and demonstration. For this, taped television is the most versatile, and, for any skill with a manual component (even doing mathematical calculations) it is probably the most effective method there is; even more effective than face-to-face demonstration owing to its replay capability. Seeing someone doing what has to be done always communicates best. But it is expensive. Less expensive but effective methods include:

- audio vision for mathematics, engineering, science;

- instruction books for most skills;

- computer aided instruction for problem solving, simulations and calculations;

- audio tapes and books for languages, interpersonal skills, etc.

The second part consists of providing students with opportunities to practice their skills and to have their work monitored. This is difficult to achieve whenever student numbers are large, but particularly so in distance teaching. For particular purposes the following are effective:

- intellectual skills that result in written work can be handled by correspondence;

- if responses are sufficiently well codified they can be tirelessly monitored through CAL programmes, with a tutor's help called up by telephone when needed;

- audible skills (including music) can be observed and corrected by telephone conferencing;

- a number of intellectual skills, such as electronic circuit design, can be self-checked by the application of standardised test procedures. Indeed, before long, home-based microcomputers will be able to simulate many electronic signal processes so that self-checking of circuit performance characteristics could become highly sophisticated;

- many, more practical, skills, however, require face-to-face supervision and so, at least until home-based two-way television transmission using the cable network is available, are not suitable for distance teaching.

Teaching in the affective domain. Probably the only fairly well understood "teaching" activity in the affective domain is advertising or salesmanship. Its role in education might be to convey to students the importance or delights of particular courses or fields of study, or, in other words, to increase students' motivation to study, though motivational factors to study and work long hours usually lie too deep to be much affected by any sensory inputs.

Television seems to be much the most effective form of communication for affective teaching, although writing and lecturing (or public speaking) can also be successful. The essence of the process seems to be to appeal to the emotions as well as to the intellect. The ability of television to show disturbing aspects of reality gives it its extra strength, even over evocative writing.

Much affective teaching however emerges with time over along periods of study, especially for degrees or other qualifications. The activity of study develops habits of diligence, self-reliance, etc., and so changes students' attitudes and values. But these changes occur as by-products of the teaching. They are rarely the overt educational aims.

## Teacher motivation and the quality of teaching.

If technology can make study more acceptable and convenient to students, it may not be able to do the same for teachers. Yet it is essential, in the long term, even if not initially, when enthusiasm to experiment is high, to ensure that the methods used are supported by the teachers who have to use them. So a further factor in education is the problem of ensuring that teachers feel that their time is well spent using educational technology, and that good quality materials and effective teaching is achievable.

An important parameter affecting both these characteristics is the number of the teachers' man-hours spent, in generating one hour's worth of student work. Table 2 (over) shows some representative figures, including some for face-to-face teaching. The larger the student audience in each case the less expensive the method per student taught. Some methods however are effective only with small student numbers.

These data clearly have relevance to the cost of each system, but they are also of significance pedagogically. Experience seems to show that educational methods that require very substantial investments of time by the teachers soon fall into disuse, once the initial pioneering zeal has passed, unless there are extra motivations for keeping at it. Improved educational effectiveness may well not be enough to persuade teachers to spend 200 hours for each student-hour (even if 1000 students benefit) when by using face-to-face methods only 2 to 10 hours would be needed. Effective motivations include (i) extra payment; (ii) seeing one's work in print - as with writing teaching texts; (iii) appearing on television programmes (effective with broadcast TV though not with video-cassettes). Without such extra incentives the quality of the teaching using technology is likely to fall away, or die, if too much time and effort is demanded of the staff when face-to-face teaching is so much easier.

## Conclusion

This chapter has not been a summary of what is <u>known</u> about educational technology. It has attempted to <u>teach,</u> at an elementary

## Table 2: Effective use of manpower

| Teaching method | Ratio of academic man-hours per student-hour of work generated |
| --- | --- |
| Lecturing | 2 - 10 |
| Small group teaching | 1 - 10 |
| Teaching by telephone | 2 - 10 |
| Video-tape lectures (for TVI) | 3 - 10* |
| Audio-vision | 10 - 20* |
| Teaching text | 50 - 100** |
| Broadcast TV | 100 or more** |
| Computer-aided learning | 200 or more* |
| Interactive video disc | 300 or more** |

\*    requires support staff

\*\*   requires several support staff

level, the understanding of a simple taxonomy of courses, educational aims and teaching strategies. The categorisations it has presented are by no means the only ones possible, but they do provide a useful language and analysis by means of which it is possible to progress, in consultation with others, from a course specification by clients or students, both to a course structure and to an array of distance teaching methods that will be educationally successful for the particular course. Space, and the use of the printed word only, has prevented this chapter adopting either of the strategies it recommends for the teaching of understanding; though the communication of understanding is certainly part of its aim. Hopefully, however, the likely readership will be sufficiently expert to have little difficulty with any of the models and concepts used.

References and additional reading

ANDERSON, R. H. (1976) Selecting and developing media for instruction. New York: Van Nostrand Reinhold.

ASSOCIATION FOR EDUCATIONAL COMMUNICATIONS AND TECHNOLOGY (1977) Educational technology: Definition and glossary of terms. Washington, D.C.: Association for Educational Communication and Technology.

ATKINSON, R., MAINBRIDGE, B. AND JENNINGS, P. (1981) Appropriate technologies for off-campus practical work. Murdoch: Western Australia Educational Services and Teaching Resources Unit, Murdoch University, Occasional Paper 7.

ATKINSON, R. C., & SHIFFRIN, R. (1968) "Human memory: A proposed system and its control processes". In SPENCE, K. W. & SPENCE, J. T. (eds.), The psychology of learning and motivation: Advances in research and theory (Vol.2). New York: Academic Press.

BANDURA, A. (1969) Principles of behaviour modification. New York: Holt, Rinehart & Winston.

BATES, A, W, (1982) "Learning from Audio visual media" in Student Learning from Different media in the Open University. (Institutional Research Review No.1) The Open University.

BATES, A. W. (1980) "Towards a better theoretical framework for studying learning from television", Instructional Sciences, Vol.9 No,4.

BLOOM, B. S. (1956) Taxonomy of Educational Objectives: the Classification of Educational Goals. Handbook 1: Cognitive Domain. New York: David McKay.

BOUD, D. (ed.) (1981) Developing student autonomy in Learning London: Kogan Page.

BOWER, G. H., & HILGARD, E. R. (1981) Theories of learning (5th ed.). Englewood Cliffs, N. J.: Prentice-Hall.

BRABY, R. (1973) An evaluation of ten techniques for choosing instructional media (TAEG Report No.8). Orlando, Fla: Training Analysis and Evaluation Group.

220

BRETZ, R. (1971) The selection of appropriate communication media for instruction: a guide for designers of Air Force technical training programs. Santa Monica, Calif: Rand.

BRIGGS, L. J. (1970) Handbook of procedures for the design of instruction. Pittsburgh, Penn.: American Institutes for Research.

BRIGGS, L. J., & WAGER, W. W. (1982) The handbook of procedures for the design of instruction (2nd ed.). Englewood Cliffs, N. J.: Educational Technology.

CRONBACH, L. J., & SNOW, R. E. (1977) Aptitudes and instructional methods. New York: Irvington.

DALE, E. A. (1969) Audiovisual methods in teaching (3rd ed.). New York: Holt, Rinehart, & Winston.

DWYER, F. M. (1978) Strategies for improving visual learning: a handbook for the effective selection, design and use of visualized materials. State College, Penn.: Learning Services.

ELSTEIN, A. S. (1979) "Problem Solving: applications of research to undergraduate instruction and evaluation." Programmed Learning and Educational Technology, Vol.16, No.4.

ESTES, W. K. (1978) Handbook of learning and cognitive processes, Vol.5: Human information processing. Hillside, N. J.: Erlbaum.

FITTS, P. M., & POSNER, M. I. (1967) Human performance. Monterey, Calif.: Brooks/Cole.

GALLAGHER, M. (1978) "Good television and good educational practice: problems of definition". Educational Broadcasting International, December.

GAGNE, R.M. (1977) The conditions of learning (3rd ed.). New York: Holt, Rinehart, & Winston.

GAGNE, R.M. & BRIGGS, L.J. (1979) Principles of instructional design (2nd ed.). New York: Holt, Rinehart, & Winston.

GAGNE, R.M. & WHITE, R.T. (1978) "Memory structures and learning outcomes". Review of Educational Research, Vol. 48.

GROPPER, G.L. (1976) "A behavioural perspective on media selection". AV Communication Review, 24.

HEIDT, E.U. (1978) Instructional media and the individual learner. London: Kogan Page.

HOLMBERG, B. (1982) Essentials of Distance Education. Hagen: Fern Universitat, ZIFF.

KEMP, J.E. (1980) Planning and producing audiovisual materials (4th ed.). New York: Harper & Row.

KNAPPER, C.K. (1980) Evaluating Instructional Technology. London: Croom Helm.

LEVIE, W.H. (1977) "Models for media selection". NSPI Journal, Vol. 16 No. 7.

OLSON, D.R. (1976) "Towards a theory of instructional means". Educational Psychologist. Vol. 12.

OLSON, D. & BRUNER, J. (1974) Learning through experience and learning through media, in Olson, D. (ed.) Media Symbols: The Forms of Expression, The 73rd NSSE Yearbook, University of Chicago Press, Chicago.

REISER, R.A. and GAGNE, R.M. (1982). "Characteristics of Media Selection Models". Review of Educational Research, Vol. 52.

ROMISZOWSKI, A.J. (1974) The selection and use of instructional media. London: Kogan Page.

SALOMON, G. (1979) Interaction of media, cognition and learning. San Francisco: Jossey-Bass.

SCHRAMM, W. (1972) "What the research says". In SCHRAMM, W. (ed.), Quality in instructional television. Honolulu: University Press of Hawaii.

SCHRAMM, W. (1977) Big media, little media. Beverly Hills, Calif.: Sage.

TOSTI, D.T. & BALL, J.R. (1969) "A behavioural approach to instructional design and media selection". AV Communication Review, Vol. 17.

TRAINING ANALYSIS AND EVALUATION GROUP (1972) Staff study on cost and training effectiveness of proposed training systems (TAEG Report No. 1). Orlando, Fla.: Training Analysis and Evaluation Group.

## 19.  PUTTING IT TOGETHER: NOW AND THE FUTURE

Tony Bates
Reader in Media Research Methods, Open University

### The Advantages of New Technology

Recent developments in technology are bringing advantages to distance teaching and removing some of the disadvantages previously associated with the use of audio-visual media.  New technology promises:

- a wider range of teaching functions and a higher quality of learning;

- lower costs;

- greater student control;

- more interaction and feedback for students.

One of the major benefits of computers and cassettes is that they enable students to develop skills, through structured activities, practice, and feedback.  Media such as television and computers provide source material which students can work on to expand their understanding and to which they can apply their knowledge. Different media provide alternative ways to reach understanding and comprehension, and in distance education, where tutor-student contacts are limited, a variety of presentation is essential. The use of media (including home kits) is essential for teaching science and technology at a distance. The introduction then of audio-visual media into distance teaching widens its scope and provides alternative approaches and the variety that are essential to student motivation and deep understanding.  The use of audio-visual media can help increase the quality of learning and reduce drop out.

For some media, costs are dropping to a level where their use makes economic sense even in institutions with very limited budgets.  A well-designed audio-cassette, integrated with the text, is a low-cost, highly effective teaching medium for individualised study, with much greater flexibility than many other media. In an increasing number of circumstances, video-cassettes have considerable educational, cost and distributional advantages over broadcast television. Thus video is now a viable proposition for a number of institutions which previously could not contemplate using broadcast television because of its high cost. The skilful use of word-processors could result in major savings on course production costs. Developments are now so rapid that any distance teaching institution needs to keep under continuous review the possibility that new technology could lead to major reductions in operating costs, or allow an expansion of activities into new areas or to new target groups within fixed cost limits.

New technology is also removing many of the inconveniences and limitations previously associated with studying through audio-visual media. Cassettes give students more <u>control</u> over their learning. This enables students to be more flexible in their study patterns, and more effective in their learning, through review, analysis, and reflection. Cassettes parallel many of the control features of books, while at the same time expanding the range of skills that can be taught at a distance. Indeed, computer-controlled video discs will provide students with far greater control than can be achieved even through books (which will nevertheless remain one of the more flexible of teaching media.)

New technology also provides greater opportunity for <u>interaction</u> between student and learning materials. With computer-assisted learning or cassettes, students can try out answers, and get <u>feedback</u> on their performance. Similarly, telephone tutoring permits feedback at a distance from tutors able to deal with a range of student learning problems or personal difficulties. Far from eliminating human contact, technologies such as the telephone and CYCLOPS make possible personal tutorial contact where otherwise it would be impossible for remote or isolated distant students.

## Limitations of New Technology

There are still major obstacles and limitations to the introduction of new technology for distance education, and these limitations have roots much deeper than the innate conservatism of education.

Distance teaching is an area of education where the educational thinking and requirements are still well in advance of the technology. In many cases, the technology has not been developed to a stage where it is yet useful or viable for distance education. Distance teaching requires technology which is so cheap, reliable, easy to use and multi-functional that it can be found in nearly every home. Apart from books, broadcast television, radio, audio-cassettes, and the telephone the technology at the moment cannot actually meet home-based needs. Video-cassettes and micro-computers are beginning to become widely available, but they are not likely to be found in most homes before the end of this decade. Other technologies, such as viewdata, cable TV and video-discs, will not be universally available until the end of this century, if at all.

Furthermore, some of the technologies are limited in their educational potential (such as viewdata and teletext), extraordinarily difficult to design for flexible learning material, and even more diffiuclt for learners to use (such as computers), not developed sufficiently to be ready for home-use (CYCLOPS), or hideously expensive to produce (such as good-quality CAL or interactive video-discs).

The variability of access to new technology creates considerable problems for distance education institutions. By 1990, access to technology in the home in Britain is likely to be something like this:

|                        | % of households |
| ---------------------- | --------------- |
| Broadcast TV and radio | 98%             |
| Audio-cassettes        | 90%             |
| Telephone              | 80%             |
| Video-cassettes        | 66%             |
| Microcomputers         | 50%             |
| Cable TV               | 40%             |
| Viewdata               | 30%             |
| Teletext               | 20%             |
| Video-disc             | 10%             |

Like all predictions, these have to be guesses, but whatever variations there may be on individual media, the point will remain that some media will be almost universally available, some media will be available in only a small number of homes, and others will be available in a lot of homes, but by no means all. The two extremes do not present major problems. Below 50% access there are two options: provide students with the technology at the distance teaching institution's expense, in the form of a home kit (which could be very expensive); or don't use the technology at all (which in most cases would be the sensible decision). When access exceeds 80% it seems reasonable to expect the small proportion of students without access to make a special effort to get the technology. It is in the intermediary range - 50% to 80% - where difficulties arise, particularly when such technologies have substantial educational benefits. Video-cassettes and microcomputers are the biggest problems in this respect, exacerbated in both cases by the variety of different incompatible formats in each medium. Access to these media, although by no means universal, is growing rapidly. Given the long period of time over which distance education courses are planned and run, the timing of the introduction of such technology is crucial. At the Open University, we now survey each year students' access to media equipment; similar monitoring is surely essential in other distance teaching institutions, since equipment ownership varies greatly from country to country.

The variability of access also causes problems of social equity for distance teaching institutions, many of which have been established to cater for those who in the past have been educationally or economically disadvantaged. It is not likely to be the case that those students for instance who do not have video-cassette players will at least have a micro-computer. On the contrary, there is likely to be a widening of the gap between those such as the unemployed, disabled and elderly, with very little technological equipment in the home; and those who are earning good money, and likely to have a wide range of equipment. In this respect, broadcast TV, radio, books and audio-cassettes are still the most suitable technologies for open access.

Another major limitation is the need to produce high quality teaching material for use on new technology. Apart from audio-cassettes, the telephone and CYCLOPS, most technologies require a high level of skill in knowing how best to use the technology for teaching purposes. Unless the subject experts are willing to master the technology themselves, professional "producers" are required to "transform" teaching material into appropriate formats. The "easier" the technology, the more likely it is to be used by subject expert and student alike, which probably explains why audio-cassettes are so widely used at the Open University. The alternative is to set up special production departments, such as BBC/Open University Productions for television and radio, or the Academic Computing Service for computer assisted learning. This however means employing permanent, highly paid professional staff, and is expensive. Furthermore, with the range of media available to distance education rapidly expanding, either professional staff will have to widen their range of expertise (probably still favouring their original skills), or the choice of media will become limited to those areas where expertise already exists. The real danger though is that the subject expert will be further distanced from the students through having to work through intermediary producers or "transformers", who will impose their own standards and requirements on the teaching materials. For the use of technology in distance education to become really widespread, the technology has to become so simple that ordinary teachers and students can use it with minimal training.

Some technologies are extremely demanding in terms of the skill and time required to design effective teaching material. Broadcast television and computer assisted learning in particular are at the extremes of cost and difficulty. This is why devices such as audio-cassettes, the telephone and CYCLOPS, which enable relatively untrained teachers to create their own materials, are so important. In some instances, such as CYCLOPS, the savings on production costs could well compensate for the relatively high cost of specialised user equipment, especially for courses with low student numbers. In the meantime, while highly demanding technology is used, there will continue to be a shortage of good designers and hence a shortage of good courseware. There will also continue to be a need for team-work, with contributions from both subject-experts and professional producers. Indeed, teams are likely to increase in size, as the range of technology expands, again adding to staff costs and the complexity of course design.

The greatest problem though is deciding <u>which</u> media to use, and the <u>different</u> ways in which each medium should be used, so that they complement one another. This is an extremely difficult area in which to make rational decisions on strictly pedagogic grounds. The previous chapter sets out some guidelines for media selection, but any such set of guidelines is hampered by a number of difficulties. Firstly, most media are multi-functional, in that several different media can each be used to teach the same thing equally well, under the right circumstances. Nevertheless, some media are clearly less appropriate than others for certain learning tasks. Broadcast television has obvious weaknesses in teaching manipulative skills; books are not very helpful for teaching laboratory techniques; computers are not so easy to use as broadcast television for providing an overview or synthesis of a subject. Yet given enough time, money and imagination, exceptions could be made to each of the above examples. This problem can only be resolved if there is a generally agreed, comprehensive and powerful theory of teaching and learning which can explain differences in how people learn from different media. It is a great pity that as much energy and investment is not put into this as there is in media production and distribution. Here surely is an area for joint research between distance education institutions.

Lastly, as already hinted, the introduction of new technology in distance education requires major changes in professional roles. While it is not necessary for subject experts to become professional producers, they should be aware of the potential and limitations of various media, and how they might be used in their teaching. Acquiring this knowledge though is no mean task, and will not happen by chance. The range of media available is now becoming so wide that it is difficult for a single person to encompass the advantages and disadvantages of every medium, yet some specialised knowledge is needed to make sensible decisions. Internal training then needs to be systematically organised for those teaching at a distance.

Another hindrance to innovation is likely to be the organisational problems caused by changing roles. Word-processing shifts more editorial responsibility on to the academic, increasing his or her work-load. As my secretary will testify, word-processor displays cause eye-strain, and using a word processor tends to make a secretary's work more demanding and frustrating than straight copy-typing, particularly when learning to use the medium. Whenever an academic uses new technology for the first time for creating teaching materials, it always takes much longer than anticipated. (A good rule is to make a maximum estimate, then multiply by three for the first time and two for the second time.) Professional boundaries are becoming blurred and overlapping. Will departments built around mainframe computers be willing and able to adapt to decentralised and local use of micros, both for administration and teaching? Will broadcast television producers be willing and able to make non-broadcast video programmes in a style that exploits the cassette format? Do you need a producer at all for audio-cassettes? How should the production of interactive video be organised, and who - in terms of professional role - should be in charge? These are all difficult issues, affecting people's careers and work-life, which need handling with extreme sensitivity.

## The Great Unknown

How likely is the following scenario? A subject expert (a senior electronics engineer), contracted by a distance education institution, sits at home (or in his office) at a computer terminal incorporating word-processing facilities, computer graphics, and synchronised sound recording. He works with the aid of an authoring system, down-loaded on to his own micro from the mainframe at the distance education institution's headquarters. The authoring system provides a checklist for unit design, such as how to write objectives, how to build in self-assessment questions and answers, how to simulate experiments, how to use graphics to illustrate material, how to lay-out the text, etc. The subject expert prepares on his terminal a draft unit (including graphics) on the design requirements of a microchip. Areas where he needs full video (with a rough description) are inserted. The whole draft programme (including typing errors) is collected together on one computer diskette and despatched during the night via the public telephone service to the main-frame computer. The next morning a course "transformer" (previously an editor or educational technologist) runs a routine, computerised check on spelling and layout, identifies the areas needing full video, and transmits the request to a video production unit (who will then make direct contact with the subject experts.) When the video extracts are made, they are called up for recording via cable on video-cassette, by the subject expert, and the transformer, each using dial-access on a switched-star cable system. After discussion between the transformer, the engineer, and the video producer, the transformer writes a short computer-program, incorporated into the general draft unit, giving guidance to students on how to use and work through the video material, including activities, exercises and re-routing. The whole unit, on diskette, video-cassette and audio-cassette is then independently checked by the subject expert and the transformer. Once approved, the video material is transferred to video-disc, and the material on diskette is transferred to the mainframe computer.

After seeing an advertisement for the course (potential students can get details of all courses through the viewdata system), a student enrols by dialing up the registry computer, via his home-based micro linked to the telephone system. He gives his name, address and telephone number, and arranges payment of fees by authorising payment from his bank. The registry computer checks that payment is cleared, gives him a code, searches for the coded course material, and downloads the material about the microchip design on to the students' micro. The student also receives by post an audio-cassette and a video-disc. He links his video-disc machine to his own micro using an interface sent by the University with the disc. Using the combination of computer, video disc and audio-cassette, the student works through the material. When the student feels he is ready, he carries out some tests, types in some answers, and despatches these to the mainframe computer, which gives him a grade, and comments on his work. He still does not understand why one of his answers was wrong. He telephones his tutor, who, with the aid of a CYCLOPS-type facility, draws a diagram explaining where he had gone wrong. He then goes round the pub, to have a drink with his mates, since he feels the need for normal company.

What you feel about such a scenario will depend on your view of adult and continuing education. The technology for all this already exists. It is quite feasible, when the technology becomes more widely available. But is it education? And if it is, how long will it take to get us there? My own guess is within 15-20 years, i.e. roughly the same time as the Open University has already been in existence.

One important feature of new technology is its malleability. Computer-based technology can be adapted to meet particular needs. In the past, distance education has had to rely on widely available mass media, and ride on the back of it. Interfaces for computer-controlled video, CYCLOPS-type developments, and software for micro-computers can now though be adapted to meet specific purposes directly relevant to distance education. There is considerable scope here for joint research and development between distance teaching institutions. Co-operative work on developments such as CYCLOPS might have resulted in its more widespread use in distance education.

Technological developments also have major implications for the role of study centres. It is clear that conventional classrooms in conventional educational institutions are not suitable for shared use of equipment, yet shared use of equipment will become increasingly important as an intermediary stage before all students have the necessary equipment in their homes. Finding suitable alternative arrangements though will require considerably more initiative and enterprise than has been shown by regional staff so far. This is partly because regional staff, quite rightly, place primary emphasis on direct person-to-person contact. This will remain important in distance education, but alternative means of contact are also essential for the many students for whom attendance at study centre is at best a major inconvenience and at worst impossible.

Another unknown is the extent to which new technology will radically transform distance teaching institutions, or whether new technology will generally just be added on to existing systems. My scenario assumed no central, full-time academics, broadcast television, books, or face-to-face tutorial contact, but up to now, new technology has rarely replaced the original system on which a distance teaching institution was based. Although audio and video cassettes are beginning to lead to a reduction - but not the abolition of - broadcasting at the Open University, text still remains central, with all the other media around the periphery. One reason for this is that people who control decision-making have existing interests to protect. My own view is that technology will remain on the periphery of distance education unless a whole institution is changed, with money moved out from some areas altogether into new areas. This may be easier to accomplish in brand new institutions or in institutions that have been less successful in the past in teaching at a distance. In those with a good previous track record, fundamental change is likely only as a result of drastic budgetary cuts or very strong external political intervention. Any institution which can move gracefully from its current position to one where new technology plays a more central role will have combined the daring of a free-fall parachutist with the balance of an ice-skater.

The greatest unknown though is what an increase in the use of technology will do to students' thinking. Postman (1983) has argued that the predominant influence of television in our lives is moving society away from valuing objective, scientific rational thinking to giving greater importance to impressionistic and intuitive thinking. My own view is that computer-based learning still tends towards convergent, "closed" thinking, while broadcast television can stimulate creative thinking. Basically, though, no-one knows. It is though such an important issue that we ignore it at our peril. Everything may be possible eventually through technology - but we should ensure that what is done through technology is what we want, no less in distance education as in other aspects of our lives.

## References

POSTMAN, N. (1978). The disappearance of Childhood. London: W.H. Allen and Sons.